CW01660809

The Struggle with the Angel

The Struggle with the Angel

A Poetics of Lloyd Newson's
Strange Fish
(DV8 Physical Theatre)

Janet Adshead-Lansdale

DANCE BOOKS

First published in 2007 by Dance Books Ltd
The Old Bakery
4 Lenten Street
Alton
Hampshire GU34 1HG

ISBN: 9781 85273 117 5

A CIP catalogue record is available for this book from the British Library

Printed and bound in Great Britain by Lightning Source

for
John

Contents

Acknowledgements

This book is the outcome of a long research process that began in 1992. The process was often delayed by urgent teaching and administrative demands arising from my post as Head of the Department of Dance Studies, then of the School of Performing Arts at the University of Surrey (1991-2002). I am grateful, therefore, to colleagues, friends and postgraduate students who have encouraged me to sustain these evolving arguments over time.

I am indebted to Lloyd Newson and DV8 for producing this powerful and demanding work – *Strange Fish*. The stage version stimulated this research process and, after many, many viewings of the subsequent video, I remain entranced. Some of the artists involved in the production of *Strange Fish* readily agreed to interviews and provided much fascinating material.

I am grateful to Clement Crisp for permission to reproduce his review of 'Strange Fish' published in the Financial Times on 31st July 1992 and to the Guardian for permission to reproduce 'Truly, Badly, but Terribly Manly,' a review by Judith Mackrell published on 22nd September 1995.

Professor Richard Cave read and commented critically on an earlier version of the text, Professor Jennifer Brown and Professor Alexandra Carter also offered comments at an early stage. John Duke has been a life-support system, in many more ways than I would wish to articulate here, while also being my sharpest critic.

The publication of esoteric academic texts is a fraught business at this time, as all scholars know, and I am deeply grateful to David Leonard, of Dance Books, for keeping faith with dance research. I also acknowledge the support of the University of Surrey in resolving problems of maintaining academic freedom in writing about the work of a living artist. It has taken four years from the completion of the text to its realisation in print, largely for these reasons. I am indebted to Duncan Lamont and Ben Williams in this context.

Janet Adshead-Lansdale
May 2007

CHAPTER 1

Intertextual Dances: Analytic Exploration

In this book I pursue the claim that intertextuality is a powerful analytic tool with wide application for the performing arts. In doing this I extend lines of argument laid out in *Dancing Texts* (Adshead-Lansdale, 1999, ed.) and provide an extended example of an intertextual analysis of a particular performance piece, *Strange Fish*. The readership envisaged includes performers, critics, and theorists of contemporary performance arts. It is directed to those engaged in cultural studies, in performance art, in physical theatre, dance, theatre, gender and queer studies in Europe, Australia and North America. Such wide application is not as improbable as it sounds since the genre of Physical Theatre, with which this text deals, has been promoted within a variety of contexts and attracts audiences from all these fields.[1] Significantly, too, the rise of the body (so to speak) combined with the death of the verbal and literary author, is fruitful territory for more thorough investigation, in its implications for the physical arts, than has so far arisen. Thorough investigation requires cognisance of dance theory where, unlike theatre and music, the 'body', if not quite in the same sense, has always been both subject and object of practice and theory.

The choice of *Strange Fish*

Theoretically, and methodologically, this text offers a contribution to the development of interpretative theory in the arts and to the analysis of performance practices. Topical conceptual and methodological problems are explored through an extended analysis of *Strange Fish* (1992) by Lloyd Newson and DV8 Physical Theatre to demonstrate the value and potential of a close reading of a performance text in a post-structuralist environment. The exposition of a particular kind of logic, an interpretative rationality, through argument and demonstration of a working method of critical practice, is as relevant to theatre as to music and to dance; as relevant to the classical theatre and the Russian Imperial ballet as to their modern expressionist and postmodernist manifestations.

Newson's dance making is interesting and thought-provoking in its own right; it is topical and highly regarded, as well as being suitably contentious for my theoretical and methodological arguments. The kind of work, and this piece in particular, was extremely popular at the time of its making (1992); it was then televised (1994), giving access to a wider public, and was subsequently made available on video (BBC/RMArts, 1993) and DVD (Arthaus, 2007). It also gave rise to extensive comment although this is largely confined to short newspaper and journal articles which, while they serve to illustrate different critical positions and themes, neither exhaust the subject nor uncover its multiple layers and complexities. They do not begin to reflect on how changes in art practices relate to changes in critical practices.

It might be argued that to focus on a single work is to make it monolithic, to imply that it is 'better' than other works and by this means to re-establish a canon of 'classics'. In fact relatively little has been written in this canonical form in dance (Beaumont, 1944; 1947). Writings which address a single dance, or even a small group of dances, are largely limited to mid- twentieth-century. The over-development of canonical studies in literature or music for example, does not necessarily imply that in-depth studies of dances have no value. It is true that I regard *Strange Fish* as valuable in its potential to repay extended study, why else would one spend many years working on it? I appreciate it for the issues it deals with and the way it deals with them. The choice of a single work is justified on the grounds that it allows me to pursue themes and methods in some depth, not skating over many works or many ideas. I can delve into the complexities of interpretative practice through an exploration of one performance text and, through such analysis and enjoyment, establish a long-term relationship with it. It is more like friendship than canonical elevation, more like healthy (and often critical) respect, than adulation or veneration.

When *Strange Fish* was first performed in 1992, the year 2000 seemed some way off. It was little talked of at the time and none of the critics made a connection between the subject matter of this piece and the approach of the end of the second millennium. In the intervening period as my research has continued it was, briefly, difficult to ignore 'millennium fever' in its more commercial aspects. Religious aspects were considerably lower key, reflecting the diminution of interest in, and of the dominance of, Christianity in the Western world. Nevertheless, reactions to events as diverse as the New York Exhibition, *Sensation* (1998), Bartlett's performance piece, *Seven Sacraments* (1998), the American film *Stigmata* (1999), an exhibition at the National Gallery, London, *Seeing Salvation The Image of Christ* (Finaldi, 2000), and the linked BBC TV programme in April, culminating on Easter Sunday, Harrison Birtwistle's opera *The Last Supper* (2000), lend support to the idea that while the number of practising Church goers in the Anglican Church in the UK has sunk to a new low, the story of the life of Jesus Christ and the institution of the Church remains a powerful and enduring part of Western mythology. More recently, with the growth of fundamentalist influences, the controversies underlying these events have become directly and politically significant. We would not, perhaps, have envisaged the savagery of the debate about the potential split in the world-wide Anglican church on the appointment of an openly gay bishop that we saw in 2005.

Stigmata (dir. Rupert Wainwright) tells the story of a girl receiving a rosary from her mother in a remote Brazilian village. The wounds of Christ appear on her body. The legitimacy of the claims made for and about her, and the involvement of the Vatican, as subject matter for the film, testifies to the usefulness of myth (here of the stigmata) as intertext for this set of issues. *Seeing Salvation* (2000) brought together 79 images of Christ, selected around several themes: Sign and Symbol; The Dual Nature; The True Likeness; Passion and Compassion; Praying the Passion; The Saving Body and The Abiding Presence. As befits the cultural moment of the end of the millennium, the emphasis was not on establishing what was, or was not, an 'authentic' representation of Christ, but on the purposes for which these images were made, and what they might have meant to their original viewers. Acceptance that context, and the viewer's position, affect the artist's representation, allowed the curator to trace the evolution of the image over two millennia and to focus on the universality of constructs of love, sorrow and pain. Twentieth century interpretations included those of Stanley Spencer (1920; 1924-26), Salvador Dali (1951) and Graham Sutherland (1953).

Not all art exhibitions in the year 2000 were respectful. Chris Ofili, winner of the Turner prize in 1998, created controversy in New York with his painting of 'The Virgin Mary', displayed as part of the exhibition *Sensation: Young British Artists from the Saatchi Collection*. As Ellison remarks, Ofili's abstract painting of the Virgin 'adorned with elephant dung' (1999) was a prime target for the then mayor of New York, Mayor Giuliani, who professed himself offended and threatened to remove funding from the Brooklyn museum. In his view the work desecrated 'the most personal and deeply held views of people in society' (one can ask of course, which people?). The style of advertising for the exhibition was provocative in advising those with high blood pressure to seek medical advice before attending. Yet the English response was very different. Searle, writing in the Guardian on the original exhibition, describes 'rich and complex [work]... gorgeous, playful parodies of exoticism and ethnicity' (Ellison, 1999).

Closer in parodic intent, and directly linked to DV8 was Michael Arditti's novel, *Easter* published in the year 2000, seven years after he had written a review of DV8 titled *At the Theatre of Blood* (1993). Like Newson, he exposes late twentieth century Christianity in a merciless and shocking manner. His novel is a challenge to believers and non-believers yet carries a recommendation from the then Bishop of Edinburgh. Its parodic fusion of the sacred and profane is a counterpoint to DV8's *Strange Fish*.

Rather more difficult to assess was Neil Bartlett's music theatre piece, *Seven Sacraments. A Dramatic Oratorio* (1998), created with his own company, Gloria. It was performed in Brighton, Southwell and London, each time with a different group of 60-100 school children, but with the same classical singers and with DV8 performers, for example, Wendy Houston, and Shared Experience associates, Jon Owen and Becky Chapman. Indeed Neil Bartlett is perhaps better known for his controversial plays addressing gay issues. It was an odd, yet convincing, juxtaposition of modern politics with religious belief, a paradoxical work which offered something at the level of primary school children while also attracting an audience of adults, many of whom made gender constructs problematic if only by their appearance.

Birtwistle explored the significance of *The Last Supper* for the third millennium in a series of dramatic tableau. He recognises that these are commodified images, already loaded with history, but perhaps no more or less a commodity for sale now than they were in the second, fourth or fifteenth centuries. Recycling myths, adapting them to fit the changing times, is a recurrent past time of ideology-creators, whether these are religious men, politicians or art curators.

Re-cycling myths has also been common among artists themselves throughout history, as revealed in a recent parallel to my own study, John Richardson's *Singing Archaeology* (1999), a fascinating analysis of Philip Glass' *Akhnaten*. Drawing on Greek mythology, he creates a work that ranges from the exposition of large abstract themes to close readings of the opera. He offers musicological detail to support his construction of interpretative statements, linking them to quite specific moments in history. These histories, which are archaeological, mythic and musical, are made directly relevant to, and reflective of each other, and of *Akhnaten*.[2]

I cite this work at several points since my own intention, like Richardson's, is to avoid the pitfalls of interpretations which tell the reader nothing about the work, but more than anyone could want to know about the author's personal history. I also hope to avoid the trap of reading *Strange Fish* simply as a response to its cultural context. I seek also to avoid the globalising tendency to sweep all practices under a fashionable (if attractive) discipline, for example of cultural studies or gender studies, in monolithic fashion without regard to their appropriateness. It would be naïve to assume that any theoretical position could be taken as some kind of universal, and applied across the Performing Arts of Dance, Music and Theatre. Each has a distinctive history and particular points of intersection with cultural practices. They can neither be separated from the wider cultural landscape, nor united in their formal practices. They currently span different parts of another landscape, that of cultural and critical theory, flowing in a multitude of ways for which intertextuality is both a useful metaphor and a practical critical methodology.

Analytic Modes

Dance and Theatre meet in the relatively new field of Performance Studies as cultural acts, events, or practices, under an expanded notion of performance which encompasses street festivals as well as theatre, sports and rituals, staged performances, individual interactions, and political discourse. Schechner's early work (e.g.1990) has been followed by constructions of Performance Studies as a discipline, for example as represented in collections of essays by Reinelt and Roach (1992) and European versions by Campbell (1996) and Huxley and Witts (1996). Berghaus (2001) is the latest. Typically, writers contributing to these texts filter performances of many kinds through the perspectives of cultural studies, feminism, and psychoanalysis creating a site for lively interaction between disciplines through the notion of 'performance'. There are specific implications of these views for Dance, since it operates primarily through the medium of movement, and through highly specified genres, and these are explored fully through my analysis of *Strange Fish*.

Dance Analysis, for its own part, has a number of historical threads. The 'classroom' analysis of the ballet's *danse d'école* or its modern counterpart, the Cunningham technique, has given rise to a form of structural analysis which bears a marked similarity to music analysis (see Jordan 2001). A broadly based Movement Analysis, on the other hand, of the kind developed from Rudolf Laban's work, owes its heritage to the European expressionist theatre. A contextualised 'discipline'-based approach to analysis, employing gender studies, or psychoanalysis, for example, ties Dance in to both Literary and Performance Studies. Ethnography links history and anthropological approaches to analysis of dance practices while post-structuralist theories of the 'text' inform dance analysis in a different way – the subject of this reading of *Strange Fish*.

In my own work in Dance Analysis, which originated at the end of the 1970s, I articulated relationships between analysis of a formalist or structuralist type and theories of interpretation, or ways of 'making sense' of what we see, which recognised the importance of the perspective brought to bear by the reader, and of the texts invoked by the work. In Adshead (1988, ed) the collected essays focused on what happens in the moment of connection that generates sensation, appreciation, and understanding, recognising that it has always depended on the interaction of individuals with the event or work or text *and* on the multiple contexts that both of these envisage and represent (p.87).

However, the absence of a lexicon of movement identifying specific meanings suggests that demonstrable codes, in a one to one relationship, do not exist. Instead, the possibility of another, different, understanding always remains. As Martin states 'the performance event can be grasped only as a process of exchange through the mutual interruption and displacement of narratives' (1998, p.39). These narrative features are at the root of the intertextual approach followed here, both freeing and constraining the reader simultaneously.

Attractive and comforting as it would be to have 'a' theory or better still, 'the' theory of dance analysis, music analysis or theatre analysis, each theoretical position is but one among many interdisciplinary traces. Neither can it be assumed that any methodology used in a discussion of *Strange Fish* is automatically relevant to the analysis of other events. Theories and their accompanying methodological constructs need to be used in as subtle a series of variations as the performance practices themselves which each time give rise to distinctive new works.

As Theatre Studies has moved further from the dramatic text towards theories and practices of Performance Studies a substantial void has appeared across which music rarely steps. Although the term 'performance' proliferates in the discourses of dance, drama and music, it takes very different forms within each of these disciplines and across them. Similarities in the use of the term 'performance' probably only extend to requiring evidence of a specific set, or mix, of technical skills (in the production of sound, voice, movement) and in the interpretative understandings needed to use them in relation to the work of named authors, composers and choreographers or in respect of work in improvisatory modes.

For musicians the concept of performance refers most usually to the act of the performer in giving life to 'music' that exists on a score, possibly including elements which are improvised in performance. For dancers it may have a similar significance in referring to the reconstruction from a 'text' of a kind, but with major differences given the very small number of complete, publicly available, notated scores, the existence of two major systems of notation and the lack of choreographers and dancers able to read either. Performance in this sense is always a doubly interpreted act, the 'text' in the sense of the movement, being taught by another and conveyed via other dancers' memories, or those of viewers or notators outside the dancing.

In modern and postmodern dance (and some forms of ballet) 'performance' takes on many other meanings in common with its use in jazz and non-western forms of music. It is more associated with the personal investment of the individual (whether dancer or choreographer or collaborators) in the creation of a fluid work than with interpreting a fixed text.[3] Connor analyses the doubled meanings of performance, as acting, making or doing something *and as* enacting or impersonating, which then entail notions of imitation, repetition and citation. These senses of performance resonate with contemporary life, 'saturated with and fascinated by techniques of representation and reproduction' (in Campbell, 1996, p.109). Not only are the resulting performances vulnerable as 'works' or 'texts' but they are also lodged in an individual's socially situated and changing experiences, seen more as events than discrete objects. More recently, ideas of the 'performative', allied to the presentation of the self in everyday life, as well as an integral part of the dance performance, have gained ground (Butler, 1990; Case, 1995; 1996).

The Issue of Genre: Situating *Strange Fish*

The subject matter with which Lloyd Newson deals in *Strange Fish* has been tackled by other choreographers in the realm of modern dance over many years. In the UK, but in the Graham tradition, Robert Cohan created *Mass* (1973) and *Stabat Mater* (1975) for London Contemporary Dance Theatre. These works could be seen as religious statements in themselves - no trace of irony was visible for example in the portrayal of Mary in the second of these works. The questioning of male/female roles, and the recognition that biological sexuality is not a straightforward guarantee of gender identity, had already encouraged a revisiting of the construction of both male and female characters in theatre and dance but it was not apparent in mainstream modern dance. By 1980 Fergus Early and Jacky Lansley, part of the X6 Collective, produced *I, Giselle,* reversing male and female roles, to an electronic transformation of the well known music by Adam (Jordan, 1992). Lansley continued to make versions of the classics, predating the more recent but much more successful works (in the commercial as well as artistic sense) by Matthew Bourne and Mats Ek. The attempt at faithful reproduction of the past has been replaced by a knowing re-appraisal of how 'the past' has been constructed to suit the teller of the story. While many versions of the classics create new steps or designs while essentially telling the same story, they can also tell different stories, using many of the same elements but in a way that makes its own techniques and prejudices visible. Such a method may involve parody, violence to the 'original', and ironic commentary as well as a re-location of the work in time and place.

These practices are highly relevant to my discussion of *Strange Fish* in which I ask how it comments on and reconstructs 'the story' of Christ. It uses well-known moments and images from the story of his life and draws on the morality found in biblical tales. Further, *Strange Fish* picks up the increasing cultural visibility and legality of 'alternative' genders. Meanwhile, and in ironic contrast, it challenges Christian views of morality at a time of discomfort for the Church. Evidence emerges of explicit homosexuality (not illegal but not accepted in the Christian Church), of child abuse and the fathering of illegitimate children. This evidence, within the higher reaches of a Church supposedly untainted by such things, invites the view that theological attacks on different forms of sexuality are mendacious and dishonest. I go on to suggest later in my analysis that Lloyd Newson's portrayal of male/female relationships is equally double-coded.

The idea of flexibility of coding is key to intertextuality and ties in closely to issues of genre analysis. Discussion of 'coding' is embedded in a semiotic approach but also in much post-structuralist theorising and it is the shift from the one to the other that is highly significant. 'Codes', understood in some forms of semiotics as constructing a direct signifier/signified relationship and an unequivocal meaning, open up new relationships, introducing irony, parody and wild juxtaposition that might initiate new traces. Genre has become problematic in recent arts debate yet the questions it raises are a vital part of analysis. Suspicion that genre categorisation might simply be a means of creating a canon of valued works while dismissing 'the rest' has long been in need of Frow's recent reassessment (2006). It is difficult in an era when the very notion of similarity between works/texts, which genre relies on, is less popular than that of difference and pluralism, which post-structuralism promotes. Post-structuralist analysis demands a highly self-conscious critical method that exposes its own assumptions, its values and its processes, in the interests of exploring the many possible constructions of meaning. Such a method, in turn, rests on increasingly sophisticated categories of difference. Pluralism does not itself deny or invalidate genre-based readings. Indeed the very idea of pluralism rests on increasingly fine distinctions being made through specifying similarity and difference, in order to establish the particularity or individuality of the work.

In a practical way, the subject matter of this analysis of *Strange Fish* contributes to recent and topical debates within Physical Theatre, as a relatively new type of performance practice, where theory is as yet poorly developed and genre categories tend to be crudely constructed. It aims to articulate a method of analysis where generic links are crucial but not dominant. The obvious links with theatre and dance are, however, many and varied, adding complexity to the process. In this context a more sophisticated analysis of a single example may prove useful.

Questions of narrative are inescapably intertwined with issues of genre in the sense that how narrative is understood at specific moments depends upon broader cultural movements of modernism and postmodernism. The debate about types of postmodernism and their relationship (oppositional or not) to modernism is similar across all the arts (Hutcheon, 1998; Usher and Edwards, 1994). These issues are far from resolved, and they are highly relevant in a discussion of Lloyd Newson's work. I ask if Newson's work shares features in this respect with my parallel example of *Akhnaten*. In illustration of this modernist/postmodernist shift, Richardson argues that '*Akhnaten*...has a powerful subtext that addresses precisely the problematic relationship between postmodernism and its modern antecedents' (1999, p.26). Glass exposes points of difference from contemporary modes of serialism, which are evident in the lack of linear continuity within the larger whole of the work. Instead, local, surface-level, structural considerations are dominant. Despite the surface level interest, Richardson also argues that the postmodern musicians he discusses 'do not conceive of what they do as politically neutral pastiche; there is always an urgent political subtext to their work just as in the postmodern dance' (p.32) if only initially to critique the organicist whole. Thus what began as an oppositional postmodernism can be seen moving into the eclectic and relational strains of recent years, while nonetheless retaining a critical edge. I explore this parallel later in relation to Jocelyn Pook's music for *Strange Fish*, since she acknowledges Glass' influence and her own music challenges convention in its use of classical, folk, and pop music elements. The political sub-text here is whether she can 'count' as a classical musician or a 'cross-over' musician – both complex and suspect categories - but sufficiently rigid for her CD 'Deluge' to be disqualified from both charts (Weller, 2001).[4]

The axis is different for Lloyd Newson but the question is similar - how far his work might be seen as a continuation of expressionist dance theatre of the late 1980s through to the early 1990s – itself an extension of European expressionist modernism of the 1930s. Whether his work is more clearly aligned to the post-war theatre of Bausch, for example, or to recent European forms of postmodernism is significant in setting up the traces of the mosaic that the analysis explores. The answer must depend on how one characterises this kind of modernism (the European theatrical kind e.g. of recent Belgian exponents, not the North American abstract expressionist version) and how postmodernism is viewed. Both lend themselves to a variety of definitional positions, most clearly revealed in the debates surrounding the concepts of narrative and discourse, which I develop further in Chapter 2.

It might be thought that questions of genre in music are peculiar to its classical forms, but there is evidence that they dominate in popular music, too, as the Pook example referred to above indicates. From these ideas I draw out the necessity of close, genre-informed, reading of selected texts if any depth of understanding is to result. Writing on his own education, the theorist of Heavy Metal Music, Walser, states that

> as a musician, I cannot help but think that individual texts, and the social experiences they represent, are important. My apprenticeships as a performer...were periods spent learning musical discourses. That is, I had to acquire the ability to recognize, distinguish, and deploy the musical possibilities organised in styles or genres by various communities...becoming a musician...is a process of learning to understand and manipulate the differences intrinsic to a style, which are manifested differently in each text and performance.
>
> Walser, 1993. p.xii

Whether from the position of a performer or a spectator I argue that there can be no escape from this detailed study not just in music but in any of the performing arts. We need to understand the discourses, the narratives that the text operates through and also to understand how the individual reader constructs particular performances.[5] These two senses are reflected in Barbara Johnson's 'classic' study *The Critical Difference*. The telling of a story, and the story of the telling, as she describes the problem, exposes two equally seductive narratives - that with which the work is concerned, and that which the reader constructs (1980, p.7). Within each of these narratives are many stories. To mention a few of those relevant to *Strange Fish* – it can be said to be 'about' Angels, Sirens, Christian liturgy, parties, AIDS, drowning, men and women. It is 'about' the fragment, the slice, the cut-up version, the violence of deconstructive methods. It is 'about' whatever Lloyd Newson and his collaborators individually think it is about, notably the depth of their own involvement; just as it is 'about' whatever the critics, and you and I, think.

Firstly it is necessary to situate Lloyd Newson and the work of DV8 Physical Theatre within the broad genre categories established by dance critics in the 1980s and 1990s. In a series of articles which sketch the contemporary mood of particular periods Constanti (1987) Burnside (1992) and Parry (1996-7) describe the range of current work in dance and dance theatre and attempt to draw out similarities and differences through the construction of category systems. While these are brief articles they serve the purpose of illustrating the application of genre concepts, revealing both in their advantages and disadvantages. They map the dance (not theatre) scene into which *Strange Fish* emerged.

Prime sites for re-evaluation of genre and style boundaries are often found in Festivals presenting new work or presenting a large amount of work in a short period, such as those of Dance Umbrella and Spring Loaded (both London events). The above articles register a ten-year shift across the British dance scene at the time at which Lloyd Newson's 'physical theatre' emerges. Burnside writes about 1980s-1990s British 'contemporary dance' and in this category she places Richard Alston, Laurie Booth, Rosemary Butcher and Siobhan Davies, valuing them as original and mature voices. Although recognising that they do not together make a 'united school of thought based on a common philosophy', she suggests they nonetheless share a 'cultural and social heritage which has influenced their absorption and transformation of contemporary dance' (1992, p.42). Their transformations are seen to share certain qualities and concerns, notably in the integration of 'the elements of production [that] separates these collaborations from the 'jarring juxtapositions of other European work' (p.42) and to have certain distinctive preoccupations which contrast starkly with North American contemporary dance and with dance theatre in other parts of Europe.

Further similarities, she argues, are revealed in the construction of a 'determined neutrality' (p.42) through

> abstraction, technical exploration rather than innovation, examination of the formal properties of dance in performance, collaborations exploring the relationship between theatrical elements.
>
> Burnside, 1992, p.31

Almost in the same breath she remarks on the conspicuous absence of the kind of 'dramatic narrative...emotional expression and sexual relations...shock tactics...political ideology...raw athletic physicality' found across the rest of Europe and typically credited to Lloyd Newson (p.31). Burnside draws up the parameters of what might be termed a distinct style, which she likens to 'the exposition, modulation and recapitulation of a musical score' rather than 'Aristotelian cathartic theatre' (p.32), in order to differentiates between each of the four choreographers. The grounds on which she does this are, for example, the degree of dedication 'to exploring the formal properties of the dance medium'. She suggests this is most obvious in the work of Rosemary Butcher where 'intellectual pleasure in their patterning and a sensual enjoyment of the smooth textures of the movement and the colour range' are most evident (p.32). This relates to (but does not match entirely) a long-standing historical tendency for dance to aspire to the condition of music rather than to become theatre, the fundamental paradox for dance, from abstraction of line and form to expression of the individual personality or the social condition.

An 'elegant and reticent aesthetic' but one based on a wider range of themes or moods is seen to characterise Siobhan Davies' 'bodies in motion', building a 'corporate psyche' rather than individual personalities (p.32). Within a world of movement, however, 'a wider world is invoked' and a 'larger canvas of human suffering' (she refers to *Arctic Heart* and *Different Trains*) than Rosemary Butcher ever creates. Laurie Booth, she argues, contrasts most obviously with the other three in deriving his movement from martial arts, physical theatre and contact improvisation but sharing the eliciting of response from 'the physical embodiment of the work and not through emotional engagement. Like Rosemary Butcher then, there is no illusion to be accepted' (p.33).[6]

Roughcut, the work by Richard Alston that Burnside discusses, is hardly typical, although sharing with his other works 'technically demanding, physical exploration' which requires 'swift, clean execution and vital energy'. She argues that his work has a greater range of reference to narrative elements, representation and literary themes than any of the other three choreographers in this group, although his most highly acclaimed pieces are 'abstract and self-referential' (p.33). Pursuing this elaboration of differences allows the criteria on which Burnside bases her stylistic judgements to emerge more clearly.

Constanti counterbalances Burnside by considering very different types of work in the 1987 Spring Loaded festival at The Place which, she argues, reveal

> two opposing schools of thought...dance which appears to be based (naïvely?) on gratuitous pyrotechnics...[and] the retaliatory movement stemming from a vigorous personal/social/political stance
>
> 1987, p.26

She refers to *Images* and *La Bouche* in the first case and Emilyn Claid, Liz Aggiss and DV8 in the second. Reluctance to let 'tragedy become beautiful' is shared by this second group. 'Hard hitting and compulsive' realism and physical/emotional risk-taking feature strongly. Unexpected shifts in the borderlines between 'witty nonsense' and 'vicious parody' make Lea Anderson's work for the *Cholmondeleys* clearly her own while sharing some of these other characteristics in its

> rich, abstract vocabulary, the secret cues and whispers are built into a weird, hermeneutic grid of movement, magically sustained by the infernal animation of Drostan Madden's music – a blend of Velvet Underground, saxophone...and accordion.
>
> p.28[7]

Nearly ten years later, in 1996, Jann Parry tries to assess what constitutes cutting edge work in Britain as the 1990s approach their end, which she does by reflecting mainly on the diversity within what she terms 'new dance'. She finds a concern with constructing narrative, a trend towards spectacle and theatre, although not in the American 'victim art' form. She sees dance at this time as not very radical, rather a 'paler, safer, softer version of experiments that originated elsewhere' whether in Butoh or contact improvisation (1996-7, p.69).

Nonetheless she constructs a number of categories within which to consider new work and spans a huge field; firstly, *ballet-derived work* as in the newly re-formed Ballet Rambert under Christopher Bruce; secondly, a category which she names by two individuals, Richard Alston and Siobhan Davies, as the creators of modernist, developed versions of established contemporary dance techniques, both commissioning music, both carrying implicit rather than explicit emotional and narrative content. The highly physical approach of what are sometimes called *Eurocrash* companies typifies a third group. Anne Teresa De Keersmaeker, Wim Vandekeybus and Claude Brumachon are seen to belong here but so, too, are circus-trained groups. She groups dancers who use *martial arts*, including Laurie Booth and Russell Maliphant, as a fourth stream; while a fifth category, of *English Eccentrics* 'includes an assortment of choreographers whose work is highly idiosyncratic' (p.71). Here she refers to vastly different individuals from Javier de Frutos to Julyen Hamilton, and including Wayne McGregor, Matthew Hawkins, Yolande Snaith, Lea Anderson, Liz Aggiss and Jonathan Burrows. '*Mature performers,*' whom she groups separately, include Misha Baryshnikov, and Fergus Early. To this amorphous group of categories she adds *Club and rave culture* (Bunty Matthias); *Text-based work* (Nigel Charnock, V-Tol and Second Stride); *Cross-cultural/intercultural* groups (Vivarta festivals, and Shobana Jeyasingh, Peter Badejo); and finally *New Technology dance* (Mark Baldwin).

Such attempts at categorisation reveal the frailty of the exercise and it is hardly surprising that it is often derided. The criteria are mixed in type, there is little apparent logic. However, Parry's attempt suggests a need for more precise analysis rather than for dismissing the exercise as fruitless, while also illustrating how difficult it is to capture trends and changes within their own lifetime. What it does reveal very clearly is that in each example a different set of genre codes operate to create different value systems against which critics (and readers) construct their own views. The very existence of such articles is witness to spectators' and critics' needs to group works in order to explain or account for them, seeing their inter-relationships as a way of understanding them. Physical Theatre, the general category into which Lloyd Newson and DV8 are usually placed, emerges clearly as a distinctive type of work of the 1980s and 1990s. From these characterisations of genre, as essentially a set of relational concepts, it is possible to expose affinities and distinctions between genres and within genres.

In an extended research study, Christine Lark situates physical theatre within the European context and narrows the focus to the emergence of a particular 1980s form in British theatre (1999). She then uses concepts of subject matter and treatment to track Newson's works. She refers to similarities between works from the level of movement detail to the grand scheme of each piece. In doing so, features emerge that serve to distinguish Lloyd Newson's Physical Theatre from that of the practitioners described by Burnside, Constanti and Parry. In sum DV8s work can be allied closely to theatre, taking the works as a group, although *Strange Fish* is an interesting exception in its attention to the musical landscape, as further analysis reveals.

It is equally pertinent to examine the genre-base as revealed in critics' writings on *Strange Fish*, positioning their own 'authorial' voices. 'This is total theatre - do anything to get a ticket' was Edward Thorpe's unequivocal critical response to the London performance of *Strange Fish*, a response that was typical across the critical community although differently expressed. To ask the question who are these critics – to clarify who it is who writes about DV8 – is to articulate a dance-specific and theatre-specific response, which varies depending on the age, preferences and long-held views of the individual. Well-known national critics of ballet and contemporary dance are cited here to examine similarities and differences in view and to analyse reasons given for these views.

How readers construct the subject of a work, and how they analyse the way it is treated, are also significant indicators of genre. In this next section I illustrate this general point and demonstrate though these critical perspectives that much is uncontroversially shared. There is general agreement about what *Strange Fish* takes as its subject matter – which coincides in some, but not all, respects with Lloyd Newson's view. But there is also significant difference in how critics see the relative importance of themes and how they describe the treatment of the material, and this emerges through discussion. Underlying the critics' perspectives are their own positions on life, art, sex and the possibility of spirituality in a consumerist, agnostic Britain of the 1980s and 1990s. It is possible to reveal these readers' genre codes and personal preferences as they influence interpretive choices by contrasting a reading which constructs *Strange Fish* as a theatre of religious parable with one which sees it as a theatre of dramatic expression, a third which focuses on a psychoanalytic reading exposing alienation, and a fourth highlighting a theatre of sexual politics.

A Theatre of Religious Parable

Jann Parry sees Lloyd Newson as a subtle manipulator, first challenging perceptions by 'tackling violent sexual relationships head-on' then more deviously,

> engaging our sympathies so that we submitted willingly to his apocalyptic vision of the human condition. *Strange Fish* is even more cunning, because we respond with laughter that dies in the throat. We giggle at the mating games of over-sexed adolescents and cringe at crashing party bore Nigel Charnock...neither we nor the players realise until too late that these cravings for physical intimacy at any price are deadly.
>
> Parry, 1992a

Tying her own response directly into this (through the use of 'we') reveals the level at which Newson gets through to an audience, even the professional critic (often thought sceptical) is swept into his narrative. Parry is prepared overall to be generous in her review and concludes that the message, however harrowing,

> is transmitted with such vigour, by such formidable performers, that hope rather than a virus surely lingers within the walls of the set. The Christian imagery, even the word 'harrowing', holds the promise (however hard to believe) of salvation from hell.
>
> 1992a

Parry (1992b) takes the opportunity in a longer article than the newspaper review cited earlier (1992a) to develop this idea, and it becomes apparent that she is a critic who is highly conscious of the religious intertexts of the piece. She expresses surprise that other critics made so little of it, and argues that

> *Strange Fish* starts with a Day of Judgement scene and continues in the shadow of the Cross, and the Judeo-Christian ethic it represents.
>
> The direction of their effortful journey implies redemption: no one is cast down, so instead of condemning sinners, this female Christ

> might be saving them. In the medieval Mystery Plays Christ harrowed hell before he rose again from the dead, rescuing righteous souls from damnation: *Strange Fish* embraces that sense of 'harrowing' as well as the word's more familiar meaning.
>
> Parry 1992b p.24

Parry specifically reminds the audience of morality and of death. Similarly, in her analysis of Wendy Houstoun's character, Parry emphasises the 'humiliation she suffers for her 'sexual "sin"' although she problematises this idea by the use of the bracketing with quotation marks. Referring to the 'stoning of a wrong-doer' is direct biblical connotation. She is one of few critics who sustains the religious theme rather than referring to it and then to a multiplicity of other themes, talking about Pappenheim hanging 'crucified', and referring to her directly as 'Christ' (p.27).

Parry is able to move away from such an immediate response to say that DV8 Physical Theatre deals in 'ambiguity' – not much apparent from the initial critical reviews of 1992 – for example in citing the image of water as something that 'both sustains and kills' (p.24). Again, in discussion of Wendy's role as siren she opens up the scene where she urges Nigel to fly, asking

> does she want to kill him or have sex with him? (Flying is, after all, a Freudian metaphor for the sexual act). When he does eventually plummet down...she ignores him...She tries again, however, towards the end of the piece, while he ropes himself to the cross – a Christian seeking salvation, or Odysseus tying himself to the mast to resist the sirens' song.
>
> Parry, 1992b, p.26

Strange Fish is, she concludes, a 'theatre of parable' (itself a biblical construct), in which 'multi-layered meaning can be conveyed through imagery, as it was to congregations who understood pictures better than words' (p.27). She is not alone; Bill Harpe in a short review of the Manchester production refers to what he calls the 'visionary' creation of DV8 in this way, rescuing it for Christianity:

> this may not be a sexual vision which the Christian Church would approve of, but it is an essentially Christian vision. [It] accepts that sex, like life, is a vale of tears. It may be a joke – and this work certainly has its very funny moments – but it's a poor joke.
>
> Harpe, 1992

Neither does Dromgoole (1992) find it much of a joke. Although not noted for his enthusiasm for physical theatre, he is nonetheless among a generation of older ballet/modern dance critics who finds much to commend in DV8s work, since it conforms to certain genre conventions allied to dramatic dance, but he finds less in *Strange Fish* than he found in previous works. Among the adjectives he selects for this work are 'brilliant.. innovative...clever...effective use of movement...superb moments of choreography' but finally states that their claim to reinvest meaning in dance is 'pointless if all there is to say are a few trite observations about how people hurt each other when desiring each other'. One of the basic sets of values underpinning his distaste can be found in this revealing phrase, referring to the female semi-naked 'Christ', saying that 'the Church is pilloried from the start'. He continues, perhaps in a sense justifying his own or others' continuing Christian belief:

> perhaps the Church is out of tune with the times in emphasising that sex is a part of marriage and family, but DV8 are wildly out of touch with the times in presenting a work about sex and relationships which behaves as though neither marriage nor the producing of children exist in fact, or in anybody's head either.

His view, which might seem essentially conservative is that 'in the natural course of things, lovers are transformed into parents', a position clearly at odds with a gay culture, and with many partnerships at the end of the twentieth century in their challenge to 'the natural course of things'.

A Theatre of Dramatic Expression

John Percival, a British dance critic of very long standing, who enthusiastically heralded and supported the British modern dance development as expressionist theatre in the late 1960s and through the 1970s, sums up Newson's achievements, saying that he

> at last provides a theatrical experience that can seriously be measured, for its physical and emotional daring, its complexity and intelligence, against Pina Bausch's work...for all its desolate picture of people vainly seeking friendship or love, the production is also hilariously funny...not an evasion of the seriousness, but an enrichment of it...this production makes most of our new-wave choreography look like kid's stuff.
>
> 1992

Edward Thorpe (1992) calls the work 'astonishing' because of its 'haunting imagery, its humour, its drama, its often frightening extremes of physicality and several visual surprises' enhanced by Peter J Davison's set, of

> a wooden wall with doors, windows, traps, hand and foot holds, ladders and ledges, creates a fascinating *mise en scene* for the non-stop action, as indeed, does the stage itself with more traps, subterranean passages and tanks of water.

Clement Crisp, also usually more than a little sceptical of new performance, applauds *Strange Fish* in no uncertain terms. I quote in full from his review since it articulates the 'unholy alliance' of postmodernist practices with extreme theatricality and expression of the pain of life. The seriousness of the work is obviously appealing, its emotional intensity is applauded, and the power of its performance is a crucial factor in Crisp's interpretation.

Strange Fish 31 July 1992 Clement Crisp

> In the six years of its existence DV8 has produced vivid and thought-provoking work that has explored the idea of "physical theatre". DV8's creations have charted areas of social and sexual politics – from the bleak homosexual desire of *Dead Dreams of Monochrome Men* to the pursuit of dreams and desires in *if only*. In everything, there has been the match of technical daring with emotional bravado: if it is not perched on the edge of the perilous, DV8 seems to say, then it's not worth doing. And if it does not challenge its theme - and its audiences' preconceptions – then it is not worthy of DV8's idealism.
>
> There has resulted a body of work that stands at the fore-front of British dance and, surely, of British theatre, by reason of the dazzling use of the ensemble's gifts – the pieces are usually a collective creation – and by the zeal of Lloyd Newson, DV8's director, to push further and further into that most dangerous territory, the human psyche. Now DV8 has brought its latest creation, *Strange Fish*, to Riverside Studios. The title is owed to the Buddhist saying that we should be as ignorant of what we are going to catch as a fisherman of what is at the end of his line. The argument concerns the nature of our quest to find someone to love (though DV8 does not believe in tame gazelles or gentle doves) and something or some one to

believe in. The staging is – and in this lies an acute fascination – exactly of our time In gauging the forms through which this quest may be understood, and the terms in which disillusion will manifest itself.

We see a boarded stage in front of a wooden facade (excellent design by Peter J Davison) which has windows, doors, a ladder and small apertures which will enable the cast to find hand and foot holds for the more acrobatic moments of the action. As the action begins, drifting mist reveals a cross from which hangs the Christ-figure of the singer Melanie Pappenheim. Through the gloom a crowd of naked bodies climb across the stage and into the facade of the building. The tiny, elf-like figure of Diana Payne Myers, a fascinating performer despite her sixty-something years, lights candles at the foot of the cross. Wendy Houstoun, that thrillingly intense dancer, whirls and falls, holding a wine-glass which she constantly fails to seize with her other hand. A door opens to reveal Diana Payne Myers worshipping a crucifix in front of a gushing wash-basin. The stage brightens to bring on other members of the cast – Jordi Cortes Molina, Nigel Charnock, Dale Tanner, Lauren Potter, Kate Champion – who mime, exchange physical babble, flirt, pick up and drop each other (in every sense) as a tango rings out.

I have detailed this opening section since it contains images which will recur throughout the 90 minutes of the piece. They are in no way shocking – though Disgusted of Tunbridge Wells may not be too happy – but they are provocative in the very best terms of DV8's creative imagination. The performance process is to confront each member of the cast – and each of us – with the failure of belief, of love, with the corruption and extinction of hope and desire. *Strange Fish* is pessimistic – in an interview Lloyd Newson quoted Francis Bacon's comment that he "believed in nothing but was eternally optimistic" – yet it takes a compassionate view of its crises and of the human condition. It is riven with moments of wild humour and galvanised both by stunning theatrical coups and stunning performances from its cast.

Speech is minimally used, notably by Nigel Charnock as the gabbling unwanted guest, desperately trying to be loved – "People are my hobby. I'm a people person" – and insinuating himself between pairs of lovers. A duet for Lauren Potter and Jordi Cortes Molina is a transcendental study in movement curving and oiling itself through bodies. Houston sticks two feathers on Charnock's shoulders, leads him to a window, and urges him to fly – and heart-stoppingly he plunges down. (Freudians will recognise the sexual connotation). Intercourse between Houstoun and Tanner degenerates into frantic masturbation by the man as a torrent of stones suddenly pour on to the stage and Houstoun starts to flail and writhe among them. The images resonate throughout the action and we make connections, and know the despair that lies at the heart of the work. The closing section Is fiercely daring. Charnock has roped himself to the Cross. Rejected by the other members of the cast, Houstoun has torn up part of the stage floor, to reveal subterranean waters. She teases Charnock. He flees from her through trapdoors but she at last releases him from the cross and they plunge into the water. Melanie Pappenheim appears, supporting Dale Tanner as if holding a Christ from a Deposition. Houstoun emerges from the water and wanders over the empty stage. She takes a glass of wine, climbs up the cross where Pappenheim again hangs, pours wine on her, kisses her, and after a desperate search for Charnock, balances herself upon the last wine-glasses. The light dies and we can take no comfort from what we have seen.

In the matter of performance, the evening is unflawed. The playing of the ensemble – the brilliant conflict and complementing of personalities; the shared sense of risk and trust; the acuteness of timing and physical response – is matched by an emotional awareness that is dazzlingly communicative. One may argue with the work's premises – its denial of faith, of the enduring power of human relationships – but there can be no argument about the astonishing force of its realisation and performance. To Lloyd Newson and his cast, admiration and gratitude. The fine score and soundtracks are, respectively by Jocelyn Pook and Adrian Jackson (*sic - actually Johnston).* Admirable lighting is by Steve Whitson. Not to be missed.

© Clement Crisp *Financial Times* (31st July, 1992)

A Theatre of Alienation

In both Parry and Crisp's writings there is more than a hint of another strand of theories of both the author and the reader derived from the field of psychoanalysis. The relationships *Strange Fish* sets up can be understood by virtue of a shared emotional vocabulary which finds expression in everyday life in bodily posture, in facial expression, in the way we move. Nadine Meisner gives a quite specific account of this kind in describing the duet between Lauren Potter and Jordi Molina in Scene 5. It starts with arms clasped and continues that way 'so there is a sense of intimacy, but also entrapment, and perhaps dependency as well' (1992, p.11). Clearly this is a meaning that is shared and which is based on the physical hand clasp which is never relinquished in the duet.

Questions of how interpretations are constructed relative to an individual sense of identity produce a paradox, that the self becomes a function of interpretative strategies. The self is as illusory as the text and as the author. The reader in this account exists within constraints of both a personal, linguistic, and social character. The importance of language, rejected by both the formalist art movement and by psychoanalysis in favour of a subjective, subconscious world, returns to pre-eminence in a new sense.

A point of interest here lies in the consistency of interpretation of the characters portrayed by the performers, and the apparent conflation of the actual people, Wendy, Nigel et al with their roles in this piece. Since Diana Payne-Myers is *not* a nun it would seem naïve to say that she is, in some sense, herself. Rather, she is using her own experience and views to create a character. Parry (1992a) refers to the 64 year old Diana Payne-Myers as the 'ubiquitous crone' and Percival (1992) as a 'game old bird'. These terms are not meant to refer directly to her personality, as known to friends and colleagues, but to a constructed character. The distance required to construct a character, rather than to identify the self with the character, sits rather oddly with Newson's view that his performers are profoundly 'themselves'.

Similarly, while Wendy Houstoun is referred to by name within the work, she is plainly not 'herself'. Watson (1992a) reads her as 'a devil who only dreamed of being an angel', as 'a regal pain in the ass', and as, literally, 'a living kiss of death'. Brennan (1992) reads Wendy as 'raw and unfinished...she wants to have her identity reflected back through others'. Parry (1992a) sees her as someone 'who should be shunned like the plague, for that is what she is *la rage*, the Black Death, AIDS'.

The specifics of the interpretative construct may vary but the deduction common to all, which Newson and his collaborators clearly 'foresee' in the making of this work, is of a character who is wicked, evil personified, by evoking stereotypes familiar to most western readers. There is no disagreement either with Watson (1992a) who sees Jordi Cortes as 'a limb-twisting serpent of lust', a reading based on codes derived from everyday sensual behaviour and its exaggeration in the theatre in many previous productions. Similarly, for Parry (1992a) Dale Tanner is 'the stud' of the group. Watson (1992a) describes him as an all-too-believable narcissist'. Using exactly the same words, Constanti (1992) calls him the man 'whose every muscle definition is a work of art, [and who] stars as a prize narcissist' just as Nugent (1992) refers to Dale Tanner 'boast[ing] to the audience about the bits of his body that he likes best, from his shoulders to the "versatile ass that is my favourite bit"'.

For most critics the men are seen to 'fall victim to their own vanity and sexuality' rather more than the women (Parry 1992b, p.25), reflecting a still-popular view that men can't control their impulses while women can, and should, otherwise they risk another stereotype, that of 'whore'. The Virgin/Whore binary is inescapable even in late twentieth century Europe where equal opportunities, harassment and discrimination legislation has been enacted. Indeed, Parry sees Melanie Pappenheim not only as 'Christ' but also as the 'Virgin Mary' (1992b p.24). I refer to her as both guardian angel and avenging angel in my own accounts. She is sensuality personified, encapsulating male fears of women as dangerous because of both their purity and their immorality.

For Constanti (1992) Nigel is 'a social embarrassment, hyperactive, a loony', his every utterance a 'cliché'. He behaves like 'a serial molester'. She introduces another analogy – likening this work to a 'ship of fools'. Percival (1992) responds to these people as a group as 'sad loners' (particularly Wendy Houstoun and Nigel Charnock) and to Lauren Potter as a 'shy, sly girl on the edge of things'.

Newson, himself, is clearly aware of the metaphoric implications of some of the images he employs e.g. in using water under the floorboards 'as a metaphor for the subconscious and for those things that are below the surface' (Meisner, 1992, p.12). Many critics were content to pick up his view of meaning. His own readings include the obviously psychological reference of sailors, tied to a post, giving rise to phallic symbolism. These interpretive strategies seem to fall within the tradition of a Brechtian dance-drama, revealing of the modern character, with the full force of twentieth century alienation strongly felt.

A Theatre of Sexual Politics

Of a different generation from Crisp, Dromgoole and Percival, is Keith Watson who has written extensively and supportively about DV8 over a period of time, championing the work in a way that would lead a reader to suppose that he identifies closely with them. He wrote the programme notes for *Strange Fish* (1992) which contained a lengthy essay on previous works and on the company's view of their mission in life. Watson starts with a clear enough commendation saying ' Dance was dead on its feet until DV8 came along' and aligns them with unusual companions (for dance):

> a decade after The Clash and The Sex Pistols had spat and snarled angry new life into rock music, stopping the safe and sentimental in its tracks, here was a brand of physical theatre unafraid of nailing its colours to the mast: political and sexy, DV8 was a gale force wind across the becalmed seas of abstraction that dance was paddling in.
>
> 1992

Keith Watson's powerful language elaborates codes from which viewers can reconstruct his logic. In summary his view is that *Strange Fish* is 'enthralling dance theatre that marries an epic sweep with personal insight'. In turn the viewer's constructs can be exposed. The viewer's ability to 'read' the codes of any dance form will depend upon their familiarity with that genre. It will also depend upon their support for, or antagonism to, the kind of world that is evoked in *Strange Fish*. More widely it will depend upon the positioning of the viewer in relation to work which comments freely upon important matters of belief.[8]

As a final analogy linking contemporary physical theatre to contemporary music through a politics of sex, I refer again to Walser's study of Heavy Metal music (1993) in which he demonstrates the significance of sophisticated genre constructs. He discusses marketing heavy metal on tour, in CD form, and on merchandise, arguing that unless these products match the subtleties of fans' ever-changing definitions of difference they are unlikely to succeed. Each version or style, within the genre, picks up different threads of heavy metal's historical texts to position itself quite precisely even while denying the need to categorise in this way. What is interesting in Walser's text is the evidence he gives to support the idea of rapidly changing forms of the genre and the dedication of its aficionados to analysing its shifts in minute detail. 'Genre is dead, long live genre' would seem to be the message.

Mirroring the increasingly fast commercial development and production time of new products, Heavy Metal condenses time shifts in its endless genre changes. It is a modernist commonplace that what took 100 years to evolve in pre-modern times took 10 years in modern times and in postmodern times, 10 days or even 10 minutes. The resulting fragmentation became evident in Heavy Metal's history after only twenty years (its start is generally thought to be in 1968) with a proliferation of forms known as thrash metal, commercial metal, lite metal, power metal, American metal, black (satanic) metal, white (Christian) metal, death metal, speed metal, glam metal (p.13), each connected to the history of Heavy Metal in different ways.

Bringing together a textual analysis with ethnographic material and cultural studies it may be possible to arrive at a more informed analysis that moves beyond global generalisation - in Walser's case of Heavy Metal and in mine of *Strange Fish* - and to some extent the field of Physical Theatre. Such a method also demonstrates the continuing importance of the concept of genre, and brings into relief its social contestation and transformation. Thus the 'ancestral' genre constructs and the 'authorial' voices of collaborators (Chapter 2) respectively serve to create several versions of *Strange Fish*, to give it form and structure in different ways. Differences arise depending upon the theory of art that prevails, the personal interests of the participants and spectators, and the constructs of genre and style operating within a group of works and among dance makers at a specific time.

A Poetics

This book adds to the literature of a transient art, framing it within emergent theoretical disciplines and research methodologies. It operates through a demonstration of the logic(s) of texture and of connectivity between 'intrinsic' details of the actions and events of a work, located within the bigger cultural themes on which it draws. More precisely, in its specific focus on DV8's work, it documents and analyses contemporary and contentious performance practices. In this Scylla and Charybdis of troubled waters there are also the rocks and subterranean currents where danger of drowning lies. Drowning, in writing in the arts, is sometimes the consequence of minutely detailed step-by-boring-step, formalist description of action, with neither cultural positioning, nor contextualisation nor justification apparent. At the other extreme the writer may drown by wallowing in an endless sea of undigested and often spurious generalisation unconnected to the work in question.

These watery metaphors are deliberate, since *Strange Fish* evokes many variations on this theme. It is a small intertextual move from fish to sirens and angels in the Greek and Christian traditions of Western Europe and one which is highly appropriate to this discussion. In a key shift from structuralism to what might be called 'poetics' Roland Barthes uses the biblical story of Jacob in Genesis 32 under the heading of 'The Struggle with the Angel' as a site of analysis and it provides me with a useful and apposite starting point given its many resonances. Barthes announces his agenda in this way:

> the structural analysis presented here will not be very pure...referring in the main to the principles shared by all those semiologists concerned with narrative...I shall allow myself...to direct my investigations towards...textual analysis...used with reference to the contemporary theory of the text, this being understood as the production of significance and not as philological object...such an analysis endeavours to 'see' each particular text in its difference – which does not mean in its ineffable individuality, for this difference is 'woven' in familiar codes; it conceives the text as taken up in an *open* network which is the very infinity of language, itself structured without closure; it tries to say no longer *from* where the text comes (historical criticism), nor even *how* it is made (structural analysis) but how it is unmade, how it explodes, disseminates – by what coded paths it *goes off*.
>
> 1977, p. 126-127

Stravinsky, in his *Poetics of Music* (1947, p.4) traces 'poetics' back to Aristotle but he also offers his own characterisation of poetics as 'making'. While his concern was with things of his own making, mine is with how we all 'make' the work we watch or dance or act in. Hutcheon, in her excellent book *A Poetics of Postmodernism* (1988), constructs 'poetics' in a way that is more relevant for our own time and which is informed by theoretical views of the modernism/ postmodernism debate. She avoids arguments of causality and instead offers 'provisional hypotheses, perceived overlappings of concern' between the arts and between the arts and theory, 'reading literature through surrounding theoretical discourses rather than as continuous with theory', and being observant of the contradictions of postmodernism. 'It is both a way of speaking – a discourse – and a cultural process involving the expression of thought that a poetics would seek to articulate' (p.14). In a dialogue with the past, which is neither naïve nor sentimental, she suggests that postmodernism 'confront[s] and contest[s] any modernist discarding *or* recuperating of the past in the name of the future...it suggests...a re-evaluation of and dialogue with the past in the light of the present'. And finally Hutcheon identifies the issues that 'define this poetics (or problematics) of postmodernism: historical knowledge, subjectivity, narrativity, reference, textuality, discursive context' (p.231).

The historical knowledge that links Hutcheon's theory to that of Barthes relates to the struggle with the angel as a familiar episode in Biblical and mythical narrative. It is a story commonly retold in the arts, entailing the overcoming of an obstacle or even, as Barthes puts it, an 'Ordeal' (often by water, or fire). In *Strange Fish* there are similar ordeals to those endured by Jacob, not only physically but also psychologically and socially. Later I pursue the analogy between Barthes' study of the biblical story and Lloyd Newson's construction of the figure of the 'angel'. Where in his tale it is Jacob who is subject and object; sender and receiver; opponent and helper, in mine it is the Angel who adopts multiple positions (Chapter 6). The significance of this compounding of roles is that

> the paradox, or at very least the anomic nature of the formulation, can be seen at once: that the subject be confounded with the receiver is banal; that the subject be his or her own helper is less usual; but that the sender be the opponent is very rare and there is only one type of narrative that can present this paradoxical form - narratives relating an act of blackmail.
>
> Barthes, 1977, p. 138

In Frow's appraisal of the construct of genre the notion of poetics also reappears, succinctly described as

> the attempt to construct a systematic account of verbal art forms: by extension, any systematic account of organised textuality of any kind.
>
> Frow, 2006, p.151

Equally dominant, and systematic, is the application of my personal politics, my own subjectivity, which means that the idea of blackmail lingers uncomfortably in my consciousness throughout this analysis, stimulated by Lloyd Newson's use of women, and in particular his constructions of sexualities and gendered identities. Woman's desire to control her own fertility, even to choose her own mate, still offends in many societies. The abortion issue will not go away, female circumcision continues, and the oppression of women through many religions remains as evidence of the need of men to control us. In the twentieth century these very obvious methods have been replaced by more subtle means of 'suppressing women, legally, politically, economically, and psychologically' (Walker, 1983, p.x). Even in the twentieth-century women have been threatened by gender nonsense of a pseudo-psychological kind. The idea that educating women might make them ill (usually with a form of psychological illness, often hysterical) is on a par with the blindness once thought to result from an excess of (male) masturbation, but with the greater malicious intent of disenfranchising half of the population.[9] Optimism and feminist intertexts have to be tempered by this other evidence.[10] Showalter (1998) demonstrates both convincingly and vividly the perpetuation of these strategies through such 'hysterical epidemics' as chronic fatigue syndrome, recovered memory and satanic ritual abuse.

The potential of blackmail and a metonymic montage of intertexts playing with, and on, *Strange Fish*, is as *se*ductive and *pro*ductive, for my purposes, as the play with Barthes' own writings. I take from Barthes, in summary, that one is 'dealing...with a sort of *metonymic montage*: the themes (Crossing, Struggle, Naming, Alimentary Rite) are *combined*, not "developed"'. If the emphasis in analysis consequently shifts to the text as 'intertextual construct, the product of various cultural discourses', as Culler describes it, the problems do not dissolve, since these discourses are themselves constantly fluid (1983a, p.85).

To create a book that shares these characteristics is problematic, given the narrative form running from page 1 through to the 'end'. By maintaining self-consciousness at the level of the metanarrative and by juxtaposing interpretative perspectives I can hope to keep the question of boundaries, focus and interpretative logic always visible and also to allow this text to 'go off', in Barthes' terms, where it will. In the parallel case of *Akhnaten* Richardson analyses systematically how Glass develops a 'unique conception of narrative structure' (1999 p.xiv). As specific critical concerns arise he addresses them. This is a structure that I used in an earlier version of this book on *Strange Fish* but one which I subsequently moved away from in order to give the *issues* a greater foregrounding and to use the work more as a springboard for critical debate than to give priority to it as a subject of analysis in its own right.

One reason for this is pragmatic. The practical likelihood is small of an entire book seeing the publishing light of day if based on one physical theatre piece of a less mainstream character than the highly regarded and controversial opera by Phillip Glass. But another reason is that I am not as convinced by *Strange Fish* as John Richardson seems to be by *Akhnaten* and do not want to give it quite such pride of place in the final account. There are things I dislike about it, although it continues to grip my thoughts. There are elements and themes that horrify me in their significance, and which another artist might have treated differently. While in itself this might be a good reason for giving it pride of place, in the end I prefer my politics to take priority explicitly over Newson's. I use 'politics' in several senses here, to refer to gender politics; to theory-of-art politics; to an openness to varied perspectives rather than a focus on the 'message'; and, ultimately, because I see the contribution this text makes as being as much about method and theory as about *Strange Fish* and as much, if not more, about the 'reader', me and you, as about Lloyd Newson and his collaborators.

The Structure of the Book

In Chapter 2, I address notions of narrative as they pertain to *Strange Fish*, notably in the positioning of the writer (me). Secondly I describe the voices that take the narrative position in the piece; the authorial and ancestral dances and sonorities that set the context; the narratives that we inherit from the body of scholarly writing in dance, and to a lesser extent in music and theatre, in theorising such works. Chapter 2 also contains material upon which (and in conjunction with the video or DVD) an analysis of *Strange Fish* might be made. I construct a narrative, which subsequently forms a reference point for a number of thematic developments in a discussion of distinct interpretative positions and debates.

In Chapter 3 I articulate a range theoretical positions, tracing a path from narrative to the notion of intertextuality. From a traditional structuralism or formalism I move to more recent ideas from deconstruction. This allows me to unpack recent writings in dance analysis, which I term 'Ancestral Scholarly Narratives', to construct an argument for an intertextual theory and method. Finally I focus on the strengths of a performative intertextuality in dance analysis. From this, practical methodologies that inform my analysis emerge, which explain the layers of analysis it produces as different traces of texts and intertexts become important at different times.

Chapter 4 marks a change of direction, from theory to elaborated interpretative discussion of *Strange Fish*. Firstly, in Chapter 4 I draw attention to the ways in which *Strange Fish* constructs masculinity starting with myth and legend of pre-Christian eras and proceeding through Greek and theological sources to extract ideas about the significance of Christ as a human male figure. Women occupy the subordinate position of the 'other' through this account as it picks up later theories from psychological anthropology. Myth and ritual become contentious concepts leading to a view of characters in *Strange Fish* as 'sacrificial victims' suffused with narcissistic anxiety.

In Chapter 5 this binary coin is flipped. Starting from goddesses and the Virgin Mary, gender-conscious theories inform associations in *Strange Fish* between fish and women in theology. Re-workings and re-constructions of history which seek to position women differently are explored in the light of a mythic inheritance of Christianity, and through the characters of Eve and Mary (in their many guises), as carried forward from the late twentieth century into the third millennium.

Chapter 6 denies these binaries and exposes the multi-vocality of theory and of themes within *Strange Fish* seeking opportunities to re-cast this sombre history in more positive terms. It exposes the depth of prejudice and the insidious character of theologies which accumulate in a reader-text-author matrix around the Siren figure. Fluid constructs of gender, more open narratives, reveal another side of the work, configured as Plainsong, as a Lament, as a restatement of cultural history based on close reading of the music, the movement and the narrative threads. Finally I lay claim that the title of 'The Struggle with the Angel' can be justified and understood at the nexus of erotic pleasure with psychoanalytic force, as embedded in the event that is *Strange Fish*.

Chapter 7 draws some final elegiac remarks together, widening the canvas to broader social and gender questions.[11]

1 It is reviewed in a widely varied spread of newspapers and professional journals and is studied in many kinds of courses at university level. Articles have appeared in scholarly journals, and a doctoral thesis has been written (Lark, 1999).

2 Richardson's is an account which is as free from jargon and complex terminology as it is possible to be in such writing and delightfully open to alternative positions. It wears its erudition lightly but it is clearly there, not hidden, not something to apologise for, but *used* in an imaginative fashion, to work at this vast and intricate 'opera', while never losing sight of the experience of the music theatre it discusses.

3 See Lycouris (1996), a recent doctoral thesis on the subject of improvisation.

4 Weller (2001) also states that her new album 'Untold Things' has 'been deemed ineligible for the classical chart' since Pook is 'neither a recognised classical artist nor a recognised classical composer' (official quote).

5 Recent outlines of responses in Dance Studies to such issues can be found in Morris (ed. 1996).

6 More recent analyses of Butcher's work and Davies' can be found in Worth and Preston respectively, both in Adshead-Lansdale (ed. 1999).

7 More recent analyses of Anderson's work can be found in Dodds, in Adshead-Lansdale (ed. 1999).

8 Viewers of this work have been known to take against it simply because it challenges long-held and valued conceptions e.g. of Christ as indisputably male. In relation to other works e.g. *Never Again* (1989) watching two men, or two women, relate strongly to each other, even to kiss, has prompted anger. In showing this work to Australian men (teachers) in 1990 I met refusal to deal with the work at all.

9 It is only recently that women have been able to complete a university level education at the most prestigious western universities. The view that women would be unable to make politically informed decisions, hence denied the vote for many years, is only just giving way to a recognition of their power to swing the political debate and an understanding that their opinions might be different from their partners. Even the revolutionary election for the UK parliament in May 1997, which returned a Labour government with an exceptional number of 120 female Members, saw few of them attain and maintain real power.

10 Denying women education and health care; preventing them from taking up a public role; chaining them to the home; reducing their view of the world to a net across the eyes, while the rest of the body is covered from head to toe, is still practised under the authority of one of the supposedly great religions of the world, Islam, and recently reinforced in Afghanistan and Malaysia. Even more pernicious is the fact that to convince women that God (in whatever mythic form) is the source of this contempt relies on women themselves accepting the myth. Foucault's contention that human beings can be persuaded to discipline themselves in this most distressing manner is fully justified by this example (1976; 1978). The energy it requires is wasteful of human resources and its outcomes cruel and inhuman, yet it continues to be supported in the name of various male Gods, and is a powerful source of women's lack of confidence and belief in their own contribution to the public world. That it continues tells us how much is invested in this unequal power relationship.

11 Material used in this text has been published in an article titled *Siren Sensualities* (Adshead-Lansdale, 2002).

CHAPTER 2

Constructing Narratives: Creating *Strange Fish*

> Narrative acts 'to engender the subject in the movement of its discourse, as it defines positions of meaning, identification, and desire'(de Lauretis, 1984, p.10).

In this chapter I draw out a discussion of narrating voices, or of who is telling what kind of story. The voices of Lloyd Newson and his collaborators are important but they are not the only voices of interest here. The reference to narrative voices in the plural reinforces two principles: firstly, that many stories can be told around *Strange Fish*, with the corollary that none of them has a claim to be universal or all-embracing; and secondly, that the story told will differ in consequence of the cultural position and individuality of the person who tells it.[1]

I make a distinction between 'authorial' and 'ancestral' voices, although the two are closely intertwined.[2] I use 'authorial' in the sense of the 'author' as historically constituted, as the original artist, but I also treat the construct of 'author' as equivalent to the 'reader' in the sense of a postmodernist 'creator' or 'constructor' of the work. On this basis, each of us has a 'voice', which becomes 'authorial' as we bring the work into existence. People engaged in making and performing the work, whether as performers, film makers, critics, spectators or theorists, speak with 'authorial' voices as do those watching and writing, whether from academic disciplines or from experience of the theatre. *Strange Fish* itself articulates many such 'authorial' voices, arising from individual characterisations, from situations that develop, and in terms of the concerns it deals with i.e. its subject matter and treatment.

In contrast I use 'ancestral' to refer to those traces of the past and of the pre-existing present which surround creative artists and the ideas with which they engage. The term 'ancestral' allows me to reflect not only on specific antecedent texts and narratives that might affect an individual's response (whether as maker or reader) but also on those narratives enshrined in the history of dance and theatre. Both are important in the creation and construction of any theatre or dance form. They are significant here as the basis of the genre coding of the text of *Strange Fish*.

I present a number of accounts of *Strange Fish*. Even if a reader is familiar with *Strange Fish* in either or both of its versions, how anyone chooses to talk about is not self-evidently straightforward. The answer to the question 'whose narrative is this?' is not simple. Lloyd Newson created one narrative for the stage, he collaborated with David Hinton in creating another one for the film, which Hinton directed, and I now create a third. What is brought to the fore is my own purpose in carrying out this analysis which, while not perversely in opposition to previous constructions, is nonetheless uniquely mine.

Which *Strange Fish*?

Methodologically, a detailed analysis of the staged version would be more than a little difficult, and combining material written on the stage version with detailed and prolonged video analysis is itself problematic. Lloyd Newson explicitly states that he wishes only to preserve the material through its adaptations for video (Gombrich, 1997). Sadly, while the video version of this work is readily available for all spectators (Newson and Hinton, 1993), the stage work is not. If the video recording had taken the form of a record of the stage performance the difficulties would be much less extreme.[3] The staged performances lasted some 90 minutes – the adaptation for BBC television was condensed and substantially re-worked to last 54 minutes. In fact, in shortening the work, the directors (Lloyd Newson and David Hinton) also set it in rather different environments, more conducive to filming. Extensive use of the back wall up to the limits of the performance space was one of the most striking features of the staged performance, giving an unusual three-dimensional height and depth with a rope used to enable performers to swing across the space at a speed not otherwise possible. When small stones cascade from the full height of the stage, and people climb, or are positioned on the wall at various levels, a specific dramatic tension is created that video cannot mimic.

Mackrell wrote one of few accounts directly addressing changes between the stage and video versions (1994) finding the video version more literal than the original, but nevertheless a 'masterpiece' of its kind. She praises the camera work for shaping the material with such 'a sure intensity' that the experience was not, as with so much filmed dance, a second-hand experience. Her own response was to be 'moved and stilled as powerfully as if you were sitting in the theatre'. Given the greater capability of camera work in capturing movement in a forward-backward dimension, than capturing movement which travels from high to low, or from one side to the other side, the re-location of some scenes to a narrow corridor, with the viewer placed at the end of it, is understandable. It also serves to create its own dynamic and dramatic tension which, it might be argued, is just as powerful as the original, but different in its signifying force. Similarly, intimate close-up shots in this emotionally-laden work have a distinct impact not so evident on the stage. Meanings are not interchangeable. Something similar, but not identical, is created.

Strange Fish was staged in several European venues in 1992 before its première in Seville in Spain in June. It was then performed in the UK, in Glasgow, Newcastle, Manchester, Londonderry and London until the end of August. Vividly as the stage version remains in my mind, it is based on one performance, overlaid now with many viewings of the video version. Although newspaper and journal reviews can be useful in recalling and commenting on the staged work they, too, were written after short acquaintance.

The 'I' in the narrative

Since I am the 'author' of this book it is appropriate that I first expose something of my own artistic and theoretical inclinations and reveal something of my personal history as background to my responses as a 'reader' and 'constructor' of *Strange Fish*. With the 'natural' reserve (or to be more precise, perhaps, the cultural reserve) of the English academic, it is sufficient to say that growing up in the 1950s and 1960s in the north of England, in a predominantly working class area which was recovering from the closure of the mills and factories of the industrial revolution, as a result of the advent of cheap fabrics from the Far East, made its own mark. The mill sirens, the smog, the working footwear (clogs), provided a stark contrast to the high quality single-sex schooling for female high achievers that I received, while both were contained within a wider framework of Victorian and puritanical religious views that were dominant in the region, in the class framework, and strongly-held within both school and family.[4] Most of this would have been shared by many young women of this particular sub-culture.

As I grew up, a passion for dance and music, the open hillsides and the Lake District in Spring, provided a contrast to industrial Lancashire, offering romance, sensuality and spirituality. An agnostic adult life followed, lived in the vivid climate of the feminist movement of the 1970s, in a variety of relationships and working in a subject (dance) which, by definition, had previously been excluded from serious study, as being evil, or irrelevant, and predominately female, therefore doubly irrelevant, is perhaps explanation enough, for the moment, of the background to some of my own reactions to such works as *Strange Fish*. Although I am now employed in the relatively secure and respectable profession of University Professor, my subject interests still speak of subversion within academe.

Since 1990 I have used examples from works by Lloyd Newson when teaching masters' degree students at my own university, and for conference papers on dance analysis, in Australia, Canada, the United States, many parts of Europe, and some parts of Asia. One reason for doing this was to conduct a kind of ethnographic empirical study to confirm or dismiss theories that form the focus for this chapter. What emerges from this fieldwork is that English-speaking, white, well-educated females aged between 23 and 50, who are knowledgeable about contemporary dance and theatre, generally share a set of values about what this kind of art should set out to achieve. In the late 1980s and 1990s they invariably placed a high value on Lloyd Newson's work.

It is interesting to note, however, that while some students who have left their own countries to study in England can place a value on work of this kind, they are often highly conscious that it would not be acceptable at home, usually because of its explicit sexuality and its openness in dealing with gender issues. Thus a further, and necessary, level of clarity can be obtained when the individual's personal position in terms of moral convictions is juxtaposed with social constraints and family positions.[5]

Postgraduate students form one, highly privileged, group of readers. They are not a monolithic group; they are not identical since individuals within the group will feel and think differently. But they will share some preconceptions about the value of higher education and the value of the performing arts. Similarly, if stereotypically, it needs only a cursory glance at an audience for the public performance of Lloyd Newson's work to see that it attracts its own following, often of gay and lesbian spectators, as many male as female in the audience, often of a wider age range and wider subject base than for much contemporary dance. If shaved heads, black leather and an ear-ring typify a particular group, they are out in force for Lloyd Newson in the late 1990s. At second glance, of course, each person will respond differently, will choose variations on the uniform of class and gender identity. Nonetheless they are a distinctive group sharing some perspectives and choices.

This is not an essentialist position, which might state that these things are of value without question, but rather the opposite. Because of our education, our life styles, our interests, we value much the same things, and accord equal weight to particular themes. For example, in this case, we share a view that works which explore the often-painful results of trying to engage in deeply meaningful relationships are 'good'. No doubt this is a reflection of the rise of the individual and of psychoanalytic thought in the twentieth century and the concomitant greater willingness of individuals to reveal emotional states. Referring further back, however, we share a historical legacy of Christianity and Greek myth. This is not to say we could all recite biblical or Greek stories verbatim, but that we connect with them in some fairly vague, or in some cases highly specific, way depending on our experience and knowledge. Similarly, our knowledge of Freud might be quite minimal, but the vocabulary and intensity of concern with emotional situations, which characterises late twentieth century life, derives much from his thinking.

While these comments refer to the *subject matter* with which Newson deals, it is also true that certain values about ways of *treating* subject matter are also shared. Thus we value work which shows, often in graphic detail, the responses of individuals to personal experiences of gender politics, in this case of both a hetero and homosexual nature; relationships which are engaged in freely, but which can become manipulative and physically violent.

Views held in common across the UK can probably be expressed with less definition than, for example, views held by London-based, urban performers of gay persuasion. Whether these positions and these places connect with each other is probably at the root of agreement and disagreement in interpretation. This interactive and intertextual matrix of relationships between individuals and culture is thus complex and multiply-layered. Into this I have to add my own (and yours, my reader's) autobiography, desires, dislikes, experiences, particularly of religion, of music, of theatre and dance, of sexualities and choices made in daily life.

It might seem odd or arrogant to place my own authorial voice before that of Lloyd Newson: it is neither, given the arguments above. This book is my construction, not his, and the very choice of structure and content already creates a personal view. In this sense, as author, I have the 'prior' voice although Lloyd Newson and his collaborators created the performance earlier in time. It does not mean that mine is more valid than any other.

Writing a text of *Strange Fish*

The following description is written from my own point of view based, as I have said, on seeing the work live, once, and many times on video. Likewise the images are my own selection of moments which stimulated the description. This account attempts to construct a description that is relatively uninflected and rather straightforward. It might serve as a guide to the spectator watching the video for the first time.

Scenes are referred to by number and by title. While being inescapably interpretive, these descriptions attempt to lay out the action in narrative terms with an indication of the main movement constructs used. Their relative lengths and position within the whole are given here.[6]

Strange Fish

DURATION	MINS	SUMMARY	TITLE
1. 0.00-3.17	3.17	Church Scene 1.	Religious observance
2. 3.17-4.42	1.25	Corridor Scene 1:	Interrupted conversations
3. 4.42-10.52	6.10	Bar Scene 1:	Intimidation, competition and co-operation
4.10.52-15.30	4.38	Bar Scene 2:	Sexual play, two against one (female-male)
5. 15.30-19.08	3.38	Corridor Scene 2:	Dissolving the self, male-female duet
6. 19.08-23.35	4.27	Bar Scene 3:	The party, the isolate and the group
7. 23.35-27.43	4.08	Room Scene 1.	On being alone and together
8. 27.43-30.00	2.17	Corridor Scene 3:	Intimacy interrupted
9. 30.00-39.30	9.30	Room Scene 2:	Pointless sex and its aftermath
10. 39.30-45.30	6.00	Corridor Scene 4:	Brief tenderness turns to violence
11. 45.30-49.15	3.45	Room Scene 3:	Baptism and absolution
12. 49.15-54.20	5.05	Church Scene 2:	The desecration of the Cross

Scene 1 – Church Scene 1: Religious observance

In the first scene of religious observance, Diana Payne-Myers faces the camera with a bank of lighted candles between her and the viewer. She is dressed in black with a black cap or scarf over her head. She looks ahead, chin slightly upturned, serious and reverential. Behind her is a large Cross on which, just visible, can be seen the outlines of a figure. Wendy Houstoun, in an orange sweater and casual trousers, drifts around at the foot of the Cross, shrouded in dim light. Scattered across the field of vision are candles, placed singly and in groups. Visible also is an effigy of mother and child. When combined with a figure kneeling in prayer, and a shaft of light shining as though through a high narrow window, it suggests a church. A melodic female voice, sometimes in solo form and sometimes apparently in two-part harmony with itself, is at first disembodied. In a closer shot it can be seen to belong to the figure clothed as 'Christ'. Once the figure moves, straining against thongs, the camera closes in, and it becomes clear that this Christ is female. This 'Christ/Siren/Angel' figure is Melanie Pappenheim, who appears in various guises later on in the piece: hence this multiple designation. Wendy Houstoun walks around and watches, apparently detached, perhaps uncomprehending, perhaps dismissive of what she sees. Finally she opens a door upstage left, letting a shaft of daylight in, and departs, closing the door noisily.

Scene 2 – Corridor Scene 1: Interrupted conversations

Wendy Houstoun and Nigel Charnock emerge from separate doors into the rather murkily lit corridor of Scene 2. They approach each other (at the far end of the corridor from the viewer), check that they are not observed, pull their sweaters up over their heads and conduct a half-bent 'conversation' in movement, bobbing and weaving, tipping towards and away from each other. Violin and accordion music, which recalls Jacques Tati and an old French café, punctuates the action with a rhythmic commentary. They conclude the conversation, straighten their clothes and 'dance' purposefully towards the camera. They are quickly interrupted: first by Dale Tanner, whom they turn away from and exclude; and then by Lauren Potter, who appears through another door and who, in contrast, is allowed to join them. They greet each other, then mince and prance together down the length of the corridor in a rather jerky fashion, reminiscent of self-absorbed teenage behaviour, into the bar.

Scene 3 – Bar Scene 1: Intimidation, competition and cooperation

In this much more warmly lit bar (Scene 3), conversation continues, the three of them teasingly gossiping together in movement, leaning against the bar, until a new male (Dale Tanner) enters and approaches, walking on his hands. They focus intently on this curious sight until Dale turns his head to look at them, at which point they gaze elsewhere, turn away from him and give every appearance of not having seen him. Nigel Charnock breaks away and joins Dale Tanner, who is still upside down but doing inverted press-ups against the wall. Using classic approach-avoidance tactics, the three surround Dale, with Wendy taking over his inverted position, casually crossing her legs while balancing on her hands. Their curiosity is now overt, as is their challenge to him. The women distract Dale, catch him unawares and mock him by their diffuse yet directed actions. They incite Nigel to demonstrate equal prowess and laugh at his failure to make any impression in the competition. One of the recurring motifs appears, as a closed door in this wall is opened. Nigel rushes through it away from the action, followed soon after by Wendy, who, with much greater calculation, pops out from a hatch to hit Dale on the head, sending him to the floor, aided and abetted by Lauren.

A further development of this action takes place when Kate Champion enters shortly afterwards. She is inadvertently tripped by Dale, then mimicked quite pointedly by Wendy and Lauren with pseudo-sexy mannerisms. She is pushed aside and hindered in relating to Dale, although she remains conscious of him, breaking away from the women to follow him when he disappears into the corridor. Her success is short-lived. Wendy and Lauren rush after her, obstruct her passage and take hold of her physically. They finally drag her backwards, push her into another room and lock the door, ignoring her screams, pretending nothing is amiss. Jordi Cortes Molina appears from another door; ignoring these events, he moves off into the bar.

Scene 4 – Bar Scene 2: Sexual play, two against one (female–male)

Molina enters the bar rather cautiously at the start of Scene 4. He balances candles on each shoulder and moves carefully along circular pathways, knees slightly bent. His reverie is broken by the entry of Wendy Houstoun and Lauren Potter dressed as blonde vamps, with short shiny dresses and blonde wigs. They approach Jordi Molina as in a game, taunting him to respond. The women are clearly in league against him, and their wild turning, falling and rolling movements incite his involvement in this sexual game. The voices mimic the action with a series of high-pitched shrieks and chants based on *na*.

A bemused Jordi follows them as though they were animals on heat, until the scene culminates in Lauren's wig being spitefully pulled off by Wendy. Lauren and Jordi, however, have made a different kind of contact and she follows him down the corridor, with Wendy petulantly bringing up the rear, no longer the prime mover.

Scene 5 – Corridor Scene 2: Dissolving the self, male–female duet

Lauren and Jordi's love duet takes place in the corridor in Scene 5, firstly against the bitter orange wall where she spreads herself across him, then on the floor, remaining in physical contact as the lighting focuses intensely on them alone, with little recognition of the surroundings – hence my title *Dissolving the self*. They slide over and around each other with tightly clasped hands, in an unendingly flowing series of movements, contained and connected to each other. They separate and join again, and she drapes herself over his shoulders, clasping him again within her own joined hands. It creates a womb-like state, reinforced by a warm orange glow of light. This comforting picture is disturbed by Wendy Houstoun who, positioned close to the viewer, has watched this scene from beginning to end before finally walking off down the corridor and into the bar.

Scene 6 – Bar Scene 3: The party, the isolate and the group; and Scene 7 – Room Scene 1: On being alone and together

The following two scenes are extensions of each other, differing in bringing the whole group of performers into interaction in Scene 6, and being restricted to one couple with Nigel and then a duo of Nigel and Wendy in Scene 7. The original bar scene is augmented by coloured lights and a low stage, through the curtains of which Nigel emerges into a scene of small groups, drinking, chatting, as though at a party. Nigel begins an obsessive monologue about being 'a people person'. Despite his professed love of people and his determination to talk to individuals, he is rebuffed by each in turn. As the action becomes more frantic, the gentle turn away of another performer becomes a leap over the bar or into another person's arms – 'anything to escape Nigel' is the message. The facial expressions of the performers brought into close-up, their bodily twitches of disdain and small steps as they move away from him, give the lie to his endless stream of modern psychological truisms about how pleased he is to see people, how good it is to relate, while he signally fails at every juncture to live up to them.

Left alone, Nigel continues his monologue on being unwanted and on loneliness. As the social scene darkens, the spotlight focuses on him, creating a white and black shadowing, his blond hair and light trousers contrasting with a dark blue sweater. He rambles on about how nice it is that some couples have found each other, describing in some detail how they hold each other, touching them and himself to show where and how (Scene 7). He approaches one closely entwined couple, Lauren and Jordi, and attempts to separate them, using every possible device, and many not normally seen – but without success. As orchestral music of some romantic, Wagnerian sentimentality begins, he tries, but eventually fails, to force them apart.

Wendy now appears and is seemingly a more willing partner, until his affection gets out of hand. His gestures become ferocious, painful and far from friendly as he presses the back of his arm across her face. The scene ends when she screams 'Stop it!', turns away and leaves him almost in darkness.

Scene 8 – Corridor Scene 3: Intimacy interrupted

In the third Corridor Scene (Scene 8), Jordi and Lauren continue their love affair sitting on a bench. In a mirror image of the previous scene, it is Wendy, not Nigel, who attempts to come between them by sliding along the bench towards them. When denied, she exerts brute force, tipping them off the bench and attempting to squash Lauren underneath. Eventually the couple manage to retrieve it and depart, Lauren perched on top of the bench, which is balanced across Jordi's back. Hearing a noise, Wendy turns to see Dale Tanner developing his muscles by practising pull-ups on the doorframe. As she moves to join him, she passes the silent and still 'Christ/Siren' figure now wearing a brown dress, standing quietly at the edge of the screen, her face turned to the wall.

Scene 9 – Room Scene 2: Pointless sex and its aftermath

In Scene 9 Wendy strips off her top and stands quite still, naked to the waist, in close-up, expressionless. She turns to confront Dale, who has followed her into another room, and the Siren/Christ/Angel figure frames her, now as guardian angel. She sings a new plaintive melody, circles Wendy and clicks two stones together before flinging them to the floor. An increasing avalanche of small stones rolls towards the camera, and around Wendy's legs. Through a mirror Dale is seen, facing Wendy, with showers of stones falling between them. As the melody resumes with slight catches of breath, Dale approaches Wendy, she places his hand on her breast and they kiss. Religious icons at crazy angles come into focus as a most irreligious scene of sexual humping takes place under Melanie's ironic gaze. With several singing voices as accompaniment, Wendy Houstoun breaks free while Dale Tanner continues to bounce up and down on the bed, watched now by both Wendy and the Angel/ Siren/Melanie.

Against a slow rhythmic pulse Wendy comes into view, lying spent on a bed of stones, twitching as more are dropped singly onto her by a circling Angel (of judgement? As the pace increases, she grinds herself into this bed of stones. In this aftermath of pain, friends gather around at the doorway while Wendy backs into a corner like a frightened animal and pulls her sweater over her breasts.

When Wendy emerges from the room, it is apparent that these 'friends' have been whispering about her and that she is no longer welcome in the group. The group splinters as she approaches. They stalk each other, and in frustration Wendy barges into each performer in turn with her shoulder, trying to grab them, forcing her pain on them.

She rolls on the floor and initiates a rolling, leaping sequence in and out of the room and down the length of the corridor, in which they all join. Just as in the earlier scene, they all avoid Nigel, finally leaving him alone. They all now flee out of Wendy's way.

Scene 10 – Corridor Scene 4: Brief tenderness turns to violence

In this silent scene (10) a tentative tenderness turns to violence as Nigel and Wendy's attempts to offer something to each other fail. She rushes after him, grasps him in a flying leap, offers her hand but withdraws it as he reaches out. She offers it again; he responds, but she slaps his hand. For the third time she offers and removes her hand and he finally turns away. She runs round him, and offers her hand for the fourth time; but when he responds she replies by hitting him around the face. In a scene of extraordinary violence they roll, barging into each other as Wendy first manipulates then destroys Nigel.

During this scene, Wendy's leaping and whirling seems unfocused, sometimes directed at nothing or at herself, an indiscriminate series of actions. As the lights flicker and fade, and a single low thread of sound begins, the sound of stones can again be heard. The floorboards rattle and fly up to reveal an open tank of water. Wendy sees limbs appear up through the water; she pounces, but fails after some struggling, to catch whatever is under the surface of the water. As she flings the boards around, she becomes aware of movement in the corridor – it is Nigel.

Closing the door carefully behind her, she approaches him with a welcome tinged with demand. Nigel retreats behind a door and a thoroughly menacing game of chase begins, in and out of doors, and along the length of the corridor. As echoes of the earlier café melodies recur, Wendy draws Nigel into a final embrace. She promptly and viciously pushes him away finally shoving him unceremoniously backwards into the tank of water. He disappears from sight.

Scene 11 – Room Scene 3: Baptism and absolution

Scene 11 is a contrast in tone, starting with only the movement of the water, melancholy singing, and the face of the singer reflected, inverted, in the water. She appears at the side of the tank as a woman in a black leather jacket. Dale Tanner enters, now ill, sunken and clearly feverish, clutching a thick coat around him. He moves cautiously along a wooden plank, dimly lit, with a bluish hue. The woman – mother/singer/Christ/guardian-Angel/ Melanie – holds him, cradles him, rests his head on her shoulder, sinks to the ground with him and sprinkles water from the tank over his forehead as if in baptism or absolution. Pulling herself along the ground while supporting him on her back, she rolls him over into silence and darkness.

Scene 12 – Church Scene 2: The desecration of the Cross

Finally, in Scene 12 Wendy Houstoun emerges from the water in a violent spurt, coughing, soaking wet and into total silence. She calls quietly 'Nigel ... Nigel'. As her call increases in intensity and fear, Wendy moves down the dark corridor lit with strips of blue light into a scene that recalls the first one, the church or religious environment. This time it is dark, its objects in disarray, with clothes strewn across the floor and Christ back on the Cross, singing an agonised discordant chant. Calling for Nigel with increasing desperation produces no result and, grabbing a chalice, Wendy climbs the Cross, pulls the singer's head back and pours the wine/water over her face, mouth and throat, and silences her by bringing their mouths together. As 'Christ' falls from the Cross, Wendy descends, walks to the door upstage left and exits, looking back into the room as the light fades, in repetition of her first exit from the earlier scene.

The Ancestral and Authorial Voices of DV8[7]

Lloyd Newson's work with DV8 emerged from a white, American/ Australian/European nexus of 1970s youth culture, notably of those interested in theatre dance as well as the popular and physical arts of the time. The experimental dance and theatre scenes in London in the early 1980s provided a challenging context for Lloyd Newson's creative endeavours. The range of work available at that time contrasted the abstractions of a fading modern dance, humanised through its contact with pedestrian movement, with the violence of a form of realism which was to lead to extremes of self-exposure in the 1990s. The simple fact of the birth of a 'new' form, called by rough consensus 'Physical Theatre', is evidence enough that Lloyd Newson, while unique in many respects, was also part of a wider move towards dramatic, gender-conscious works which sought to challenge accepted beliefs. The term 'theatre' was deemed inadequate, as was 'contemporary dance' - both by critics and performers.

For some years the work of DV8 has been seen as ground-breaking and the company has been credited with contributing to the revival of both theatre and dance practices in Europe.[8] Physical Theatre claims a European heritage that is distinctive and different from anything current in North America. This extension of the Expressionist theatre and modern dance movements from the early part of the twentieth century is peculiarly European in character in its focus on the intensity of emotion and on the use of images, words and movement, separately and together, in dealing with personally and socially relevant, and politically intense, subject matter. Classical theatre and ballet have not been immune from this shift - it is embodied in expressionistic treatments of traditional subject matter in these forms, too.[9]

Lloyd Newson was born in 1957 in Australia and, while studying psychology at Melbourne University at both undergraduate and post-graduate levels, he danced in the Modern Dance Ensemble, an amateur group with release and improvisation interests (Parry, 1990). He has worked in Europe for over 25 years creating powerful socio-political pieces which address issues such as sexuality, politics and homophobia. These works are generally created in collaboration with composers who often work directly with digital technologies.

Newson's meteoric rise to fame is reflected in the number of awards he has received, including the Prix Italia for the television version of *Strange Fish* with David Hinton, in 1994.[10]

Newson came to the UK in 1980, studied briefly at the London School of Contemporary Dance and joined Extemporary Dance Theatre (EDT) in 1981, producing a company piece alongside another newly emerging, and equally controversial choreographer, Michael Clark. EDT was one of the small companies to emerge in the mid 1970s from the burst of activity at The Place following the first performances of London Contemporary Dance Theatre in 1967. The associated School produced graduates with ambitions to spread the gospel of modern/contemporary dance across Britain. From a start at the Edinburgh Festival in 1975 EDT grew to become a well-respected middle scale company, to which Emilyn Claid was appointed Artistic Director in 1981. Her appointment heralded a change of direction for the company arising from her links with experimental dance and commitment to politically-charged work. She had also been instrumental in the founding of the X6 Dance Space and of New Dance magazine. Newson produced *Breaking Images* in 1982, and *Beauty, Art and the Kitchen Sink* (1984), and three workshop pieces in 1983 and 1984. Emilyn Claid also commissioned works from other new dance choreographers such as Jackie Lansley, for *Speaking Part* (1981) and Fergus Early, for *Napoli* (1982). While Newson might have been impatient to move on, he was already in the only mainstream company with such experimental ambitions, which he acknowledges in interview with Solway (1985).[11]

Following a Dance Umbrella appearance with *Bein' Apart: Lonely Art*, Newson started his own group, DV8 (deviate) Physical Theatre in 1986, as an independent collective, with, among its stated aims, 'to re-invest meaning in dance'. *Strange Fish*, one of some 15 works produced by Lloyd Newson is a suitable focus for these discussions for a number of reasons. It can be taken as in some sense representative of this newly emergent genre.

Lloyd Newson sometimes refers to his own work as 'Visual Theatre' which serves to place the emphasis on the visual as much as the text-derived image. All theatre is visual, one might argue, and to this extent it does not move the debate on, but it does open up a gap between the work of DV8 and the many other kinds of theatre that have adopted the term 'Physical Theatre'. Many groups operating in this field start more obviously from a range of texts, or a text, even while they may improvise and move far away from such starting points. In a rather crude sense some Physical Theatre pieces may involve rather more standing around and speaking than DV8s work usually does, and fewer developed, dance-like, sequences. Whether this warrants a new descriptive genre term is debatable, but it raises the often spectacular 'visual' dimension of Lloyd Newson's dance/theatre to a platform alongside the visual arts.

In fact, writing on recent performance art and physical theatre forms has emerged from many directions, some with a more obviously visual arts emphasis. Adler and Pointon (1993) writing about the human form and visual culture since the Renaissance, reveal a broad sweep of multi-disciplinary interests among their contributors. Such studies share with dance and theatre a keen interest in how representation functions. Representation of what, is the first question, of how recurrent subject matter is tied to particular treatments as structured by notions of genre and style at different moments in time. The second question is how historical threads of narratives or ideas, which have become the subject matter of art, interface with an author's personal experiences, both of life and of the traditions of each art, and the shared cultural history of all the arts.

In the 1990s there existed competing, even mutually exclusive, positions on what was 'new' and of value in the contemporary dance scene, and this provides the background to the development of Physical Theatre as a genre of performance, as described in Chapter 1. The network of connections, of threads, that link different versions of these forms to prior and current events and to Lloyd Newson and his collaborators in 1992 is the issue here. The obsessions, commitments and methods of those around Lloyd Newson are made manifest in choices of event, movement and setting creating visible traces of existing and new genre and style. What is interesting is how they are deployed, changed, re-structured, de-constructed, and often defied, in *Strange Fish*.

The position of the 'author' as historically understood is still contentious. Lomas locates the reduction of art to biography as the danger in this arena, and one for which there is ample evidence (in Adler and Pointon, 1993). It takes many forms, from the assumption that what the artist as a person says of her/his process and purposes must be true, to the idea that the way the artist lives must be what is represented in, and must necessarily explain, their art. Biography can be a way of trivialising art (most frequently that made by women); it 'relegates it to the private domain of a singular life history' with little wider significance; thus it 'obscures the actual work of self-presentation' that the artist is engaged in (p.5). The whole issue was made highly visible by Tracey Emin's bed, submitted for the prestigious

Turner prize (London, 1999) where, as Lomas says of Kahlo, 'her body is a site where political concerns intersect with personal ones' (p.19). Soiled underwear and the mess of everyday life presented as 'art' (definitely in inverted commas) shows how far the debate has come and we can no longer assume, or treat innocently, the relationship between artist and work. It cannot be denied, but its detailed tracking raises many interesting problems.

Early philosophy of art theories explicitly distinguish between the author, the text or work and the reader and conceptualise the construction of meaning predominantly in terms of one of these positions. In some sense this is why the terms exist, to polarise these positions. My argument is that performers are readers and readers are performers, in ways I shall explore. Similarly, critics and scholars are both 'readers' and 'creators' of *Strange Fish*. Oscillating between two positions, I deny extreme manifestations of the infamous 'death of the author' but I also deny the other extreme that preceeded it, that 'true' perceptions of the work must be the same as those of the creators.[12] The rise of individualism from classical through to romantic views of the author has been moderated through the nineteenth and twentieth centuries to the point where credit is directly given to the artist, and only to one individual, even in collaborative work, i.e. most usually to the choreographer and not the performer in dance.[13] In earlier parts of the twentieth century it could be said that even within Diaghilev's theatrical collaborations the composer held pride of place, closely followed by the librettist and visual artist and, bringing up the rear, the choreographer, the last in this very clear hierarchy.

At the modernist extreme, in more recent times, the 'work' has come to be regarded as an exploration and celebration of the medium in which it operates. The work is seen as a very human exploration, but one which, sharing something with a God-like position, denies the personal engagement of the author just as it denies that 'meaning' is constructed by anyone in particular.[14] The politics of human interaction, most frequently revealing the pain and conflict and the alienation of modern living, has provided a thriving agenda in the post-war years. The alienation and subsequent artistic fragmentation of purposes and forms that brought the twentieth century to a close has shattered what few unities remained. Discontinuity is evident in the chance happenings of a performance art event, the random juxtaposition of improvised practices and the breaking of boundaries between schools of thought and artistic styles.

However, these categories of classical, modern etc (while useful for analytic purposes) cannot in the end be separated, nor can individuals be slotted precisely into only one of them. Classical ideas continue to exist alongside modernist tendencies in life and in art. Central European Expressionism can be traced through a variety of manifestations as it transmigrates into a postmodernist form, and this is the subject of the next section.

The Expressionist Narrative

Newson's relationship to the expressionist tradition is revealed in his deep concern with the legibility of dance. His relies on his collaborators to 'reveal something of their inner selves', to the degree that the performer may feel 'totally exposed and vulnerable' (Newson, 1993, p.13). He challenges the modernist idea of the construction of emotional archetypes by making reference to the real, auto-biographical element of these performers' lives. The detail of an actual individual's personality is not generally a feature of expressionism which tends instead to favour the universalisation of emotional experience. In this sense Newson reflects work of a postmodernist character in the 1980s which more typically draws on autobiography without reserve.[15]

Among traces of expressionism that may not be immediately obvious in their relevance to a reading of *Strange Fish* is Newson's inheritance of an actual European expressionist dance movement in his native Australia. This tradition owes its origins to Gertrud Bodenwieser's move from Austria in 1938 in the face of difficult political circumstances, her subsequent world tours, and her establishing of a new life which took *Ausdruckstanz* to the Southern Hemisphere.[16] She continued to work within expressionist philosophies, pursuing belief in the dramatic power of dance; her quest for the right form to give expression to issues of contemporary relevance; and the rejection of traditional dance techniques in favour of the idea of the dance dictating its own form and vocabulary (Grayburn, 1990; Vernon-Warren & Warren, 1999). These are ideas familiar in the writings of John Martin (1933; 1939) on the American modern dance, and in the dances of Martha Graham and other exponents of the art in the US. They provide concrete evidence of the vigour of the internationalist movement in the modernist arts at that time (Connor, L. 1997).[17]

Newson's work, however, is much more than a re-articulation of 1930s expressionistic ideas. He has expressed interest in constructing stories that might serve either stage or film and which function through metaphor and allegory (Parry, 1990). Far from taking existing stories as the *basis* of his work he states that he 'start[s] from an idea and then look[s] for texts with which I can have a *dialogue*' (my itals). He also refers to starting from an image – a clue that seems to inform *Strange Fish* in its use of the Cross.[18] Newson *re-works* ideas within the framework of a topical 1990s political agenda in a form which uses *many* media, including words. Thus he creates a mode of expression that deliberately flouts the highly valued integrity of expressionist dance – its central concern being for expression through movement alone. It is however, a version of an expressionist agenda, albeit somewhat distorted by postmodernist concerns, which explains and ultimately legitimates Newson's aim of creating in the spectator the feelings of the choreographer, and thus completing the communicative loop in a satisfying fashion (satisfying at least in Newson's terms). Although invited on more than one occasion to contribute directly through interview to the writing of this text Lloyd Newson declined (Gombrich, 1997).

Autobiographical fragments published in interviews with Solway (1985); Parry (1992); Meisner (1992) and Newson (1993) reveal Newson's view that what dance can do best is to deal with 'a very personal investigation' rather than 'social and political themes on a larger theoretical level' (Newson, 1993, p.13). And yet when challenged by a feminist accusation of sexism in his works he takes up the victim position, saying 'everybody in my pieces were victims...we're using the work to explore issues which caused us unhappiness, brought about by our own abilities – as gay men, women – to play underdogs and accept that' (O'Toole, 1992). But in recent political argument, and in feminist and post-colonial theory the notion of difference would be more important than the shared one of victimhood. The experience of homophobia is different for men and women, and for different age groups; victimhood is different for varied shapes and sizes of people, and for black and white people. Newson seems to underestimate this response and to essentialise the experience, a position which is entirely consistent with his expressionist and social realist views on art.

There is a curious relationship between representations of the self and the real-life or off-stage self here. Critics tend to assume that the actor is playing him or her self picking up Lloyd Newson's statements.

> Wendy Houstoun asks Nigel Charnock to fly; she wants Dale Tanner to be able to stand in a handstand for longer than is possible.
>
> Meisner, 1992, p.11

Newson constructs a personal narrative *for* the dancers based on a psychological analysis and a concern with spirituality:

> Wendy has lost faith, she's lost friendship, she's lost one of the people she wants as a friend, Nigel, largely through her own actions, she has isolated herself. In her desperate need for friendship she has actually alienated herself to the point that she has lost all sense of belief and faith.
>
> Meisner, 1992, p.12

Newson has given an account of himself in a series of interviews often repeating particular stories or views from one to the next. In an interview with Jann Parry in1990 he appears to reject distinctions between art and life in a desire to deal with deeper life issues. Ellen Cranitch quotes Newson as starting by 'consider[ing] how people are drawn to death through desire'. She lists influences including Edward Albee, Jeanette Winterson and French and Saunders (presumably from his own testimony), and primarily in *Strange Fish*, the Greek myth of Ulysses and the Sirens. Cranitch quotes Newson thus:

> I am fascinated by what the voice represents in that tale – both beauty and destruction – there's a parallel with AIDS here, being attracted towards an ideal of love or beauty regardless of the implications.
>
> Does the very striving for meaning in our lives, for deep and intimate relationships, actually hinder our chances of achieving it?
>
> Cranitch, 1992

Richardson's story of the construction of a libretto for the opera *Akhnaten* and the selection of archaeological (in both the sense of being literally available and in the Foucauldian sense) makes the analyst of *Strange Fish* aware of the relatively inarticulate position adopted by Lloyd Newson in comparison (1999). An easy conclusion might be that Newson simply does not research his works in the same depth as Philip Glass, which we may never know since he is reluctant to talk about it, or that the subject matter is not so resonant in its history or amenable to this kind of analysis, which is clearly not true.

The link to Foucault lies in Glass's willingness to let 'documents speak for themselves, preferring not to impose on them their own interpretations' (according to Richardson, 1999, p.11) but to show 'how things are fabricated' (p.11). Self-consciousness about the historical and archaeological process is evident in his comment on *Akhnaten* that there is no new textual material in this work. This is an interesting idea for a newly constructed opera, one that Birtwistle (2000) shares, both resonating with Foucauldian theory (Foucault, 1969). It raises the question of whether this might also be said of *Strange Fish*. It might be supported in so far that neither invents an entirely new or modern story but is based on narratives long known.[19]

Glass constructs links between the character of Akhnaten and others of the same era, particularly his family, to Moses, and to twentieth century figures. It is possible to see these figures and the period anew as in retellings of the Oedipus story through Freud and Lacan. Recent egyptologists interweave theories with the history of the archaeology of the region. Glass employs minimalism as (for him) a positive response to the non-everything-else of musics of the time – clearing a space in which new voices might be heard – creating a postmodernist poetics, according to Richardson. This is the space of the offspring of serialism in music, when additive and subtractive procedures of the late 1960s and early 1970s dominated New York arts in many forms, mirroring interests found also in dance. While it would be stretching the analogy too far to see Lloyd Newson as closely concerned with either serialism or minimalism, what Glass and Newson share is the problem of how to deal with familiar texts, how to use the same methods of representation as other cultural expressions yet maintain a critical distance. Both operate within the known, using powerful historically-rich images, and yet seek to critique these images.

The Voices of Collaborators

The importance of the dancers' individuality and personal commitment is reflected in Newson's choice of collaborators, ranging widely in experience, age and physique, but each capable of meeting the challenge of working to develop movement that is distinctively their own, yet appropriate to the theme. Newson makes reference particularly to Diana Payne-Myers' 'fragility and her age' (Meisner, 1992, p.11), illuminating his general principle (rather oddly found also in Balanchine's views) that 'dancers are not pigment, they are living and feeling, and you can't deny, no matter how you try, the humanity on stage (p.12).

Diana Payne-Myers, who is over 60 years old, has played a significant role in several of Newson's works. She is sometimes abused, exposed unmercilessly, yet this is not what Newson speaks of. Instead he says he has reservations about eighteen year olds telling him about life (in dance) and wants to 'look at how older people's lives are revealed through their movement' (Meisner, 1992, p. 11). But the movement that he wants to see is hardly pedestrian in character even though it draws on everyday action and gesture.

He states that the quality of the work is seen to depend utterly on the sensibility of his partners. Newson himself says 'our work is only ever as good as the people involved, only as deep and profound as they are' (1993, p.12). In a practical sense the commercial and financial pressure to make more works to a strict timetable inevitably might raise the question of how profound they can be, and this in turn reflects back on the performers. Characters begin to repeat themselves – notably Wendy Houstoun and Nigel Charnock's characters across several works. This is not surprising if there is any 'authenticity' in the person's life, and it is to confuse art and life. Works, too, can become formulaic, yet the consistency of view and political position that we might think desirable for an individual's sanity is not what modernist 'art' prioritises in its urge to make it new. So it might be argued that it is problematic, possibly mischievous, perhaps even an abdication of his own role, for Newson to place this burden of responsibility upon his collaborators and performers.

First and foremost he requires his dancers to be highly competent technically. While these dancers would not fit a standard of 'technique' where such a concept equates with a perfect Cecchetti style or a Cunningham style, the techniques he uses exist and are well recognised in the genre type of Physical Theatre within which he works. He states that dance graduates are probably not suitable partners in this enterprise and uses actors, gymnasts and people whose life experience may (he suggests) be broader and who are willing to challenge accepted conventions. In turn, some critics readily accept *Strange Fish* as 'part dance, part theatre, part musical and part gymnastic display' (Whetstone, 1992).

In an interview in 1993 Newson talks of the collaborative process of making pieces, starting with detailed preparation transcended by the 'physical truth of movement [which] is much more complicated and cannot often be captured by words or discovered until you are in the studio with dancers' (p.12).

Parry (1992b) refers to the three and a half months spent improvising and shaping material to create collectively this thing called *Strange Fish*. Yet the performers' openness to improvising and to taking responsibility, which he cherishes, has to be balanced against his statement that 'ultimately I do make the decisions, set exercises and edit material' (p.12). His view of his collaborators and their responses reveal him to be conscious of the power he is playing with. He says 'I have tried to create a company that allows me maximum power while at the same time enabling my own performers to question' (Newson, 1993, p.11).

A further complication arises in the re-working of the stage version for video, requiring a shifting of perspective for all the collaborators and clear direction from Newson and Hinton. One of the composers, Adrian Johnston, reflects the uncertainties of the group about the 'flattening' of the work on video, and their anxieties that the camera can trick the viewer so that impressive physical feats may simply be illusion (1997). Clearly an overall view and focus is necessary to bring such complex projects to fruition but this itself may imply a style of leadership at odds with the ideology of the collaborative process. This longstanding debate has coloured both practice and theory in devised theatre for some time.

The harsh reality of 'collaboration' is that practical and financial concerns, and the wishes of the prime motivator, dominate. One artist, in this case Lloyd Newson, obtains the funding, and selects and discards collaborators to suit his vision. Adrian Johnston, did not feel able to insist on sections of the music remaining as he wrote them, although changes would be discussed between them. Newson clearly has the over-riding decision-making position.[20] One of the performers who seems able to question Newson and retain her integrity is Melanie Pappenheim, herself a powerful performer. Her interests in folk and religious music as well as her classical training and achievements as an artist perhaps contribute to her status.[21] She reports Newson's working processes as 'heavy duty games' undertaken with great intensity, drawing out material from the collaborators (1997). In this instance he was dependent upon Melanie Pappenheim to work out the dramatic sequences on the Cross in the early part of the work, while also constructing the music with Jocelyn Pook directly on to tape. To be able both to sing and move in this way is a skill restricted to few performers. While Newson was obviously responsible for selecting her, rather than other possible performers, she in turn is very important in the construction of the scenes involving the Christ/Angel/Siren figure and in the precise interplay of these threads of character(s).[22]

Melanie Pappenheim was able to resolve arguments about the inclusion of *Lullaby*, when Jocelyn Pook's desire to retain it conflicted with Newson's wish to discard it. Pook is equally ready however, to acknowledge that his suggestions, from a non-musical perspective, were often very useful. The strength of his vision and his willingness to produce examples of music which he thought might be appropriate as a starting point led to valuable interplay (Pook, 1997). By her account most composers only stay for one show with Newson partly because of his lack of understanding of the compositional process and his inability to compromise.

The song cycles Melanie Pappenheim had already created elsewhere and that she continues to make with Jocelyn Pook, for example for the Brighton Festival (1991; 2001) reveal a shared interest in semi-staged and movement-rich performance that presaged their collaboration in *Strange Fish*. It is these two, of all the collaborators, who share an interest in palindromic verbal and musical structures and in polyrhythmic constructions, of which an earlier composition, *A Man, A Plan, A Canal, Panama* is an example. Their interests are common across classical and popular music as part of the postmodernist linguistic self-consciousness. Language or, more precisely, techniques for 'playing' with language, tease the listener and make her/him question their ability to understand it. The creation of a 'soundscape' is how Adrian Johnston describes the outcome (1997). These compositions draw on a shared western cultural history which triggers emotion at a generalised and perhaps subliminal level, similar to the use of music in advertisements. But under this surface are the endless reverberations of the Christian mass and of sets of beliefs which it represents.

The collaborators in *Strange Fish* were hardly new to the process of collaboration or to working with each other. Jocelyn Pook's musical experience includes working with her own quartet as well as on theatre shows, initially at Lancaster University where she worked with dancers, actors and musicians. Both Wendy Houstoun and Lloyd Newson were for a time with Ludus dance company in Lancaster while Adrian Johnston worked at the Lancaster Playhouse.[23]

Like Pappenheim, Pook is eclectic in her interests and in the range of her work. Both might be said to be postmodernist in their willingness to move across genres and to bring elements of different histories into relationship.[24] Pook acknowledges the influence of Steve Reich, Philip Glass and Michael Nyman (1997) and is sometimes characterised as a 'romantic pragmatist' (Gray, 1997) or alternatively as rock and roll's 'classical' voice and praised for an astonishing musical journey through the centuries and across cultural boundaries. Gray asks what it is that makes Pook's compositions 'classical' as opposed to 'popular' and suggests that

> it has less to do with the new technology she blends with more traditional chamber orchestras and voices than with her *modus*: Pook's music combines formalism and ingenuity with a radical and imaginative edge.
>
> 1997, p.39

Rather rudely her music is sometimes termed, by those who like their arts 'pure',

> a melting pot of pseudo-spirituality...technically adept and traditional sounding – sufficient to pass, in these shifting times, for a contemporary classical recording
>
> Lebrecht, 1997, p.21

However, Jocelyn Pook's interest in eastern vocal sound and music is neither recent nor short-lived. It can be seen in her work with *Three Mustapha Three* as well as in the sources she refers to for particular works. The eclecticism of her references is indicative of an open palette of sound. Her CD *Deluge* links two millennia – the year 1000 and the year 2000. Using sampling techniques she mixes music from Hindu, Christian, Jewish and Islamic sources to create 'spacious, slow moving' works which have been likened to a modern requiem, 'speaking of post-nuclear death as well as the death of love' (Searson, 1997, p.51). To work between *Meat Loaf* and medieval meditation with *3 or 4 Composers* on *Still Ringing* (1997) is quite a feat. For her first UK tour in 2001 she brought together violins and viola with keyboards, baritone sax, a re-designed quanun and singers whose combined talents covered Iranian singing, Tamil and Carnatic music, combining all these threads with sculptural installations.

It is also typical of a recent trend in music composition (a postmodernist trend and therefore dismissed by some) to 'plunder' (if one does not like it) or make fascinating use quite deliberately (if one does) of familiar, historical, musical texts. As with the music of Philip Glass, Jocelyn Pook's music works because 'it relates the immediate to the remembered, the perceived to the pre-configured, the actual to the known, experiences to the experienced' (Richardson, 1999, p.53). These are elements construed by the receiver, and located in relation to other elements of the performance and of one's own history and life experience. It is fair to say that Glass's music is in fact more about re-examining past techniques than inventing new ones, as is that of Jocelyn Pook. They are not alone, since the popularity of Chaconnes of Pachelbel, Nyman and others also reflects growing interest in the late twentieth century in pre-classical forms of western music - a form of millennial angst or nostalgia perhaps.

The overlapping interest between dance, music, theatre and film that links Pappenheim and Pook is also shared with Adrian Johnston. Johnston and Pook have known each other since 1989, had common musical experiences and an affiliation to certain compositional techniques, for example, in manipulating musical fragments by digital processes; and in creating effect by illusion and allusion rather than attempting to construct narrative. Jocelyn Pook's 'score' exists only in note form, with brief melodic lines articulated. The music is made on computer and only exists in that form. Adrian Johnston produces the soundtrack on an 8 track recorder. He creates with a computerised system which can translate the result into conventional music notation. Although he studied English Language and Literature at Edinburgh he also became involved in theatre co-founding a small scale theatre company, *The Shadow Syndicate* in 1984.[25] He is very much aware that he came late into the collaboration on *Strange Fish* after Lloyd's attempt to work with another composer, Guy Michelmore, failed (Johnston, 1997; Pook, 1997).

The result in the case of *Strange Fish* was that compositions that Johnston had created over a span of four years and for different purposes with various other musicians were re-worked for this piece. These rather random processes produce a score that takes on a coherence that clearly was not part of the agenda of the artists concerned. It is, however, archetypically intertextual in its method. The history of music composition is also one of constant borrowing of themes and material from the composer's own previous work and from that of contemporaries, if without the ironic level of quotation present in the late 1990s. Johnston expresses directly a pleasure in mixing styles and contrasts this with what he perceives as Jocelyn Pook's more coherent and unified way of working, but he also voices unease at the way Lloyd Newson feels free then to 'just throw it around...so it has an arbitrary feel to it...its been completely broken up to serve that [end]' (1997).

In Johnston's testimony there is both the pressure to create something new, in the modernist mode, and a parodic 1990s re-using of material. He quotes a particular example of music for the bar scenes in *Strange Fish* being a re-working of a version created for a performance of *Richard III* in Glasgow at the Citizens Theatre. This tension between the drive towards the 'new' and 'unique' expression and a postmodernist re-working, possibly a sense of 'pastiche', is very much part of Adrian Johnston's awareness of compositional process.

Questions of ownership and of allegiance to a work or a person abound in these dilemmas with Lloyd Newson requesting that Johnston compose new material specially for this purpose. The dichotomy between Lloyd Newson's artistic vision and his need to control the production and the need (unmet) of collaborators to share more fully in this is clear. The composers felt that they had contributed fragments that were un-related and did not produce a meaningful thematic thread, and while that might be entirely reasonable their own need for coherence and structure still emerges. Melanie Pappenheim produces that thread to some extent both in her role in the work and by virtue of her experience and her personality. It is in this sense that Newson may be correct in saying that the works are only as good as the people involved.[26]

The Musical Landscape of Strange Fish

The titles and sequence of events of the 14 scenes of the staged version as the composers gave them, are as follows: Jocelyn Pook wrote tracks 1, 3, 4, 5, 9, 13, and 14, and Adrian Johnston tracks 2, 6, 7, 8, 10, 11, and 12.

1. On the Cross	2. Secret society	3. Blonde terrorists
4. Jordi's Dance	5. Knot dance	6. Good body
7. On the outside	8. Zoo Story	9. Stone song
10. Stone games	11. Water creature	12. A drowning
13. Lullaby	14. Hell, fire and damnation.	

This account provides the material from which I develop further interpretative narratives of my own, particularly in Chapters 4, 5 and 6. It is vitally important in an intertextual reading of this kind that the traces are made visible. Among the nostalgic forms relevant to the music of *Strange Fish*, as well as to the action, is the *Lament* which has historically taken a variety of musical and poetic forms, inspired by mourning rites for the dead or ritual leave-taking (bridal laments). It serves to ease the mind and to give voice to a lyrical expression of regard, as well as acting as a ritual aid, and reconciles the dead to their new condition (Grove, 1980, vol.10, p.407). Its melodies are characterised by their narrow compass, held within a tetra-chord or pentachord. This remarkably consistent ceremonial form balances the involuntary cry of grief (the 'planctus') and the deliberate framing of a message (the 'discourse') representing crisis and order respectively. I return to the 'cry' in modern psycho-analytic terms in the final chapters of the book. The Planctus becomes a refrain that punctuates the musical discourse as it becomes formalised.

The Lament flourishes in folk forms in Mediterranean areas in Europe, and in Hungary. In many cultures lamenting is a task entrusted to women.[27] The obsessional qualities of the Lament are found also in Monteverdi and Purcell where it becomes a site of excess, a deviation that must be overcome. There is an obvious link here to the nostalgic longing for Christ found in *Strange Fish* and in the compassion for human suffering that Melanie's 'lament' evokes.

Likewise, Plainsong, as a melodic thread through *Strange Fish*, structures the musical ideas of Scenes 1, 5, 9, 11 and 12. The improvisatory vocalising, typical of Plainsong, is inescapably associated with women in the later form of the lament although this contradicts normal plainsong practice of earlier centuries where it is predominantly sung by men. The voice is

> transformed into a kind of musical instrument, a sonorous line without words and unsupported by any orchestral sound [which leaves the moment] shockingly bare of other sound.
>
> Abbate 1991, p.4 [my insertion]

This exposed sound creates a voice that compels on its own, that has the capacity to move without speech. This description by Abbate (1991) of Delibes' *Lakme* might have been written for Melanie's song on the Cross. As I explore in Chapter 6, it is not seduction by the plot that it recounts but seduction by the power of the voice. Broken fragments of the same melody (which Pook and Pappenheim employ later) can suggest in themselves a fragmenting of that story and loss of control, while maintaining a continuing sonority. Melanie Pappenheim's vocalising and Jocelyn Pook's music do exactly this.

Plainsong, a form of European music dominant for eleven hundred years is evoked. But it is only *evoked*. In any event, since Grove (1980, vol. 14) warns against the temptation to make even the original manuscripts fit theoretical systems devised at the time, it seems far too dangerous with this late 20th century parody to attempt such an act. It is also rather irrelevant, if fascinating, since my point is more to do with the power of this soundscape and the way in which performers draw on its extensive history, to construct a text which speaks to the god-less world of the late 20th century, than with its accuracy or fidelity to particular modal models.

With that warning in mind it is relevant to note that from AD400 Plainsong played a major role in the Western Christian Church, and provided the basis for early harmonised music (AD900-1500) as well as for later harmonised music up to Palestrina and Byrd. Within music history and analysis there is extensive discussion of medieval classification systems and in particular of the 9th century, when heptatonic modes of Western liturgical song (Greek models of modes, tropes and tones) were brought into direct relationship with modal, non-Latin Byzantine modes. The Carolingian synthesis that was constructed (theoretically) resulted in a post hoc attempt to fit pre-existing plainchant to newly emerging models, thus

> the modal ethos of the Middle Ages...was that a mode has inherent expressive properties and extramusical associations...[itself an idea] of classical origin.
>
> Grove, 1980, vol. 12, p.398

Like other classical systems, it constructed its own highly technical gendered terms. Among its sub-rules, was a requirement to function in 'authentic-plagal pairs', which were male-female or master-servant based (Grove, 1980, vol. 12, p.399).[28]

Romantic fashion continued to use modes to create associations with native rural and archaic practices and they appear in folk song although in smaller number than formerly. It is now widely accepted that there are close associations between the European term 'mode' and technical terms in Asian musical cultures from the Arab-speaking Middle East, and also with Japanese forms via the Indian sub-continent. This history is important for my discussion of *Strange Fish* since the origins and character of the music speak clearly of this statement of Plainsong.

> It lie(s) partly in established Jewish synagogue practice of the apostolic period, partly in new developments within early Christianity itself and partly in pagan music at the diverse centres where the first churches were established.
>
> Grove, 1980, vol. 14, p.800

By the fourth century Constantinople came to dominate, following the three vibrant religious centres of Jerusalem, Antioch and Rome. Their various traditions were linked by the common framework

> of the universal liturgy; the ceremonial of the Eucharist Sacrifice; the House of the daily Divine Office; the division of the year into the Christmas and Easter cycles; the development of a local Proper

> of the Saints rooted in a time-honoured international calendar of saints' day; the division of officiating functions among a priest, deacon, lector, soloist, chorus and congregation; and the spectrum of liturgical texts, classified as prayers, exclamations, lessons, sermons, psalms and hymns.
>
> Grove, 1980, vol. 14, p.801

In summary 'Plainsong' is a term applied to the large body of traditional ritual melody of the Western Christian Church; Plainchant and Gregorian chant are commonly used as synonyms. Given the long history and extreme complexity of plainchant 'the skills of cultural psychologists and ethnomusicologists are as useful as those of the palaeographer and philologist' in tracing their history and significance (Grove, 1980, p.802) and they are linked together in my analysis in the interdisciplinary discussion of the Siren figure (Chapter 6). Free treatment persists in the late C19 and C20 centuries e.g. in musical examples of Vaughan Williams and the music of Satie selected by the choreographer Siobhan Davies for a contemporary dance, *Plain Song* (1981). The link between these fragments at least provides a preliminary clue to the evocation of 'other worlds' that the melodic lines of *Strange Fish* give rise to. Jocelyn Pook was clearly aware of both the idea of 'modal entities' as a guiding principle and of the cross cultural links.[29]

Music functions in Liturgy in the perpetual commemoration, or re-enactment, of the Last Supper in the Eucharist (the Mass in the west). This renewal of the Eucharist is the theological essence and the most important and significant of the liturgies (cf Divine Office).[30] The Psalmodic character of Plainsong derives from the fact that it was taken from the Psalter, and set as prose. Families of plainchant, each with its distinctive modal idioms and characteristic sound profiles, produce melodic phrases associated by tradition with certain musical and liturgical contexts.[31]

> The plainchant mode, then, is at bottom a collection of traditionally related melodic idioms and of established procedures for selecting and ordering them, literally, putting them together, *compositio*. Composition of this sort is sometimes called a patchwork, quotation or centonisation process, terms shared with Homeric scholars and with philologists concerned with medieval literature and oral epic...[which] includes the use of improvisational and irrational elements that transcend any fixed rules.
>
> Grove, 1980, vol. 14, p.804

Jocelyn Pook and Melanie Pappenheim's music reflects this history strongly despite its late twentieth century position. It is itself a patchwork of quotation and includes improvised elements. They acknowledge their starting points in the requiem mass. However, in making the music for *Strange Fish* they worked without recognisable language, and with an awareness of both folk and religious texts, as well as a theatrical interest. Their use of prose rhythm provides another direct link to the Plainsong period.[32]

While this borrowing or re-using may occur at the level of melodic fragments it also occurs in the construction of sections within a whole. In Glass's *Akhnaten* the Chaconne – a cyclical, slow stately, dance, using ostinato or ground bass – provides the constant against 'the shape-shifting melodic and harmonic material it underpins' (Richardson, 1999, p.63). The Chaconne, like Plainsong in *Strange Fish,* signifies a meeting of east and west in modern thinking, 'harmonic cycles tied in even cyclical chains impart to the music a sense of stasis and rhythmic vitality that we recognise both from Western popular music and non-European musical styles' (p.68). These musical structures can be regarded as intertextual in the sense of the traces they draw on, and Pook's freer use of them even more so.

However, it is not just the musical sources that inspired Lloyd Newson. He also provided some of the words that Jocelyn Pook set to music, including a German text for *Stone Song*. In working on *Strange Fish* with Lloyd Newson she created vocal sections and gave them titles, often related to discussions with him; *The Knot dance*; *Stone song; Lullaby* and *Hell fire and damnation.* Pook also refers to themes in *Strange Fish* that are different from the later interpretations by critics, for example of the *Lullaby* scene which has been seen as an AIDS story, with a shivering dying man. But the ideas that were discussed during the process of making the work were to do with the 'fear of falling asleep when you're a child' (Pook, 1997). In my own account I draw on ideas of baptism and absolution making a third narrative voice for the same scene in Chapter 6.

Although not party to all of Lloyd Newson's thinking, Pook was aware of the variants in the role that Melanie Pappenheim took, of the Siren alongside the Christ figure, but also of a figure representing a conscience, which I term a mixture of guardian Angel and avenging Angel. On some occasions Newson was clear about the kind of sound he thought would convey his characters and narratives and at other times his collaborators felt they were working in the dark (Johnston, 1997; Pook, 1997).

Jocelyn Pook's multiple talents enable her to sing or play fragments herself and work with them before making a final version, which either she or colleagues record. This is how she worked with Melanie Pappenheim, sometimes working directly onto tape. The technology can be quite basic, as in the technique of recording a section, usually a vocal line, and playing it backwards, then adding instrumentation to it. The sections called *Lullaby* and *Stone song* were created in this way although the final tracks were sung entirely by Melanie Pappenheim. Jocelyn Pook also created tracks specially for the video version, of which a striking example is the music for the bar scene for Lauren Potter, Wendy Houstoun and Jordi Cortes Molina (Scene 4).

The musical narratives that exist as threads in the mosaic of *Strange Fish* are clearly highly significant in its analysis. So, too, are narrative threads that come from the dramatic narrative and here I offer a similar account that points up the tradition that underpins expressionist theatre bearing in mind the earlier exposition on expressionist narrative in this chapter.

Dramatic Narrative Tendencies

It is instructive to cite two views on the structure of *Strange Fish* to illustrate the point that the structure of the drama is itself *con*structed and linked to genre ideas before embarking on a discussion of where the narratorial voice may lie, how the settings affect the narrative, and how the characters themselves write the narrative. Parry argues that *Strange Fish* has

> a coherent choreographic logic, rather than the cinematic or collage assembly typical of performance and physical theatre work; its visual and kinetic images are rigorously organised to convey meaning, not to stimulate day-dreams.
>
> Parry, 1992b

Brennan (1992) is less convinced. She hesitates, finding that it 'hovers... between a connecting narrative and a collage of instances'.

Strange Fish self-consciously asks the reader to address the question of who is telling the story, if any single person and whether it is only one person. The narrator is conventionally seen as a reliable, external, prophetic, voice but in *Strange Fish* a number of subject positions are adopted and individual voices can be traced, noting to whom they belong and how they interact. The narrating voice encourages a reader to identify with one or other participant while recognising that the reader herself chooses to engage with some voices and not others despite, and whatever, the text suggests.

Scene 1 seems to engage the reader as if from Wendy Houstoun's point of view as she moves around the foot of the cross and behind the penitent figure kneeling in prayer, but the singing voice encourages a sympathy with the figure suspended on the cross. In Scene 2 the active subjects are without doubt Nigel Charnock and Wendy Houstoun in private, inwardly focused, interaction. Despite the increasing number of participants in Scene 3 it is Lauren Potter and Wendy Houstoun who seem to be controlling the viewers' perspective although increasingly the reader becomes aware of the camera director, particularly in the rapid movement of Scene 4.

In Scene 5, while sympathy with the lovers is generated, the reader cannot forget that Wendy is watching from the foreground where the viewer is positioned. This is what generates a cynical view of the proceedings.

From the start of Scene 6 there is an atmosphere of waiting while being sociable, a rather unfocussed gathering into which Nigel enters, and from then on his level of anxiety puts the reader directly in his position. This is intensified in Scene 7 in close-focused events where Nigel attempts to get in between other couples. Wendy's slap in the face feels like a slap in the reader's face, not just Nigel's when she forces him away. In stark contrast, Scene 8, in which Wendy is as isolated as Nigel was in the previous scene, does not generate the same sympathy for her as it did for Nigel. Rather it is seen from Jordi and Lauren's point of view as they establish their own relationship.

In Scene 9 where Wendy and Melanie (the latter in the role of the Angel) are present, the narrator role seems to reside more with Melanie as observer of the futilities of human intercourse. Scene 10 shifts the focus back to Wendy as active director of events although it would be difficult to sustain a line that one's sympathies are with her, rather it is Nigel's suffering that speaks loudly. Melanie's position seems to focus Scene 11 as she supports the sick figure, here again in the role of the Angel. Wendy is literally the person who vocalises the text in Scene 12 but against Melanie's singing voice, and it is not clear that either is a dominant narrator.

Narratives can be derived not just from a sense of the position of narrator but from the location of scenes. ***Church scenes*** are two in number in *Strange Fish*, strategically placed at the beginning and the end of the work, setting the mood and creating a sense of opening up the work and then of completion. The very framework of a church calls up notions of dignity and humility; of reverence and recognition of one's insignificance; of belief and prayer as against agnosticism and atheism; of judgement, of facing up to one's sins and shortcomings. The most obvious and immediate contrast between the first and last scenes is in the atmosphere and mood.

The ***Bar Scenes*** (Scenes 3 and 4 and then the party scene, Scene 6) emphasise the agenda of sociability, desirability, mixing with others, meeting and parting, competitiveness, personal success and distress. The original bar scene is later augmented into a party scheme by coloured lights and a low stage and the emphasis shifts from small groups to the larger group.

Corridor scenes, as in Scenes 2,5,8 and 10 draw on a different set of texts. Corridors are places for casual meetings, for passing others with barely a glance, or for furtive, secretive and intimate moments. There is an element of danger in the narrowness of corridors, the possibility of confrontation and the threat of not being able to escape easily. Each scene carries different significance within this agenda as the title and subsequent action reveal. The idea of Corridors seen as places of potential threat, binds Scene 8 to Scene 10, whereas Scenes 2 and 5 emphasise more positive and enjoyable aspects of relationship.

While a *bar* is an open environment from which escape is possible, and a *corridor* explicitly raises the question of escape, other ***smaller rooms*** carry a more intense message. Scenes 7, 9 and Scene 11 take place in intimate settings, the first in a social space, but one confined by the use of lighting; the second in a 'bedroom' and the third around the sides of a water tank in an enclosed space. There is greater possibility in these environments for deep and genuine communication whether agonised or joyful.

The location of scenes, and the environments that are thus created, offer another baseline and a straightforward way of comparing events and assessing shifts in mood and narrative. The actions of individuals and their presence as distinct characters, too, contribute to the dramatic narrative.

Wendy Houstoun plays the part of quintessential observer and malicious influence. She is often alone, certainly alienated, but makes constant efforts to disrupt the relationships of others and to manipulate outcomes, as in the Bar scenes and in observing the social interaction of others. Her own attempts at intimacy seem always to be doomed. First conniving with Lauren Potter and then attempting to destroy her is one of Wendy's specialities. In Scene 4, Molina's self-absorbed sensuality is shattered by their predatory, circling, teasing game. It is Lauren who succumbs to the male, not Wendy, here, or ever, in this disturbing piece. Her own failures lead to further frantic efforts on her part to disrupt the relationships of others, particularly the lovers.

Group relationships reveal the underlying desperation of these individuals. Their interactions range in tone from compulsive emotional dependency when Lauren and Jordi get together (Scene 4); to the compulsive mindless sex of Wendy and Dale (Scene 9); to the utterly terrifying demonstration of emotional need between Wendy and Nigel which ends in violence (Scene 10). Even loving consolation is marred by the bittersweet sadness in Scene 11 of baptism and absolution between Melanie as Angel and Dale, the dying sufferer. Intimidation and competition (Scene 3) with the group lending approval is compounded by the party (Scene 6) where unkind acts continue. Neither is there mercy, in the judgement of the group in Scene 9's aftermath of sex; no sympathy, no pity. The ultimate betrayal is the Judas kiss that Wendy forces on Christ/Melanie – since it leads to death.

At this very obvious narrative level several types of structure emerge, all of which are problematic in the context of a post-structuralist analysis. In Chapter 3 I return to questions of narrative.

Conclusion

In practice, a conventional view of dance narrative rests on ideas of structure which operate at a number of levels, from the large scale organisation of extended periods of time, e.g. Acts/Scenes in a ballet or opera or movements in a symphony, determined both by narrative convention and musical structure, to smaller sections, even down to the progression from one note or movement to the next. It is common in both opera and ballet that the action pauses while what Abbate (1991) calls a reflective or contemplative scene occurs. In addition to virtuosic celebration there is the chance for lyrical and poetic reflection. Meditation on some recent action (e.g. commitment in love to another) and elaboration of its significance, may typically be the subject matter. As Abbate says of opera, and I would add that this is as relevant to ballet, these texts 'must be denatured by fragmentation and nonsensical repetition' and are created to bear such acts (1991, p.68). However, these texts are also deeply embedded in contemporary life and relate to it in a multiplicity of ways (Foster, 1996b).

The outer framework of an opera or ballet is often established by change from large group sections to solo recitative or aria sections, the equivalent of mime sections in ballet based on a conventional series of gesture/signs, which carry the action forward, and dancing sections, in which the formal vocabulary is on display. These sections convey mood, construct aesthetic qualities, and demonstrate the virtuosity that locates opera and ballet within their own traditions. Distinctive refinements of this model can be found in imperial classicist, neo-classicist and modernist ballets. What Kirstein calls 'legible virtuosity' (1971, p.4) is built by emphasising events, by re-stating ideas, by showing hierarchies.

A conventional view of music would suggest a close link to narrative only in the case of programme music or opera. But by extension the sweep of any music can be made to connect to a course of events and emotional states, for example as found in discussion of much C19th instrumental music. This idea is carried forward in a more abstract form where tonal 'events' take place, themes are seen as 'characters' albeit in a purely musical drama.

Abbate argues that narrative in music is not only an event sequence and way of reading but also 'a characteristic way of speaking' (1991, p.48). This view depends on a distinction between story and discourse, the latter being the work of an ordering intelligence, the narrator assembling the events, while the story is a projection of some specific object or tale, a reader or writer's assumption spun out of discourse. This also ties in with the finer points of technical discourse which identify the characteristics of individual composers or of groups of works based on elements of musical language used.

Abbate stresses that 'narrativity' has to be understood as a metaphor in music given that it is not possible (nor would it be desirable) to establish a one-to-one correspondence between musical elements and dramatic events. It operates as

> an analogy between certain linear elements of music...and the events in a dramatic plot; that is, music has been perceived as enactment, as analogous to the event-sequences of theatrical or cinematic narrative.
>
> p.x

It is a matter of recurring debate whether this affinity of dance and music serves the interests of either. The effect on dance and music of 'miming' the dramatic narrative tends to be crude. Such mimicry or 'mickey mousing' also misses the point that it is the uncertainties of dance and musical interpretations that are such a vital source of pleasure, not its story-telling capacities. Even where there are narrative links, neither dance nor music is 'acting out' or 'representing' in any exact sense what might have been spoken of in words. Each may act as a voice that 're-speaks' an event in its own way. Music has its own complexity, as Abbate argues when she says that 'certain gestures experienced in music constitute a narrating *voice*' (1991, p.19). This narrating voice is not an imitation of the singing voice but is 'marked by multiple disjunctions with the music' and therefore it is not an encoding of events or of human emotions but 'a rare and peculiar *act*'. Thus the emphasis moves from a structuralist narratology to ideas of performance and enunciation.

If, within post-structuralist theory, the rise of the reader has been at the expense of the death of the author (meaning, here, the choreographer, not myself as author of this written text) it is a further development to posit a resurrection of the author (choreographer) within a re-worked post-structuralist position. To resurrect the author is to recognise, and articulate more clearly, the self-evident position that a work is 'made' by a particular person, or group of people. Choreographic intention, as well as a reader's perception, has to be understood as arising from each person's psychological and cultural position, while recognising that the work itself is already positioned culturally and sub-culturally.

Adler and Pointon's reflections offer a similar position on this subject:

> conscious decisions have been made about self-presentation, and about the construction of narratives which relate the body of the artist to the body of work.
>
> 1993, p.4

And in a post-structuralist environment it might be argued that the representations made by an artist are inescapably, and interestingly, a crucial reflection of his/her existence and choices. Whether conscious or unconscious they are indubitably the reflections of a particular individual.

In separating out story narratives from musical narratives, Abbate raises the idea of distance, or disparity between 'the musical fabric and the phenomenal objects it is said to express' (1991, p.26). She asks if music can 'possess narrativity without the distance engendered by discursive formulation' (p.26) and what this would be like. This detached voice is most clearly seen in film, which through the shooting and editing process, constructs distance and makes its own distancing methods evident. This is key to any analysis of the video version of *Strange Fish*, adapted specially for the medium and with the close collaboration of the film director, David Hinton. The idea of an authorial narrating voice is difficult to hold on to in the plethora of positions revealed in this work.

Strange Fish, like all theatre works, required a large number of people to bring it to performance and later to video. Their voices, positions and narrative constructions are the subject of this chapter. So, too, are the voices of readers and the messages of the text. Although separating voices as I try to do here is open to the criticism that it sustains or reinforces distinctions between the maker of a performance and the spectator, it is necessary for detail of analysis and, in return, it openly recognises all those who actively engage with the work.

Stories and narratives constructed by individuals bear some relationship to ideas about myth. Doniger sees myth 'on a continuum of all the narratives constructed of words - poems, realistic fictions, histories' (1998, p.7). Myth shares with talk of art the idea of narrating an experience. Talking about art, like making it, requires an ability to distinguish different uses of conventions in relation to different materials and techniques within certain types of dance. It is essentially an activity undertaken with hindsight allowing the reader/ viewer to recognise characteristic ways of selecting and organising elements of the medium. In *Strange Fish* there is no linear story but episodes which follow each other. Characters have voices, to some extent their own, but only in a limited sense. The narrating persona are not clearly identified, voices shift. This preference for episodic form with no obvious logic for the order of the events constructs a piece not determined by 'narrative' in Aristotelian form even though its closure matches its opening. As Frow comments, the question of who is speaking 'is still the most difficult and the most interesting of textual questions' (2006, p.58).

1 A useful introduction to theories of narrative can be found in Porter Abbott's recent text (2002).

2 An interesting debate could be developed here about this inter-relationship and the sense in which all authorial voices are to some extent ancestral, and vice versa.

3 Even the choreographer, apparently, does not possess a record of the stage version although some rehearsal footage exists.

4 A wonderfully evocative construction of this period and place can be found in Jeanette Winterson's novel, *Oranges are not the only fruit* (1985).

5 This is much more so with Asian and Far East students than with those from North America and probably should not surprise us.

6 It was my intention that the descriptions of each of the scenes that follow would be layered with images taken from the video to show precisely which moments I allude to. It was not possible to obtain permission to do this, much to my regret. The possibilities of dance analysis based on new technologies would be greatly enhanced since without such material the reader has to return to the video to locate the actual moment. The video has recently been re-issued on DVD.

7 Parts of this section have already been published (2004).

8 Along with a small group of companies including Theatre de Complicité.

9 As in the work of de Valois for the ballet.

10 Lloyd Newson and DV8 have received more than 20 awards since 1987, including the Evening Standard Ballet Award in 1989 and the IMZ Dance Screen award in 1990, both for *Dead Dreams of Monochrome Men*; Digital Dance Production Award in 1988; Prudential Award in 1992; recently the Prix Italia in 2005.

11 A more extended account of the works, produced by the company, their subject matter and treatment, can be found in Lark (1999).

12 The long history of views that we inherit on this subject has produced widely different conceptions. In the classical attribution the author might be thought of as someone *through* whom God works, a vehicle, a vessel for inspiration from another world (as in Moses receiving the Tablets from God). The human being is neither credited, in the sense of owning the work, nor accountable for its content or impact on others. From these ultimate spiritual truths, history shifts to the theorist of romantic persuasion who might attribute the 'origin' and 'meanings' of a work directly to its maker, the original artist in the garret.

13 Again, woman as muse, as in the traditional ballet choreography world (Lynn Seymour for Macmillan etc) puts us firmly in our places, since the named creator is the male, just as God created the world and Adam was the first man, woman his helpmeet etc etc.

14 In a form of social realism typical of the mid-twentieth century the purpose of art and the intention of the artist was to show the horrors of the 'real' world e.g. to reveal the personal impact of the cataclysmic events of two world wars between 1910 and 1950.

15 In this he has been likened to Pina Bausch, Jan Fabre and other European choreographers of recent years.

16 Bodenwieser's life in Austria, her tours and influence in the Southern Hemisphere is documented in a number of publications including Grayburn (ed), 1990.

17 Connor, L., in an analysis of the history of newspaper criticism in the US points up the modernist links across the arts as early as 1927 (1997).

18 There are also references to him starting with a scenario, or score or narrative in *Strange Fish* but on inspection this is a very cursory document with no more than brief outlines of scenes e.g. 'Secret Conversations - Nigel enters, joins Wendy, Dale makes partial appearance'. Some titles that work their way through the entire process and which seem as relevant to the final version include the 'Blonde Terrorist section'. These descriptions were not made available to the collaborators, however, when they began work (Johnston, 1997; Pook, 1997).

19 In that Glass probes his subject matter in an archaeological depth that Newson does not, they are quite dissimilar in my view.

20 On the other side of this dilemma is a marked lack of confidence on some of the other artists' part, notably Johnston, revealed in an unwillingness to expose himself as a solo artist until he feels more certain of his own voice (Johnston, 1997).

21 Since 1986 Melanie Pappenheim has created theatre/music pieces in collaboration with both classical and rock musicians, theatre directors and choreographers. Typically she will take dance class with the performers during rehearsal periods, continue with yoga and be very active physically in the improvising and working process (Pook, 1997). What she represents is the increasingly common crossing of boundaries within performance practice, between music and dance, theatre and 'performance'.

22 Melanie Pappenheim has an impeccable musical background, as a choral scholar at King's College, London, studying German and Music. Unusually, she studied as a mature student, and both prior and subsequent musical experiences have taken her to Brussels and Italy as well as to Germany. Her range of singing experience covers lieder, early music, and the music theatre of Kurt Weill.

23 Jocelyn Pook trained at the Guildhall School of Music and Drama and has worked as a string part arranger, as well as a performer. Her commissions include the music for two Derek Jarman films. She writes music for television programmes and has created the soundtrack for commercials e.g. for Orange telephones and for television series. Her work, like that of Michael Nyman and Phillip Glass is published by Chesters.

24 Pook is a member of a group called '3 or 4 composers' who collaborate on compositions, and of 'Elektra Strings'. This group of six women work on Music performance/theatre projects as well as pop bands. She has associations with medieval themes through the music group 'Dead can Dance'. Her performance experience in 'Elektra Strings' includes work with *Eurythmics, The Communards, The Manic Street Preachers; Meat Loaf; The Stranglers* and *Style Council.* Her commissions for DV8 include *My Body, Your Body* (1988); *MSM* (1994); and for 'O Vertigo Dance Company', the piece *Deluge* (1994).

25 He has had regular commissions for theatre scores from the National Theatre, RSC and Citizens Theatre, Glasgow. He also makes scores for silent films and has performed throughout Europe and the USA. Originally he was a drummer, bassist and keyboard player. Recently he has scored feature films e.g. for Michael Winterbottom's *Jude* (1996) and *Welcome to Sarajevo* (1997) and has worked with Stephen Poliakoff.

26 The practical realities of free-lance composition mean that a composer may be working on several projects simultaneously, and the pressure from a choreographer, who tends to work intensively and exclusively on one project at a time, creates an obvious difficulty.

27 Old Testament verses of Lamentations of the prophet Jeremiah have been set many times from the C15th onwards, used specifically in Holy Week. Typically they have waned from the sixteenth century onward. Lamentations are not peculiar to the Christian Church but can be found for example in Jewish songs of mourning.

28 By the C16th polyphonic music using eightfold modal systems was well established. The 12 modes of the later C16th were then overtaken by the C19th major/minor system, sometimes seen as a reduction to two modes.

29 There are 74 pages of text on modes in Grove (1980), much of it highly technical.

30 Rules were established for the music for different sections of the Mass e.g. introits and alleluias.

31 It might also be possible to see the melodic fragments of *Strange Fish* as a para-liturgical chant, *Cantio* (Grove, 1980, vol. 14, p.817) a form which enjoyed considerable popularity during the C14th, C15th and C16th and which was frequently used in liturgical drama. But it can also be interpreted in the light of contemporary rhymed prayers and devotional verse poetry cultivated in southern Germany, Switzerland from late C13th to C17th in which the favourite subject matters included, among others, the Cross and the Virgin Mary, both ideas which dominate this piece.

32 One of the complexities of this analysis is that there is more than one version of the music. The tape that was on sale at the performance was of the stage version and I use that version for some illustrations because the musical melodic theme is elaborated in more detail in this longer version. The score that was recorded for the video version shares many features with the stage version but differs also. Since my point is not concerned with the differences between the two (no video version of the stage performance seems to exist) I shall make it clear to which I refer but in general I take a stance that accommodates both. In common, crucially, are melodic phrases, the tonal atmosphere and the structuring through time.

CHAPTER 3

From Narrative to Intertextuality

> Both axes of intertextuality, texts entering via authors (who are, first, readers) and texts entering via readers (co-producers), are ... emotionally and politically charged.
>
> Worton and Still, 1990, p.2

In this chapter I aim to steer a course through historic conflicts in the theory and practice of arts criticism and scholarship. These conflicts are present in the debates between traditional arts theory and newer forms of cultural and critical questioning – between a passion for emotional engagement on the one hand, and text-based structural analysis and the cultural construction of meaning on the other. Dance, music and theatre share a cultural and critical environment. Their many forms overlap, although their methods in both theory and practice are quite distinct.[1] Most particularly, I am concerned to trace a shift in analysis and interpretation from conventional story-telling narratives to intertextual or, more generally, post-structuralist narrative constructions. In this chapter I articulate these changing positions in the context of the performing arts, and specifically in preparation for the analysis of *Strange Fish*.

The idea of narrative is not only relevant to the literary and dramatic arts. All writing, all research tells stories, linear or otherwise, and is subject to the same conditions (Usher and Edwards, 1994). There are parallels to be explored, for example, between dance 'languages' (styles and genre of dance) and verbal languages, both at the level of dialect within a language, and at the level of trans-national linguistic similarity. Nonetheless, it is obvious that musical and choreographic processes are not based on the same kind of reasons and evidence that underpin scientific debate or everyday communication. There is a very different analogy one can make, with dance as the *poetry* of language, not its everyday communication. Hence the relevance of poetic concepts, of 'art' and 'cultural practices' and of the conventions of each highly specified stylistic form, which intervene in the process of communication.

In all cases, however, narrative is underpinned both by ideas of the 'story' or 'tale' and by theories of structure. The performing arts disciplines have shared the twentieth-century evolution of such theories, although each art takes on its own character. All, however, have developed styles that include an intensive focus on form or structure, and from which 'formalist' or 'structuralist' criticism has evolved to match. Structuralism, it is often stated, claims a quasi-scientific authority, a claim that generates unease in many fields. Performance texts are open, not closed; they use a flexible system of signification, and can certainly be discussed logically and cogently but perhaps not 'scientifically'. Threads of connection can be debated, and an interwoven fabric of readings created. None could claim some final empirical validity.

Such a claim would invalidate other insights of post-structuralism, those that expose the significant position of the person who constructs an account – the reader, spectator or participant. Individuals who make, perform and read these dances become of critical importance. In Eco's terms, this simply says that a reader is always envisaged in the writing of texts, just as I sit composing this on a word processor, thinking from time to time of potential readers, adjusting the way I express ideas with particular groups of people in mind. The co-operation of the reader does not 'pollute the structural analysis with extratextual elements' but is an inescapable and rich thread in the analysis (Eco, 1984, p.4). This presages the next section, which traces some complexities in the move from structuralism to post-structuralism.

From structuralism to post-structuralism

My interest in this question arises because Newson's own account of his work poses problems for the idea of open accounts of interpretation typical of the post-structuralist critic. He seeks a guarantee of communication that is not easy to satisfy, and urgently needs to convey his own meaning. In an interview with Levene he suggests that this is a very real difficulty in working in dance, 'partly because images are ambiguous', since there is 'no dictionary to which you can turn to that says "this means this"' (1992, p.24). The idea of a one-to-one correspondence between images and emotions or ideas is far removed from many strands of current post-structuralist thinking on meaning. Watson shares Lloyd Newson's approval of art with a message, and posits popular (and far from postmodernist) universals, saying of preview performances of *Strange Fish* in Budapest, a month before the premiere at Expo 1992 in Seville, Spain:

> it works as an ironic sign of the times as Hungary struggles to come to grips with the momentous changes of the past two years. It wasn't planned that way, but the secret of any powerful message is the ability to translate into any time and place.
>
> Watson, 1992a

The existence of 'a' message, conveying such specific meanings, typical of a strict semiotic and cultural approach, might initially be seen to be at odds with a recognition of the importance of the reader, and of the freedom inherent within the play of artistic codes.

There is a continuum of terminology that needs to be unravelled in tracing notions of form in the arts to the complex technical language of the structuralists and post-structuralists. The similarity and confusion of terms reflects, of course, a truism: that all are concerned with form or structure. By the same token, such similarities can conceal the fact that perspectives vary markedly between theorists, and from time to time. Structuralism can be confused with formalism, a kind of analysis that neglects thematic content and concentrates on the work's internal forms, codes and conventions.

The linguistic associations of structuralism encourage an emphasis on the structures that produce meaning, rather than on the meanings themselves, and on the norms and conventions that in turn produce meanings. At the other extreme, those such as Marxists who construct social and political explanations can be accused of 'biased reading', of 'neglecting the distinctive themes of a work in order to find in it manifestations of a structure or system prescribed by their discipline' – in this case, to find a social structure (p.20).

And somewhere between these positions it can also be argued that theorists working from psychoanalytic or sociological standpoints can be seen as structuralists in their interest in 'the text's relation to particular structures and processes' (Culler, 1983b, p.21). That structuralists can be concerned with paradox and play, or with rigidity and mechanical operations, or with the experience of the reader, leads Culler to suppose that structuralism is an 'indeterminate radical force' (p.22).

If distinctions between structuralism and post-structuralism are so difficult to determine – unless the former is seen crudely as a series of systematic, scientific projects attempting to develop grammars (Culler, 1983b, p.22) while the latter only focuses on 'the way in which this project is subverted by the workings of the texts themselves' – then the question of what is 'in' the text remains open. Culler asks

> is it so rich a plenitude that no reader can ever grasp it all? a determinate structure with some gaps the reader must fill in? a set of indeterminate marks on which the reader confers structure and meaning?
>
> p.73

Further potential confusion with other theories of structure arises in relation to 'social formation' or, as Giddens develops it, 'structuration'. The originality and usefulness of Giddens's structuration theory has been challenged, but in his own terms it is 'a conceptual investigation of human action, social institutions, and the interrelations between action and institutions' (Bryant & Jary, 1991, p.210). Structuration theory, first articulated in 1976, claimed 'to determine the conditions which govern the continuity and dissolution of structures or types of structure' (Giddens, 1976, p.120). His analysis was that structuralism's weakness is to regard the production of social relations as a mechanical outcome, rather than as an active process; while the problem of philosophy of action lies in dealing only with production, not with structural analysis. Giddens attempts to reconcile these difficulties, to supersede deficiencies, showing how 'social structures are both constituted by human agency, and yet at the same time are the very medium of this constitution' (p.121).

Through this characterisation it is possible to link social and aesthetic structures to recognise the continuum and continuity of experience that allows us to connect the largest social organisation to cultural practices of many kinds. Hence it becomes possible, for instance, to connect culturally dominant views of sexuality in certain sub-cultures to the works of DV8 and to the details of events in *Strange Fish*. This is becoming accepted practice in analysis. For example, Desmond argues that

> if dance styles and performance practices are both symptomatic and constitutive of social relations, then tracing the history of dance styles and their spread from one group or area to another, along with the changes that occur in this transmission, can help uncover shifting ideologies attached to bodily discourse.
>
> 1997, p.33

Giddens's preferences lie with a Wittgensteinian view (and with that of Garfinkel) on the nature of language and the relation of language to social life. In this manner, through Wittgenstein, one can make a full circle back to David Best and his art/life views. Best argues that

> it cannot intelligibly be supposed that what is expressed in language are independently existent, non-linguistic thoughts and feelings. Without language such ideas and feelings could not even *exist*.
>
> Best, 1992, p.114

Following on this argument, unique expressions are moulded into the language of *Strange Fish*, each evoking a range of traces of other texts. At a higher level, as Bryson argues:

> when, in the grand narratives of modernity, the nature of the object being described (the emergence of pure form) comes to converge with the critical framework through which it is approached (formalism), the results can be both highly persuasive and at the same time severe in the limitations imposed upon criticism.
>
> In Desmond, 1997, p. 70

Possibly one of the most-cited phrases in post-structuralist dogma has been Lyotard's 'incredulity towards metanarratives' (1984, p. xxiv) and it bears repetition and reiteration in this context. It reflects the dominance of science as a discourse in the twentieth century; a discourse that legitimates itself and refuses to see other disciplines that take a narrative form as anything other than 'fables, myths, legends, fit only for women and children' (p.27). Lyotard sees this narrative domain, into which the arts have been seen to fall apparently naturally, as equally complex. Popular stories in themselves bestow legitimacy on social institutions and follow a rhythm, a 'metrical beat of narrative occurrences' (p.22), which can be accorded the same dignity as other narratives.

In slightly palindromic fashion, Lyotard describes this as part of the 'proclivity to define the conditions of a discourse in a discourse on those conditions' (p.30). Palindromes appear in *Strange Fish*, and it, too, can be said to define the conditions of its own discourse through a (dance, theatre) discourse on its own conditions. In the discourse of *Strange Fish* the music cannot be separated from the movement, any more than the narrative structures can be ignored; and thus the perspective taken on analysis in each art must be exposed. Since *Strange Fish* operates as both a theatrical narrative and a musical elaboration of themes, compounded by danced expositions, an analysis requires understanding of each of these performance modes of structuring.

There is disjunction between dance and music in their current modes of analysis. Ayrey and Everist (1996) identify the dominant

American images of 'forensic surgery' that continue to characterise the musicologist's task. Schenker's concern with dynamic and flow has been replaced by a structuralist, cold and dogmatic account – growth and process as against architectonic structure; the biological against the architectural; the justifiable (i.e. scientific) against the metaphysical. This is not directly appropriate either to dance or to theatre in their recent forms, relating more strongly to analysis of some forms of modern ballet and contemporary dance.

However, Ayrey's wider concerns in music analysis can stand for the whole field of performing arts. He states that while the open text may initiate limitless commentary, such proliferation occludes the works and becomes analysis about analysis – what he calls 'this flight into postmodernism' (p.127), leaving the work untouched, with the result that 'their analytic fallout is elusive, even evasive'.

> Fissures and blindness in structural analysis attest to the value of self-reflective commentary and to the necessity of the recent turn to metatheory. But it would appear that an awareness of the provisional and contingent nature of all statements about music, of all positions, is increasingly paralysing the impulse to analyse.
>
> Ayrey in Ayrey and Everist, 1996, p.129

An intertextual reading raises these underlying theoretical and value positions to a level of awareness where they can be examined in relation to the text. Firstly, however, it is necessary to sketch how post-structuralist approaches manifest themselves in the detail of analytic methodology. I consider therefore the deconstruction of narrative before characterising the typical narratives of dance analysis and proposing various intertextual approaches.

Deconstructing narrative

The idea of narrative rests on structure – traditionally, that there be a beginning, a middle and an end. A series of events guides the reader, often in well-worn ways, to follow the 'story'. Interest in the regularities and constraints that appear in creating units larger than the sentence (a kind of equivalent to 'paragraph' dance structures) has led to theories of structure or of combining elements, which in turn relates to the topic of discourse (see the discussions of genre in Chapter 1 and of structure at the end of Chapter 2). Knowledge of the conventions governing how links are made between elements and between small wholes and context is a necessary condition of successful communication about art practices. These conventions are the material of constructions of genre, and of discourse analysis.

Like dance, 'any music with sequences of events – thematic ideas, harmonic processes, cadences, instrumental exchanges – in short the substance of all common practice in Western music, can be said to be narrative' (Abbate, 1991, p.45). Classical dance forms draw on exactly the same notions of thematic ideas and harmonic processes, and add their own known positions that start and end phrases (like cadences), common groupings of dancers (instrumentation) and formulaic sequences of events (structures of melody and harmony). On this basis, all dance and all music could be said to be narrative, if not 'narrating' in the sense of storytelling. The outcome of such formalist analysis is a description of structures rather than an 'event', unless it is then used to intertextual ends.

The structuralist/modernist world is epitomised in the work of Susan Sontag, for whom the very idea of interpretation is contentious and odious. Interpretation is contentious since it is 'traditionally thought of as resolving textual difficulties through careful comparison and combination of scattered passages' (Leitch, 1983, p.ix), and odious in the terms of Sontag's famous essay *Against Interpretation* (1961, 1987) since it seeks the 'content' of the work in terms of what it 'means' or 'says'. Sontag is particularly vehement about Marxist and Freudian approaches, labelling them as 'aggressive and impious theories of interpretation' (p.7) that are reactionary rather than liberating – the 'revenge of the intellect' against immediate experience. 'Our task' she says, 'is to cut back content so that we can see the thing at all ... to show *how it is what it is*, even *that it is what it is*, rather than to show what it *means*.' And finally, in total agreement with Roland Barthes, if for different reasons, she places the emphasis on 'an erotics of art' (1961; 1987, p.14). Seen in the context of the rise of modernist American art, with its concomitant formalist criticism, Sontag's response was perfectly understandable, and was a view commonly held across all the arts at that time.

Contemporary deconstruction, however, subverts the idea that we can say 'what it is', or that 'immediate experience' is unmediated. The position of deconstruction suggests that the work of interpretation is to question 'its' intrinsic features as well as the language in which its discourse is constructed. Deconstruction is sometimes seen as a method that contradicts the coherence and completion of structuralism, acting as the 'menace from within' (Leitch, 1983, p.26), an expression that itself rests on a metaphor of light and dark, the founding metaphor of Western philosophy. Similar concerns are found in theories of dance interpretation (Adshead-Lansdale, 1994; ed., 1999), while Pople takes the matter further in music, saying that

> analysis has come to be seen as one form of discourse or metadiscourse on music ... promoting analysis itself as a kind of theory through which a range of possible meanings can be described, prescribed or circumscribed. At the same time, and perhaps ironically, the interpenetrating of analysis and theory – so evident in the explicitly scientistic wave – has revealed theory, too, as a construction.
>
> 1994, p.x[2]

This is an important move, since it suggests that both theory and narrative are simply texts, with no claim to be 'the' text, thus opening up interpretative possibilities. Indeed, according to Leitch, prior to any act of structuring, and by extension, of narrating, whether by maker or critic, there is a deconstructive act – out of which interpretation acts 'to delimit and arrest *play*' (1983, p.36). 'Movement' becomes crucial, in this 'play' on Derrida's 'play' of differences, in an effort to express ideas of fluidity, the loss of certainty and de-centredness that deconstruction provokes. Language itself loses stability. Leitch makes the point that 'all facts, data, structures, and laws are assembled descriptions'. There is always only interpretation, and he goes on to say that

> all interpretative orderings, whether logical, psychological, historical, dialectical, thematic, rhetorical, or structural, are acts of willed mastery. Interpretation drives to control, insists on order, demonstrates authority.
>
> 1983, p. 58

Sontag's cherished detachment – objective and formalist – is revealed firstly as an impossibility and secondly as a deception, since it assumes the ability of individuals to negate their own positions and perceptions.

Derrida talks of the distancing methods of contemporary theory, and in particular of the value of the 'structuralist invasion' as one that cannot be relegated to history, since it is 'a conversion of the way of putting questions to any object ... the literary object' included (1978, p.3). Derrida, referring to structuralism's 'anxiety about language' (p.3), and with his usual play on words, states that the 'question of the sign' cannot become simply a 'sign of the times' (p.3).

The history of ideas is already couched in language – language itself is seen as the origin of history.

Sarup suggests that 'by challenging access to the present, Derrida poses a threat to both positivism and phenomenology' (1988, p.38) – if there can be no unqualified presence, speech cannot be prior to writing. The immediacy that would be necessary for this to be the case cannot be shown to be there. Thus Derrida refutes the emphasis of linguistics that speech alone is what we should study – that writing is merely an unfortunate appendage, if a useful scapegoat. Turning the tables, speaking could be seen to be a second-hand form of writing, rather than writing seen as an inferior form of speaking. There is a direct parallel here with the way movement and dance are often talked about, as the Sontag quotation reveals. It is as though the 'innocent' and 'immediate' movement response were of far greater value than the 'constructed', 'formulated' 'writing' of the choreography or of a reading.[3] Similarly this, too, can be reversed, and an argument made that the choreographed form is of greater value than the naïve movement response where this is seen as the equivalent of unconsidered speech.

The idea that the word, speech or movement is prior reveals a hierarchical commitment to some ultimate essence, whether in the word or movement – to the transcendental signifier that anchors unquestionable meaning and that is somehow anterior to these discourses. Derrida's position is that this, too, is a fiction, and that a failure of structuralism is that it does not put these oppositions into question. In contrast to the prioritising of speech as immediate truth, Derrida argues that writing is the precondition of language. It is conceived as prior to speech, with 'writing' as the name of the 'structure always already inhabited by the trace' (Sarup, 1988, p.45). By analogy, choreography may be construed as the structure, already inhabited by the movement trace, and a series of other textual traces ranging from philosophical and religious ideas to works made by the same and other choreographers, and to everyday movement that it may evoke.

In a useful summary, Sarup (1988) highlights the key themes of deconstruction: firstly, as found in the close reading of texts; secondly, in attention to the nature of metaphor; and thirdly, to metaphor in the context of political and ideological struggle. In Derrida's view of language there can be no one-to-one correspondences; the signifier does not yield up a signified directly, but they continually break apart and re-attach in new combinations (p.35) in a manner deeply threatening to Saussure's model of language. If meaning is not immediately present in a sign, but 'scattered or dispersed along the whole chain of signifiers ... [it produces] a kind of constant flickering of presence and absence together'. To 'read' is to 'trace' this process (pp.35–6). In turn, a 'trace' – a track or footprint – is an imprint of something absent, and by analogy each sign is inhabited by the trace of another sign, traced through all those that have gone before 'to form a complex tissue which is never exhaustible' (p.36). These notions of trace, absence and flickering presence are central to the construct of intertextuality.

Deconstruction is then

> a method of reading a text so closely that the author's conceptual distinctions on which the text relies are shown to fail ... inconsistent and paradoxical use [is] made of these very concepts within the text as a whole.
>
> Sarup, 1988, p.37

The text falls by its own criteria, unsettled and shattered. Thus it challenges the common philosophical notion of an immediately available area of certainty, a moment of pure expression.

The subject of the next two sections is the distinctive manner in which recent scholarship in dance and music has positioned itself in terms of these theoretical arguments.

Ancestral scholarly narratives in dance analysis

Systems of dance analysis have traditionally constructed their classifications and articulated their codifications directly from the highly specific expressive needs of the dance of a particular time. Some elements capture the imagination at certain times, and others at other times, rising and falling in interest, in consequence of shifts in philosophical, cultural and art practices. The pull of the artistic moon is reflected throughout its history, drawing dance first closer to its theatrical face and then to its abstract face of line and colour as a visual, musical art.

An important explanatory thread for Lloyd Newson's work can be found in the antecedent model of the middle-European theorist Rudolf Laban and that of the Central European expressionist dance. This is just one example of the complex inter-related discourse systems that combine dance movement with ways of thinking about it. Like Delsarte, Laban embraced a wider mysticism rather than a theology of a Christian God. His theories of movement and of its shaping and dynamics are derived from these ideas; they both structure and are structured by the concepts of choreutics and eukinetics that he created.

Dance is constituted both in verbal language and in its own 'dance languages'. These dance languages have technically specific vocabularies and physical counterparts, e.g. in systems of dance technique. A Laban-based movement analysis is sometimes regarded as a universally useful system. Since all dance forms have some connection with elaborated movement, it has been taken as a tool capable of use in the analysis of all and any dance and movement forms.[4] This seems to me to be a globalising and colonising tendency that cannot be supported in either political or epistemological terms.

A shift can be seen from what might be called Laban's romantic organicism to the pseudo-scientific Labananalysis which his American followers developed (Bartenieff *et al.*, 1984). In Europe, Preston-Dunlop, even in the most recent of her publications on Laban (1999), has promoted a view of his work that downplays the significance of a particular kind of mysticism as well as of his possible Nazi involvement (Karina and Kant, 1996, 1999; Moore, 1999). According to Moore, esoteric philosophy was a *crucial* underpinning for Laban's choreutic theories, while Karina and Kant argue that he was deeply implicated in the Third Reich. Desmond points to this 1980s shift in dance studies towards understanding the conditions of production and reception of cultural practices and away from the 'excavation' (as she terms it) of the text (1997, p.3). Cultural study, like feminist theory, encompasses a myriad of approaches and subjects. It perhaps shares with feminism, however, a focus on political engagement and the analysis of power.

Although the following account cannot pretend to be anything more than a crude sketch, the point that movement theory is highly art- and culture-specific is worth illustrating further through reference to selected movement theorists prior to Laban. In England, John Weaver (1673–1760) chose to analyse movement on the basis of the action of the body, cadence (time) and figures (Ralph, 1985). He grouped movements as 'steps', 'positions', 'sinkings', 'risings', 'springings', 'fallings', 'slidings' and 'turnings', but also analysed 'rules' for expression through gesture and facial expression (1706). His works told stories of ancient times (such as *The Loves of Mars and Venus* (1717)) and were driven by reaction against existing manifestations of dance, which were primarily performed as entertaining interludes within a narrative. He was moving from a heavily stylised, rule-governed form towards a more fully expressive and radical mode of expression.

Subsequently Carlo Blasis (1794?–1878) capitalised on a long line of writers to document systems of movement analysis drawn from *Commedia dell'Arte*, based on geometric lines and on set positions of the feet, legs, body and arms, to construct a kind of alphabet. He was also concerned with body type in relation to the style of dance, e.g. in devising the categories of 'serious', 'demi-character' and 'comic' dancers, matching physical characteristics to types of movement and in turn to types of human character, at a time when expressiveness of this kind was valued (Blasis, 1828; Poesio, 1993). Blasis thus was working to and with a set of cultural practices that Weaver might have found very strange – ones peculiar to the Italian context.

Overlapping in time, François Delsarte (1811–71) in North America approached the construction of movement discourse very differently. He analysed movement in relation to specific expressive purposes of rhetoric (speech used in theatrical declamation) and argued that the careful and deliberate manipulation of spiral curves, successional movement, the oppositional and parallel character of movement, ebb and flow, control and relaxation, were essential to the expression of emotion. Despite the problematic nature of belief in religious systems at that time through the sceptical questioning of modernism, his own theory was tightly based on a metaphysics of a trinity of life, mind and soul.

The relevance of these vignettes is that the terms in which Delsarte, like those earlier theorists/performers, couched his movement analysis were interdependent with his expressive ends, his personal philosophy and beliefs. Further, these expressive ends are only understandable as part of a particular cultural group's activities in that time and place. These ideas continue to be used; in this case, Delsarte's work served as the American source of expressionist ideas in dance, deeply influencing Duncan and many American modern dancers (Ruyter, 1979). These ideas become traces, interacting with other newer ideas as time passes, linking nineteenth-century representationalism through the discourse of rhetoric to the modernism of the twentieth century. An evolution into the abstract expressionism of American modern dance was then transposed to the UK, Australia and New Zealand, and in subtle ways remains relevant to Lloyd Newson's particular brand of physical theatre.

In other words, the language and concepts of analytic frameworks are themselves culturally specific and need to be examined closely in terms of the assumptions they carry. They also are embedded in, and construct, the art associated with them, as Foster (1996) demonstrates in tracking the use of the Pygmalion story in eighteenth-century ballet. Many such constructions rely on metaphoric connection rather than a physical link, making imaginative construction as significant as an intertext or as a physical movement. By this, Johnson means

> a pervasive mode of understanding by which we project patterns from one domain of experience in order to structure another domain of a different kind ... through metaphor we make use of patterns that obtain in our physical experience to organize our more abstract understanding.
>
> 1987, p.xv

Metaphor is structured, not random, if not amenable to a traditional and transcendental, propositional formula. It can be more powerful, by virtue of its partly hidden nature at several removes from the actual dance movement, than literal description of movement, which at least exposes its structures. Analysis based on metaphoric allusion is common, although often disguised, in writings on dance – it can be both powerfully evocative and seriously misleading. In the following brief survey of selected recent dance texts, one axis of concern lies between the metaphoric and the physical descriptions of dance, while the second axis links the formalist and cultural poles.

Desmond roots dance theory securely in cultural studies, asking such questions as 'How does dance signal, enact, or rework social categories of identity?' (1997, p.2). In dealing with the physicality or materiality of the body, dance is distinct from visual or literary arts. Strange Fish draws quite explicitly on a number of shared texts, which it presents and simultaneously challenges, often subverting that to which they refer. The proposition made here is that the spectator's understanding and experience of these myths and ritual practices (and of others that are absent in Newson's work and that may, perhaps, be even more significant) are as important as those identified by Lloyd Newson and his collaborators. Strange Fish, it is argued, does more than invite the reader to use these constructs – it urges the reader to do so, since in many senses they are unavoidable. Few readers could escape these allusions in parts of the world where Greek myth and Christianity have impinged. To put it even more strongly, these myths might be said to function as obligatory intertexts in any reading, since it could well be argued that some common elements exist for readers in all European countries and in the remaining and former colonies of Western nations (Riffaterre, 1990). As Gottschild Dixon (1996) also argues, in relation to the Africanist influence in American culture, these are not unattributable, subliminal, unconscious matters.

Dance and the narrative of the written text

The 'absence of presence' (as in Derridean mode) and the lack of concern with bodily matters of dancing and choreographing reinforces the legacy of historical and religious convention in which dance is used by scholars as a rather nice (or sometimes very nasty) metaphor or symbol of eternal purity (or sensual wickedness and licentious behaviour), not as actual, if transient, embodied performance practice.

In *Gendering Bodies/Performing Art: Dance and Literature in Early Twentieth Century British Culture*, Amy Koritz (1995) examines the shared concerns of literature and dance as revealed in the social milieu of British culture in the early part of the twentieth century. She is largely interested in challenging the dominance of literature over dance, and attempts 'to provide an analysis of the relationship between dance and literature that reconfigures their relative importance to an understanding of this period' (p.1). She reads this history through themes of the devaluation of the performer combined with the acceptance of women on stage; the influence of literature and painting on reception of the performing arts; and the divisions emphasised between the artist and the work through extreme versions of modernism. Locating the power of ideologies in both the literal and metaphoric body of dance highlights again the problem for dance scholarship of being part of an endlessly recurring disappearing act, pressed into the metaphoric and ideological service of the artistic and gender hierarchy in other more dominant art forms.

Taking over a language in which the notion of 'text' dominates is not entirely helpful to this disappearing body. Having long been known for its ephemerality rather than for its fixity, dance might be seen to acquire a spurious stability by its association with the idea of text. While 'dance' may be valuable in other disciplines in which it has been used to open up the idea that anything may be seen as a text, the very idea of text is odd for dance unless it is reinterpreted.

Randy Martin uses choreographic structure to 'inspire the rhetorical structure' of the writing, as in *Critical Moves. Dance Studies in Theory and Politics* (1998, p. 56). The association of dance with narrative is doubly complex – dance refers always outside the work, unlike music, by being in some senses located in an ordinary body while this body is not at all ordinary. A complex set of referents is put in train. Martin's overreading concentrates 'on the identification of context and social' constructs (1998, p.58), fluidly slipping between narrative and nonnarrative (that which is outside the text). He argues that the 'internal movement of dance narrative, what moves the plot on ... rests on the mobilization of what is nonnarrative in dance' (p.61). This challenges any idea that structure is somehow internal to the dance, a matter of formal principle.

Dance and narratives of formal analysis

There is some justification for the fears that remain that in dance, as in music, our subjects may dissolve into others, particularly into cultural studies. Some dance scholars (in actuality those whose first academic discipline was not dance but music or sociology or literature) have sought to extend research in dance in terms that were, first and foremost, recognisable to scholars in other fields. This is to accept the brutal logic of the institutionalisation of knowledge, that recognition elsewhere is more important than the integrity of critical enquiry. Nonetheless, new perspectives are of enormous value in allowing dance scholars to perceive and work at the tension between a more open and a more closed view of interpretation in dance, and between real and metaphorical bodies in art discourses.

Gay Morris's *Moving Words. Re-Writing Dance* offers an outline for further development that is open to 'intertextual, interdisciplinary work' (1996, p.10), bringing together essays on Analytical Strategies; Body and Gender; Histories Reconsidered; and Cultural Crossings. It is one of the few collections to span such a field of scholarship, and it reflects the shifting position of dance studies during the 1980s and early 1990s. The debates about formalist analysis as distinct from historical or cultural analysis are continued, with some essays (e.g. Siegel's) emphasising the former over the latter. Those that seek to explore questions of meaning do so in different ways, from Jordan's analysis of the structuring of the dance to 'reveal elements of social meaning' (p.4) to Franko's rooting of the key to dance expression in the 'visceral, intuitive aspects' (p.5). Current debates on the relationship of language to theory and analysis are explored by Foster and Satin, and questioned, where their application might be uncritical, by Thomas (p.6). Writing dance history into cultural history is Manning's significant agenda, while, along with other authors, she applies feminist theory in particular.

Ethnographic and anthropological approaches to dance analysis are found in writings by Erdman, Ness and Novack. These writings are sensitive to the limitations of objective description in a cross-cultural environment. Critics who point to the ethnocentric trap would now look to the culture under study to understand its concepts: so, too, the movement analyst, I argue, must look at the terms in which movement is made and described in that culture or dance style, in order to construct an analytical language. Movement, and the understanding of it, is no more universal than any other cultural practice – the myth of universality is one that holds back the development of dance scholarship. The idea that dance can communicate without recourse to language, a thesis beloved of modernist (dance) theorists, is wholly flawed.

Dance as theory in motion

A rather more literal view of 'literature as dance' and of the 'performance in text', as they term it, is taken by Ellen Goellner and Jacqueline Shea Murphy in *Bodies of the Text; Dance as Theory, Literature as Dance* (1995) in their drive to establish a 'theory in motion'.

In sum, this collection, partly of solicited contributions and partly of previously published material, identifies both 'bodies' and 'texts' as problematic in dancing and dance writing. Goellner and Murphy themselves, in the introduction to the text, called *Movement Movements*, clearly see their enterprise as stimulating debate on 'the interconnections of dance and literature' (p.x) – as re-invigorating literary studies, much as film and cultural studies might, by providing a 'fresh and relevant perspective' (p.1). The themes they address are the now familiar ones of dance and its relationship to political systems; dance and gender; dance and the body; dancing bodies and theories of writing. Distinctions are made between dance *as* text and dance *in* texts. The ideology of the editors is to 'let the essays demonstrate possible ways that scholars can fruitfully combine dance and literary interests' (p.x). This greater openness to methodological diversity is very welcome.

One reviewer termed this 'gesturing towards a performative epistemology' but an epistemology that is made problematic by the 'self-erasure' of dance at the moment of being danced (Lepecki, 1995, pp.68–9). As Lepecki asks, what kind of body inhabits this text? And his answer is a fearful body, an over-hygienised body, a determinedly cultural body where discussion of agency is paralysed. Lepecki's potential solution is to bring together the ideas that

> dance is trace and its writing a theatre of memory and meaning; and that the sexuality and the expressivity of the body in action are fertile breeding grounds for revolutions.
>
> 1995, p.70

Goellner's and Murphy's assessment (1995) of the state of dance theory and methodology points to the search for 'a theoretical language of its own', developing from the time-worn study of history, aesthetics and movement analysis, with some anthropology, that has typified university courses. They note the contribution that Susan Foster's *Reading Dancing* made, in its 'study of the poetics of dance and the semiotics of the meaning-generating and meaning-subverting forces in choreographic works' (p.2). In the UK there has also been a greater emphasis on the openness of meaning and the alternative constructions of meaning from the mid-1980s.[5]

Susan Foster's edited collection *Corporealities: Dancing Knowledge, Culture and Power* (1996a) combines metaphor with physicality, as dance takes centre stage in a text that uses an altogether more adventurous method. 'Choreography' is inverted to serve as a metaphor for cultural theory, extending its tentacles to embrace the larger world, in nice counteraction to the usual direction of traffic described above, *from* literature *to* dance. 'Text' and 'gender, power and identity' are dull ways to convey the excitement that this collection of presentations generates. As the authors say in the introduction:

> bodies do not only pass meaning along ... they develop choreographies of signs through their discourse: they run (or lurch, or bound, or feint, or meander...) from premise to conclusion; they turn (or pivot, or twist...) through the process of reasoning; they confer with (or rub up against, or bump into...) one another in narrating their own physical fate.
>
> p.xi

Metaphorical as this may be, it turns on its head and makes fully evident the ways in which dance is still used as absent metaphor by other disciplines. In Foster's text, relevant disciplines are subjected to revision through a choreographic method in which it is dance that provides the thematic concerns and the rhythmic phrasing. The subject of dance studies reveals its experience of dealing with ephemeral and real bodies. Here the body is seen, tellingly, as the

> critical bridge among disciplinary and political interests. It stretches in multiple directions, collecting with a powerful sweep of its arm distinct methodological and theoretical orientations, instantiating the interstices among distinct perspectives and providing an anatomy for dialogue among them.
>
> p.xiii

In summary, Foster's application of these principles in readings of ballet narratives offers a more sophisticated form of analysis, which 'examines each moment's action as the embodiment of representational strategies ... it dwells on choreographic choices' (1996b, p.xv).

The ritualisation of movement and of theories of movement

Also relevant to the idea of structure is theorising from studies of ritual. There is much about *Strange Fish* that is resonant of ritual, not least, though not only, in its direct reference to Christian liturgy. The sociologist Tony Giddens would find support in the anthropologist Catherine Bell's idea that 'the construction of social beings is simultaneously the generation or reproduction of culture' (1992, p.76). Bell further links this to ritual, arguing that

> it is in ritual – as practices that act upon the actions of others, as the mute interplay of complex strategies within a field structured by engagements of power, as the arena for prescribed sequences of repetitive movements of the body that simultaneously constitute the body, the person, and the macro- and micronetworks of power – that we can see a fundamental strategy of power .... Ritualization is a strategic play of power, of domination and resistance, within the arena of the social body.
>
> Bell, 1992, p.204

This notion is not exclusive to ritual theorists. The music theorist John Shepherd argues that 'as discursively constituted, music can evoke and refer to, give life to, our corporeal existence' (In Solie, p.51) and makes quite precise links between physiological states and our interpretation of the world:

> sound, the basis of music ... reflects and articulates the internal physical properties, the movements, and the surface textures of the bodies that generate it .... it is further shaped by the structures,

> movements and surface textures of the physical objects that reflect it. Sound is shaped and shaping, structured and structuring.
>
> 1993, p.52

In dance scholarship, Foster's readings of ballet narratives serve to demonstrate how 'corporeality ... enabled the graceful negotiation and perpetual reaffirmation of ... hierarchized social roles' (1996b, p.32).

In part this offers a theoretical position from which to explain how the actions of the participants in *Strange Fish*, while outrageously exaggerated in some sense, impress themselves upon the reader. They do this by the process of ritualisation, by intensive repetition, by condensation of meaning into painful and political force as Chapters 4, 5 and 6 demonstrate. Hence whether these discourses are conducted in words or in physical-theatre practices, some interesting effects are created. Foucault's broadening of the idea of 'discourse' from the ordinary sense of an ordered exposition, to accommodate an exploration of the very grounds on which language is used, can be applied as fruitfully to dance and theatre as to verbal languages.

In an interesting example of the complexity of dance narrative, Martin analyses Bill T. Jones's *Last Supper at Uncle Tom's Cabin/The Promised Land.* He argues that this form of narrative dance not only refers to events 'but also orders them' (1998, p.62). It comments on 'its own situation of reception and production, particularly against dance critics' temptations to contain the politics of a given dance'. By the interweaving of historical and fictional narratives the boundaries between life and art are effaced. Finally, if this piece 'imagines a resistance ... it also mobilizes through the dancing ... an imaginary terrain in which a social-aesthetic totality is momentarily displayed' (p.63). These are Martin's four levels of overreading. This piece, like *Strange Fish*, 'profanes what is sacred in art, namely, that its distance from life be maintained' (p.84). If 'the relation between public and private spheres is itself a political construct' (p.95), then issues are mapped on individual bodies. Wendy Houstoun's shift from unfeminine bitch to glamorous vamp' and to vicious witch is a perfect example of this.

One can illustrate in greater detail the complex but ritualised integration of everyday social interaction, language and danced forms by taking a scene from *Strange Fish.* In the third scene, Bar Scene 1 (*Intimidation, competition and co-operation*) and in Scenes 6 and 7 (*The Party* etc), one might say that it is *anti-social* beings rather than social beings who are constructed; but the point remains that we see them as beings engaged in social intercourse. We understand their behaviour because we understand such concepts as 'intimidation'. In the bar scene, two women attempt to trip the third female and to exclude her from the Wendy/Lauren friendship – but more than that, to prevent her from relating to the males. They mock and cheat her at each turn – an essay in how social beings are constructed in dance/movement terms. In reverse, the selection of movement itself constructs these relationships. The social context is revealed in the soft and warm lighting, in the informal postures that individuals adopt, in the light and teasing mood that is established. By staring at newcomers and ceasing conversation, their rather unfriendly curiosity is made clear. The most revealing elements of movement that make up this picture include leaning idly against the wall, crossing the arms and taking up a slouched posture – exaggerating gestures that carry quite unambiguous meanings in everyday life. It is simultaneously somewhat naïve and light-hearted, but also cunning and vicious. The 'political' overload of these gestures is very striking.

Echoes of these themes are found subsequently in Scenes 4 and 10. Understanding of the nature of these relationships is structured by culture while continuing to structure a culture that has evolved around equal numbers of males and females. This culture states that jealousy is permissible, that irresistible need might result in seducing another's partner, in turn justifying normally reprehensible behaviour. Simultaneously a hard and unscrupulous mode of personal communication is rationalised, even made funny and entertaining through the fine nuancing of movement. In the party scene (Scene 6) the harshness of such treatment is exposed more than the humour of personal need, in the refusal of every other participant to attend to Nigel's distress – there is no human kindness here, and self-interest triumphs. In both scenes the movement simultaneously uses conventions already known and creates these and other conventions anew. This analysis can also be seen as a brief example of what Desmond describes as

> how the use of the body in dance is related to, duplicates, contests, amplifies, or exceeds norms of nondance bodily expression within specific historical contexts.
>
> 1997, p.29

In other words we identify these actors as people of a certain age, having a certain set of interests, with distinctive attitudes to gender and social interaction, with particular psychological needs, and finally located as late-twentieth-century London artists who have a strong political and sexual critique to make.

Social bodies are 'constructed' by these ritualised means, and *Strange Fish* is revealed as an active site of dispositions, manoeuvres, tactics, techniques and functions. It is a shifting network of power relations, not a fixed one. It is this argument that I use more widely in dance analysis, demonstrating that movement and other elements are the very constituents of the structure of the dance and yet are constructed by it at the same time. They are its culturally constructed power base. The *plie* of ballet, for example, is not a value-free bending of the knees, however much the term is taken up by modern dancers (and even Bharata Natyam dancers in the late twentieth century) in an attempt to stress the commonalities of multi-cultural dance forms. The *plie* is already imbued with 250 years of history, and takes its cue from a society more obsessed with the form of its manners than with the content – hence its elaborate gesturing and forming of steps, which correspond to Western European conventions of a particular time and place.

Intertextuality: methodologies

In this multi-vocal world full of competing histories it is inevitable that one area of contention concerns the choice of critical perspectives to adopt on DV8's performances. They can be interpreted within at least two distinct critical traditions: the more recent and multi-faceted, post-structuralist theories and practices, as well as an earlier twentieth-century expressionist tradition – traditions that are sometimes thought to be mutually exclusive. Sally Gardner (1994–5) polarises the debate about the mutual exclusiveness of the expressionist or humanist position, placing it against the postmodernist or contingent position. Gardner's interest lies in her own dancing experience, which seems not to fall as conveniently within one or other of these traditions as writers tend to assume. She investigated the issue in a practical mode by performing a reconstruction of Mary Wigman's *Pastoral* (choreographed 1929) and following it with an improvisation of her own.

However, replacing the emotionally charged female body of Wigman with a more pedestrian, 'factual' body only reinforced the conclusion for Gardner that each is entailed in the other. Her argument is that 'different kinds of dancing create or implicate different kinds of dancing subjects' or, expressed in reverse, 'how different kinds of "thinking" about subjectivity can change the way dance is practised'

(1994–5, p.73). This does not remain simply as a bodily entailment, in some way separate from the dance form, but, I would argue, incorporates an entailment of the dance-movement forms in which these bodies or subjects participate.[6] Although modern dance epitomised a striving for individual identity, which led to a concomitant diversity of performance practices, in turn it produced its own 'universalised' forms based on distinctive, clearly specifiable conventions which are readily recognised across the English-speaking contemporary dance world. Gardner argues that once the dancer is

> absolved of the singular task of binding together specific bodily movements and specific meanings [she] is free to observe the looseness and the non-essentialness of the bonds between movements and their possible signification.
>
> p.75

Cogent (and post-structuralist) as this argument is, the direction it travels is less relevant to Lloyd Newson than to her own work. Looseness and ambiguity of meaning are not what Lloyd Newson seeks. A less extreme polarisation can be constructed through what Johnson terms a 'descriptive or empirical phenomenology', which attempts a 'geography of human experience' (1987, p.xxxvii). Such an approach does not stop at description, but constructs a powerful 'explanation' of the process of making semantic connections while not insisting that any one set of connections is right.

Given the binding together in *Strange Fish* of music and dance, I return briefly to recent positions in music scholarship. In music the purity of abstraction has been very seductive. Ayrey's and Everist's (1996) re-visiting of analytical strategies and musical interpretation announces its purposes as being 'to demonstrate and reflect on the interpretative results of analysis', thus continuing to lay claim to an order of events – analyse first, interpret afterwards – that until recently was uncontentious, at least in music. Recent texts reflect a struggle with the 'ontological and epistemological status of music interpretation bridging metatheory and structuralist assumptions of disinterested formal enquiry and context' (p.1). In sum, there is a new level of recognition and self-consciousness, where the minimum that can be expected, they argue, is that 'strategies of interpretation are acknowledged and clear' (p.2), although the nature of the relationship between description and interpretation is not clear.

Samson (in Cook and Everist, 1999) shows how music functions in this more open interdisciplinary field, making metaphoric alliances in different ways at different times (with mathematics in Greek and medieval times, and with language in the Renaissance–Baroque eighteenth century) to create a musical mimesis and rhetoric. The limitations of these systems, like those used in dance scholarship, lie in their very metaphoric character, since translation in a literal sense is not possible. Analogy may be a powerful tool but it remains analogy, not a systematic analytic tool. In recent theorising, however, the concept of intertextuality emerges even within the depths of formalist analysis, and can be seen in an interest in palindromic structures in chordal relationships.[7] Whether this is the same notion of intertextuality that is used in literature is something that needs debate. When used in music it seems to be a less open concept, where texts are linked from within to contextual information, as in 'intertextual correspondences'. This is closer to source criticism, where notions of influence continue to be evident (Worton and Still, 1990). It is a version of intertextuality in which late works illuminate early ones and early works point to meanings in later ones. This can tend to become an extended literary analysis closely related to the written texts with which the music connects – hidden analogies and correspondences – rather than the problematic juxtapositions arising from the experience of the work as implied by intertextuality. The music theorist Kofi Agawu uses intertextuality rather differently as 'forcing an engagement with other texts (musical, literary, as well as critical)' and in the sense of the play that is set up by Kristeva's codes. He asks how 'intertextual resonances interrupt and thus help to define narrativity',[8] showing that intertextuality makes for a less direct narrative – enriching, building 'an intricate web of relations around text and intertexts' (in Ayrey and Everist, 1996, p.237). This is more clearly in line with literary notions and with the account of intertextuality that I offer.

It is my contention that theories and methodologies, or practices, of intertextuality can be used to demonstrate how different interpretations are possible, how they might be prompted by a range of texts and traces of texts, and how they can be constructed by viewers or readers. No two re-tellings of a story are the same, as Doniger (1998) points out. This in turn leads to a demand that we understand how different readers are differently placed or situated and how they draw on historical and cultural accounts in order to create stories. The same person may construct different stories at different times, or if situated within another cultural group. We might ask if there are commonalities within groups – do gay men tell stories of relationships in a way that is common to them but different from that of gay women or heterosexual men or women? Labels such as these are treacherous in any case, since 'gay men' are not a heterogeneous group. But if the categories are refined, for instance to London-based 19–25-year-old male gays or heterosexual females, we begin to have a more precise specification of who is doing the reading. It may also be possible to ask what would be evident in a work such as *Strange Fish* that might tell the reader that those involved in its creation approached it from a specific gender perspective. Equally, one can ask how such identity positions would be reflected in a reading. Replacing the heterosexual world-view, like the colonialist world-view, with another world-view does not make the reading any more valid, although it may be much more interesting or more fashionable, or more challenging for readers in the early twenty-first century.

The construct of 'intertextuality', I argue, is helpful in several senses. Firstly, it is a method of tracing the inter-relationships of actual people, hiding behind and reflected in the terms 'author', 'text' and 'reader'. Secondly, it can identify and clarify the potentially conflicting sets of genre coding that add other layers to the possible modes of interaction – in this case between the choreographer, the dance and a spectator of *Strange Fish*. Thirdly, intertextuality can point to the wider significance of the body, since talk of 'bodies' serves to highlight their previous absence in critical writing and their metaphoric use elsewhere.[9] Fourthly, intertextuality focuses on the social and cultural representation of embodied human beings, since it looks outside the conditions of dance discourse to its interaction with other discourses.

On the interaction with other discourses, Desmond suggests: 'recent work ... is beginning to foreground theoretical concerns which ... focus on the ideological underpinnings of aesthetic practices' (1997, p.1). Martin is careful to insist that while politics and dance share 'movement', they have to be 'specified' as distinct cultural practices, and not collapsed one into the other. Through analysis of certain social scenes in *Strange Fish*, a 'theory of politics' can be said to be visible, if such a theory is understood as ways of treating 'participation generated through the gathering of bodies' (Martin, 1998, p.9). Certain scenes make the identification with a 'particular political movement' visible. It is possible to see how a 'sense of space and time is generated through social life' within a theatre piece (p.35). Translated into physical theatre, politics asks what is mobilised rather than how resistance operates, and, as Martin argues, this 'may be a more constructive framework ... in which to value and evaluate social change' (p.13).

Fundamentally, this debate about the relationship between types of critical strategies (or meta-narratives) when applied to dance analysis challenges the idea that we have to adopt one or another, quite distinct, critical method. It invites instead the construction of an intertextual web of methodological traces. In particular, *Strange Fish* seems to demand further analysis of this kind, since it hovers in angelic embodiment over the borders of expressionist theatre as it trespasses into postmodern territory of a more open set of strategies. There are sometimes contradictory themes, and together they render the work capable of generating, and allow the reader to construct, a matrix of free-floating, and only sometimes interlocking, interpretations.

Strange Fish draws on massive and constantly recurring themes in Western culture, notably from Greek mythology and stories of the siren; from Christian ritual and practice, notably the Crucifixion; but with a glance towards Buddhism also, in a manner that inter-relates these themes. Its subject matter is not dealt with in separate episodes in turn within the work, nor are its elements associated in a random fashion. They recur, each reiteration irrevocably changed by virtue of what has happened in between.

The title itself evokes the protest song 'Strange Fruit' (which one headline writer actually used at the start of a review, whether by mistake or deliberately is not known). It is a common first allusion for people familiar with Billie Holiday's songs. It tackled racial hatred in 1930s North America, an obvious parallel for the treatment of women or gays in *Strange Fish*.

If these themes are to be productive for the reader, to become fluid and rich intertextual seams, approaches to the work have to draw on a vast range of 'bodies of knowledge'. Relevant disciplines include theology; history of religions; Greek mythology; psychology and psychoanalysis; anthropology; feminism and queer theory; semiotics of performance; and dance and music analysis.

Succeeding sections of this book separate out threads of approach, and I argue that, while disparate, they are each relevant to *Strange Fish*. I have aimed to re-unite them in the final discussion of the siren figure to illustrate their interlocking character and the intertextual nature of the methods applied in analysis. 'Re-unite' is a rather misleading way of describing the outcome of an intertextual analysis, since the themes exposed and perspectives adopted through the book may be brought into relationship without the process leading to unity. I use the phrase ironically, to question it and to illustrate the endemic character of such ideas in language about art and the difficulty of avoiding such metaphors.

From this challenge, however, flows a series of questions about how decisions are made about which kinds of theories, from which domains, might be fruitful. As the preliminary statement in Graham Allen's recent text (2000) states, intertextuality is employed in structuralist, post-structuralist, semiotic, deconstructive, postcolonial, Marxist, feminist and psychoanalytic theories, and has been applied across a range of literary and cultural texts. Constantly at the forefront here is my argument that theories and practices are in fact interrelated: they co-exist, infiltrate each other, are entailed one in the other through time. How they do this at particular moments, and in response to, or in anticipation of, new art is what is of interest and what is explored in practice through this analysis. As Meinhof and Smith point out, 'the demarcation of the limits of the linguistic, symbolic or discursive realm cannot be quickly and comfortably settled' (2000, p.7). Theories are intertexts, too.

A clearly emerging answer to this question is to take the lead from the practice, or the text itself. The discourse that *Strange Fish* creates is largely concerned with power and sexuality. Foucault's articulation of relationships between sexuality and power and their dominance in discourse from the nineteenth century onwards have made a huge contribution to our understanding. It is now well recognised that modernist discourses assumed an essentialism that only a cultural history can challenge (Foucault, 1976). Scientific absolutism has been the dominant trend in understanding sexuality, posited as the same anywhere and everywhere – a biological urge, a force that can barely be controlled. Hydraulic imagery dominates scientific sexology, just as it does the literature on the 1930s–1960s modern dance. Reproductive sexuality, and the allocation of contrasting attributes to male and female on the basis of biological difference, form the underpinning for both, right through to Lloyd Newson's work; hence the particular relevance of theories of sexuality and gender to this analysis.

There are examples in other domains that offer more challenging positions that are worth elucidating here. De Lauretis's view of semiosis, as the 'bodily engendered' production of meaning, representation and self-representation' (1984, p.298) drawing theories of Freud and Peirce together, is unusual since these theories are often quite distinct, and in some senses distant. She does it to articulate the joining of the psychic to the social, inner and outer worlds, to demonstrate the constructedness of subjectivity. The dynamic nature of these processes is what attracts de Lauretis to a view of sexuality as a process of sexual structuring.

> Sexuality appears as a semiosic process in which the subject's desire is the result of a series of significant events ... that are contingent upon a personal *and* a social history; where by history I mean the particular configurations of discourses, representations, and practices – familial and broadly institutional, cultural and subcultural, public and private – that the subject crosses and that in turn traverse the subject, according to the contingencies of each subject's singular existence in the world.
>
> de Lauretis, 1994, p.303

The constantly changing intertexts of sexuality within the framework of Christian belief are particularly relevant to my arguments. As Weeks argues,

> there is a struggle for the future of sexuality. But the ways we respond to this have been coloured by the force of the accumulated historical heritage and sexual tradition out of which we have come: the Christian organisation of belief in sex as sacramental and threatening, the libertarian belief in sex as subversive, the liberal belief in sex as source of identity and personal resource, all rooted in a melange of religious, scientific and sexological arguments about what sex is, what it can do, and what we must or must not do.
>
> 1985, p.5

Just as other binarisms have been called into question by sociology, anthropology, psychoanalysis and Marxism, so too has the assumption (taken for granted) of two sexes, female and male. Instead of positing a morally 'right' way of living, an essentially heterosexual one of fixed positions where the homosexual is by definition 'perverse' and 'unnatural', it is possible to see shades and variations within relationships. None can be said to be more right than any other or even true for all time for an individual. Weeks explores the history and the politics of constructions of sexuality in his extended text (1985) in much the same way that dance theorists, among others, have expanded notions of their subject matter – in that each responds to the openness of post-structuralist theorising.

It is because of the affinity of dance and sex in cultural construction over two millennia, linked in a powerful nexus, that I refer to these arguments, as well as finding good reason in *Strange Fish* itself, in its representations of gendered behaviour. It has taken argument throughout the whole of the twentieth century for a political sexology to open up the question of the 'naturalness' of male/female sexuality and of gender positions as we inherit them primarily from Christian dogma. Equally it has taken the whole century for dance to be seen as an acceptable art, rather than as a form of prostitution. One clear example of the shared territory between dance and the female gender is the privileged role both have had in the twentieth century in expressing or negating 'the natural' and of expressing sexual urges. Neither can ignore psychoanalytical constructions of expression, repression and desire. Neither can ignore the feminist and gay agenda, the questions of identity they give rise to, or the styles and subjectivities to which contemporary scholarship has given birth. It has taken the whole of the twentieth century for writing to emerge that demonstrates lucidly that dance is 'uniquely adept at configuring relationships between body, self and society through its choreographic decisions' (Foster, 1996b, p.xv).

I use both Lyotard's arguments and Wittgensteinian language games to deal with these questions. Both arise from philosophers whose European roots remain in evidence and whose work ties into later deconstructive strategies in a productive way. Since I also use theories of expression in art, which have similar roots, and yet turn them to deconstructive ends, this link is apposite in a further sense. 'What we have here is a process of delegitimation fuelled by the demand for legitimation itself' (Lyotard, 1984, p.39). A hierarchical notion of knowledge gives way to a 'flat network of areas of enquiry, the respective frontiers of which are in constant flux' (p.39). The loss of a universal metalanguage is compensated for by 'knowledge that legitimation can only spring from [our] ... own linguistic practice and communicational interaction' (p.41).

Thus our ever-changing processes of structuring, as created through and in linguistic practice, serve to make life harder for the analyst. David Best (1974) describes the Wittgensteinian position on 'family resemblances' as useful for opening up philosophical debate in order to counter too rigid a drive towards 'defining' complex ideas – in this case, ideas of performance, movement and dance. But he also warns that a theory of family resemblances is not a 'universal panacea' (p.31), nor an excuse for lazy thinking, nor a means of avoiding difficult issues. Neither does he use it to support a modernist position where the arts can be detached from life. In a move that shares much with post-structuralist thinking, he also argues for an understanding of the arts as culturally-embedded practices, both in conditions of their creation and in responses to them (1992, p.xiv).

In consequence, the fact that many post-structuralist positions challenge a notion of a single truth and open up multiple interpretations of art does not relieve us of the responsibility to work at what such accounts might comprise, and how they might be (differently) constructed. It is not an 'anything goes' fall into extreme relativity or into subjectivity, but a recognition that there is more than one 'truth' and that the responsibility for constructing these truths lies directly with us. It follows that the moral or ethical implications of these positions, too, lie securely in our domain and cannot be escaped. The kind of rationality that this requires is interpretative and recognises its own presuppositions. This is to take a different view of 'interpretation' from those who discard it in the belief that it carries an assumption that 'a truth' can and should be found.

As Lyotard expresses it:

> most people have lost the nostalgia for the lost narrative. It in no way follows that they are reduced to barbarity. What saves them from it is their knowledge that legitimation can only spring from their own linguistic practice and communicational interaction.
>
> 1984, p.41

Between this 'meta' level of theorising and the immediacy of the dance, there is another structuring framework, which arises from the way academic disciplines are currently shaped. Disciplines themselves are subject to historic change and there have been many contenders over the years claiming relevance to the performing arts, from anthropology to zoology. Some are seen to be particularly significant for different threads in an analysis of *Strange Fish*, as Chapters 4–6 demonstrate. Putting them into play together can, as Lyotard suggests, promote an argument that has the advantage of making visible the

> flexibility of its means, that is the plurality of its languages; and its character as a pragmatic game – the acceptability of the 'moves' (new propositions) within the established rules; the other to the invention of new rules, in other words, a change to a new game.

It is not that attention to formal structures within the performing arts is no longer interesting or necessary, but rather that in turn 'the principle of a universal metalanguage is replaced by the principle of a plurality of formal and axiomatic systems' (1984, p.43).

Anthony Giddens, who looks at disciplines from a sociological perspective (or from several sociological perspectives), is interesting on this point. The attraction of his work lies in revoking a history of Cartesian dualism: he shares a now commonplace critique with many others, from philosophers of art such as David Best (1992) and from critical theorists such as Jonathan Culler (1983b). Giddens might be describing the difficulties that dance scholars face when he surveys his methodologies, because he too draws upon an eclectic range of sources: from sociology, anthropology, history, philosophy, politics, geography, linguistics and other disciplines. The danger of being ignored or dismissed for not being identified with one discipline in depth is evident in attacks on him for not providing a single, fully worked-out position, for not interrogating specific concepts sufficiently within a narrow enough frame of reference. His many affinities with structural conceptions in other disciplines serve to de-centre his own subject of sociology. In the same way, a conception of dance that draws on a number of disciplines de-centres both dance and the disciplines that it adopts. The widespread unease that is created in the face of constantly shifting alignments of disciplines reveals a continuing desire for linear and clearly distinguished forms of knowledge, despite the fragmentation of late-twentieth-century life.

Barthes, like Foucault and Giddens, has been described as 'conducting a series of promiscuous relationships with the discourses of his day' (Knight, 1990, p.104), from which one might conclude that trespassing across the conceptual borders of other people's discourses, like trespassing over their land, is never popular. Giddens, again like Foucault, is also *praised* for his critical appropriation of many other theories through which he engages with different national traditions in North America, France and Germany. He has an ability to synthesise or fuse these traditions. A denial of the monolithic knowledge structures of bounded disciplines nonetheless carries the danger of creating another monolith in the process. Boyne's suspicions illustrate the pitfalls well. He challenges Giddens for his

> deployment of ideas from structuralism and post-structuralism [which] has tended to be somewhat piratical – he has taken what he wanted without any real concern for where it came from or for the value of it within its proper context.
>
> In Bryant and Jary, 1991, p.65

To my mind this is a 'respectable' yet 'disrespectful' tradition that I am happy to carry forward. One specific methodological issue that has to be confronted here is that of the appropriateness or validity of linking insights from anthropology, history of religions and psychology with those from dance analysis. The absence of established relationships between these disciplines within their own contexts makes their use in dance problematic. Indeed, scholarship in dance, mindful of internecine struggles between other disciplines, has not tended to bring research methods together from disciplines that are uneasy bedfellows in their own worlds. This reluctance reflects the danger for the dance scholar, who is already at one remove from these disciplines, of applying (or mis-applying) methods with which the scholar has less than a full engagement. It can be an invitation to be dismissed, to be seen as a trespasser in areas of which one is ignorant and, sometimes more importantly, in which one is uninitiated. Indeed the high fences and burglar alarms protecting theories of modernist art, no less than the art forms themselves, were constructed explicitly to ward off such cavalier invasions. In theoretical terms, conventional epistemologies construct quasi-religious bodies of knowledge for which the initiation of the novitiate is an apt parallel. It is deeply ironic that epistemology should have adopted a metaphor of the body (as in bodies of knowledge) when its methods and theories explicitly deny such corporeality. Here, intertextuality is used to justify picking up traces from many places if they offer a contribution to a mosaic that contributes to a reading of *Strange Fish*.

The intertextual point is that the texts relevant to *Strange Fish* bear traces from the immediate present, as well as the supposedly dead past. If it is obvious that 'all texts contain traces of other texts', a more sophisticated version of this idea focuses on 'the interactions between texts, producers or texts and their readers' lifeworlds' (Meinhof and Smith, 2000, p.3). There are several threads of intertextuality and of gender politics operating both across the argument that the book makes and within the work. Each of these referential strands, and their interaction with each other, is compounded by my own response to the 'texts' that are *Strange Fish*. The account that I construct spans pre-history to the present moment in its intertextual references. It illustrates both the constraints on interpretation and the potential for endless re-interpretation. How the spectator, or reader, contributes his or her own intertexts to 'create' the work (in a highly specific sense) is also the subject of debate. My choices figure here: yours would change the narrative. In consequence, interpretations can be defended yet still be fluid. Paradoxically it allows the reader to 'create the text' and simultaneously to 'read the text as it wishes to be read' (Eco, 1979, 1984, p.9). Or, expressed in another way, it is 'a tool which cannot be employed by readers wishing to produce stability and order, or wishing to claim authority over the text or other critics' (Allen, 2000, p.209).

Performative intertextualities

An unusual study by Linda and Michael Hutcheon brings the medical and the operatic together, reflecting on the stories of illness and death represented on stage. The Hutcheons see the body as the point of intersection of nature and culture, and thus of the medical and human sciences. Opera is read as the 'nexus of the singing body as the representation of both pleasure and pain, as desired and desiring as well as sick and suffering' (1996, p.10). It is the popular clichés that make it onto the stage.

Opera has historically been obsessed with death, sometimes with grief and loss resolved by tragic catharsis through violent death, stabbings and suicides. What is revealing of the period is how it deals with disease, health, death, love. An analysis of *Strange Fish* can be informed by such an approach. As music approaches the human condition, the visual arts also demonstrate new interest in the representation of the human body as a shifting domain. Adler and Pointon reflect on the artist's body as well as on the bodies represented by their art (1993). Their collection of articles challenges this normally invisible body, and seeks to relate its concealment or visibility in a specific sense to the work of the artist. Frida Kahlo's medicalised imagery provokes a new language to express bodily experiences, archetypically the work of the 'choreographer'. Thus the same themes may be pursued across these disciplines.

Gender concerns focus around vocabularies of sound and movement that might represent male and female characters, or more subtly, femininity and masculinity – a semiotics of gender, a set of conventions – and a construction of sexuality through images and discourses. Desire, eroticism and sensual pleasure are the life-blood of both arts and are constructed in different ways as genres and times change. However, the position of dance scholarship is very different from that of music. Ignored and deprecated as an art for women (or queers) with a literature to match, the largely female exponents and theorists of dance have been only too grateful to be noticed, only to be taken over, appropriated often for male (and yes, often queer) purposes. Music, too, has also had to fight off charges of effeminacy, with the scientific detachment of abstraction through formalism becoming an attractive solution. The association of music with mathematics is itself revealing of many things, not least a desire to be utterly abstract and respectable; while, vice versa, music becomes the acceptable emotional face of scientific and mathematical logic.

De Lauretis illuminates the functioning of gender within the workings of subject discourses, and her constructs can profitably be applied to the techniques and structures adopted by choreographers and composers to support the idea of a performative intertextuality (1984). She argues that narrative acts 'to engender the subject in the movement of its discourse, as it defines positions of meaning, identification, and desire' (p.10), and this is a crucial proposition. Her method of analysis of semiotics, feminism and cinema resonates, as I demonstrate with *Strange Fish*. She uses a method in which the same 'concerns, issues and themes return, each time diffracted by a different textual prism, seen through a critical lens with variable focus' (p.11).

One major 'diffraction' is that of gender bias. Its wide relevance in dance can be exposed quite simply in asking why is it, given that all the main pioneers of modern dance in both Europe and the US, and some of those of modern ballet of the twentieth century, were women, that there are virtually no women running major companies or employed as choreographers? The list of post-WW2 choreographers in the Royal Ballet and Sadler's Wells (now Birmingham Royal) Ballet makes interesting reading. The names of Frederick Ashton, Kenneth Macmillan, Anthony Dowell, Peter Wright, David Bintley, Ashley Page and William Tuckett come to mind without difficulty for ballet;[10] and for modern dance in England since the war, Kurt Jooss, Christopher Bruce, Norman Morrice, Robert Cohan, Robert North and Richard Alston (the exception here is Siobhan Davies). Given that the progenitors were Marie Rambert and Ninette de Valois; Isadora Duncan and Martha Graham; Doris Humphrey and Mary Wigman, this at least bears investigation.[11]

Absent structures such as these can constrain and yet simultaneously liberate the moment of reading, an idea that creates a dynamic process of interpretation in which what is presented collides with what is absent, and what is said presupposes what is not said. In a similar way, Lloyd Newson can be said to be both rebellious and conformist in shattering valued ideals (kicking over the traces) while hiding behind convention (covering his tracks) in order to appeal to wider audiences in a cynical, postmodernist strategy of commodification of his work.[12]

These texts and intertexts can be seen not only as historical threads that are raised to a level of consciousness where they intervene in the experience of the work, but also as structuring the performance. Underlying these recent writings are notions of interpretation as performance, as an imaginative act on the part of a reader or spectator which itself constructs the 'performance'.[13] 'Performativity' and particularly its links to 'queer' need to be elaborated in the face of the relevance of both constructs to *Strange Fish*. Sue Ellen Case (1996) is helpful here. Instead of a 'live' performance created by stage performers, actors and dancers, we have in *Strange Fish* a virtual performance (on video), a series of screens and no real bodies. The identity of both 'the performance' and 'lesbian' is presently under siege from charges of essentialism. Case refutes this charge, referring to de Lauretis's work, and constructing her own argument that these constructs are not only linguistic but also social. Materialist, political discourses are inscribed in the physicality of the body and its experiences. 'Queer performativity', she argues, has been constructed as 'iterations of power contested at the sites of gender identification and legal, medical discourses concerning sexual practices' (p.13). Reading and writing seduce against the values of traditional performance. She says that, despite the politically inspired gay and lesbian movements, AIDS and activism, the notion of performativity

> circles back to written texts, abandoning historical traditions of performance for the print modes of literary and philosophical scrutiny. Queer, then, moves identity to readership, and 'performativity' imbues writing with performance.
>
> Case, 1996, p.17

Outside referents, the actual lived physical body, and the codification of movement in political ways remain significant. The challenge to writing to become performative echoes the discussion in Chapter 2 and earlier in this chapter about the impact on other disciplines of dance as a metaphor; but, as Case observes, it also serves to re-establish the dominance of writing over performance (p.20). In 'reimagining' a 'fleshly zone of performance', Case offers a 'corrective to transubstantiation' (p.108). The basis of her argument is that gesture, bodily movement and corporeal action together create social reality. They are not simply reflective of some pre-existing state, or inscribed with the values of others, but are created in the act. If Butler's arguments are valid (1990), then the individuals who feature so largely in *Strange Fish* are themselves 'performing' their various gendered identities, while also constructing a 'character' who exists only in this work, and is specially created for it. It doubles the complexity of everyday performance of gender.

Strange Fish portrays, in an ironic, parodic and subversive manner, the dangerous games people played in the 1990s. Issues are at once on the surface, immediate, superficially satisfying and often humorous, but simultaneously deeply disturbing. That he makes us laugh as we feel the pain is testimony to Newson's skill as well a reflection of the reader's own emotional positioning. That 'we' (many spectators) share this response demonstrates that there are cultural texts with which we are familiar and whose significance we understand. We understand them as performances, not as writing. The extent of this sharing is highly variable and the experience and specific of understanding them will be articulated differently by each of us. The level at which these ideas are picked up, on the other hand, may be dependent upon the interests and choices of the reader as well as the extent of the reader's experience of such practices.

The spectator thus may experience a similar series of ordeals to those that *Strange Fish* sets up and within which individuals react in various ways. These ordeals are psychological and social, as befits the late twentieth century, rather than explicitly moral, although a continuing moral agenda speaks through these other dilemmas. The decision to belong, to decide to which sub-culture one wants to be attached, is a more self-conscious choice than in previous centuries. The individual is far removed from any external control, given the much-vaunted freedom of movement in the late twentieth century. From the loosening of borders between countries (at least within Europe) at the literal end of the scale, to the limitless possibilities of the Internet at the other, we are given private access to previously unimaginable sources. On this argument, many governmental and social controls can be evaded. Against this utopian freedom looms political manipulation on a global scale, ethnic cleansing in the Balkans and in Ruanda; 'Big Brother' in the form of smart cards, and a database on each member of the population, which means there is no freedom at all and every movement, every transaction, can be monitored.[14]

Informed by a postmodernist sensibility, this 'knowingness dissolves commitment into irony', as Auslander puts it (1994, p.9); and with it come texts of alienation, of detachment and loss of moral responsibility, tied to the impact of recently developed electronic technologies.[15] Adopting the observer-role on life, watching it on a screen rather than living it in the flesh, accepting the impossibility of 'real' communication, encourages the absence of care in real-life encounters and leads to a tolerance of the incoherent multiplicity of texts, tracks or traces in analysis. Within *Strange Fish* another sort of observer develops alongside Wendy Houston: the Siren/Christ/Angel/Mary who observes Wendy – the observer observed – while the viewer/reader as observer is intercepted by the producer David Hinton.

> Videography reinscribes dancing in another medium that, although not a mere reflection of performance, can, by its assimilation of the active looking that editing shots from different angles allows, introduce an awareness of how history is written.
>
> Martin, 1998, p.35

We are both parasitic upon these views and yet have some responsibility and contribution in choosing how to see this relationship, once we become aware of it. The deferral of conclusions thus suggested aligns analysis of this work with Barthes's later theory in its refusal to settle on meaning. The central problem remains: how free are we to choose our intertexts? Themes of sexuality, profanity, sociality, circulate and are differently foregrounded at different moments in the piece. Together they make what Martin refers to as 'a complex and differential economy of narrative temporalities in which stories that reference different scales of historical time and experience can be told and exchanged' (1998, p.104).

Conclusion

In summary, the application of particular theories to dance, music and theatre is not without difficulty. Choice can appear to be arbitrary at one extreme, or to be an attempt to colonise an unsuspecting victim at the other. What the rationale might be for choosing any particularly theory is exposed to question, requiring the writer to answer whether it is driven by random choice, historical tradition, an argument about theory, current fashion or personal inclination. The process of choosing, and the validity and appropriateness of choices made, in this treacherously open post-structuralist field becomes fundamentally the subject of this book, in demonstrating how theoretically informed choices for both structural analysis and methodologies for interpretations can be constructed based on imaginative engagement with performance practices.

The structures and pre-existing narratives that provide a limiting framework are those perceived to be most relevant to *Strange Fish*. They derive from myth, from threads of a psychological anthropology; and from theological matters with a historical approach to understanding Christian symbolism integrated into this story. From the twentieth century, feminist and queer theory contribute to the narrative, assisting me in re-constructing *Strange Fish* in terms of both its power structures and its gender relations. My purpose is to expose how different thematic approaches imply different structures, which in turn produce different semiotic structuralisms, and thus how each exposes different traces of meaning. These chapters demonstrate how an emphasis on different types of contextual frame, and different interpretations within each frame, changes the possibilities of understanding. Interpretations operate both with and against history as we have learnt it and, in this process, create their own structures, indissoluble from meaning.

There are many different ways in which I can attribute meaning to *Strange Fish*, some of which are illustrated later where I pursue moving and constantly shifting themes loosely pinned together through such ideas as 'Sacrificial victims – male and female'; 'The Siren: intertwining texts' and 'Re-interpreting the Christ figure'. Themes such as these are heavily loaded with interpretative elements and with fluidity of method. They are based on decisions already made about how this work might be organised or structured, yet in turn they affect and change this organisation as they proceed.

Given Lloyd Newson's ironic juxtaposition of texts in *Strange Fish*, the construct of 'intertextuality' is potentially rewarding. Using this literary construct, words, sounds, music and movement are brought into relationship with design elements of scenic proportions, all compounded by a vast range of mythic and religious ideas. Not only might an intertextual approach help the reader to locate some of the diverse and ever-multiplying traces that *Strange Fish* itself presupposes, but it may also help to identify some of the texts that individual readers might construct in the process of interpreting works. It allows the reader to hold these diverse threads in relation to each other.

In parallel, the method employed in writing this account attempts to mimic the 'continuous centrifugal' and 'centripetal' movement of the reader towards, away from, and around both *Strange Fish* and the context or culture to which it refers (Ruffini, trans. de Marinis, 1993, p.68). These shifts of position are sometimes in harmony, and often not, in the case of any particular reader. As Ruffini argues, in the spaces created between a multiplicity of texts and traces there is the opportunity – indeed, more strongly, the demand – that each reader should engage in this process of constructing meaning by unravelling what seems to be implied by the work while simultaneously creating his or her own threads. O'Flaherty (1980), in a rather practical and even prosaic way, provides a justification for raiding the 'toolbox' of theory in order to address specific problems appropriately, and in order to distinguish between how one goes about it and how one justifies what one has done (p.3).

The relevance of an intertextual view of theory is that 'a text is not an autonomous or unified object, but a set of relations with other texts ... every text is an intertext' (Leitch, 1983, p.59), and thus a constantly fluid series of traces is set in motion. I arrest them in this text in order to capture a moment that strikes a chord and to explore types of narrative construction. The postmodern world recognises the existence of epistemological boundaries only in order to challenge them, leap over them and dissolve them. My own position is one of responding wholeheartedly to the idea that in these interdisciplinary or interstitial cracks lies the possibility for expansion of critical thinking and for the creation of new insights.[16] It is a view more closely allied to Derrida's and Kristeva's notions of text and intertext than to ideas of narrative logic or of historical influence.

1 The analogy, theoretically, lies in Wittgensteinian notions of family resemblance.
2 However, most notably in music, a concern with the character of the sound analysed through distinctive systems seems unshakeable, since 'bringing analysis into the orbit of recent developments in intellectual history has not displaced its traditional concern with explanation and technical description' (Pople, 1994, p.x).
3 This irritating habit of placing so many words in quotation marks is justified by the need to make all of them problematic.
4 Laban-based in this case, but the argument applies to other movement analysis systems.
5 Since American domination of dance theory is so evident, I draw attention to early British attempts to move the discipline on in my own writings e.g. Adshead (1980, 1981) and Adshead (ed., 1988).
6 A further comment is necessary because this entailment does not imply that it is the only possible entailment. Others may be constructed.
7 For example in Schoenberg's music (Ayrey and Everist, 1996, p.19), an obvious link to Jocelyn Pook's score for *Strange Fish*.
8 In the *Nachtmusik*, Ayrey and Everist 1996 (p.235).
9 Such discourse can be unhelpful in so far as it sustains a distinction between minds/souls and bodies, as well as suggesting that they are somehow detached from cultural practices more widely, neither of which is tenable.
10 Bland (1981) on the first 50 years of the Royal Ballet lists 287 works performed in this period (1930–80) made by 55 choreographers. Seven of these, i.e. 13%, were women, who accounted for 49 works, some 17%. If de Valois is excluded because she ran the company

and could ensure her own contribution of 33 works better than anyone else, then the remaining group of 6 women choreographers made only 16 of the 254 works, i.e. 6%. They were Margaret Dale, 1; Celia Franca, 2; Andrée Howard, 7; Bronislava Nijinska, 2; Sara Patrick, 1; and Lynn Seymour, 3. The three Directors since de Valois have been male: Frederick Ashton, Kenneth MacMillan and Anthony Dowell until Monica Mason in 1992.

11 In 1996 the Rambert company published its celebration of 70 years from 1926 to 1996 (Pritchard, 1996). After Marie Rambert, all its Directors have been male: Norman Morrice, John Chesworth, Robert North, Richard Alston and Christopher Bruce. Of the approximately 340 works performed in this period, nearly 80% were choreographed by men. Women who produced 4 or more were Andrée Howard, Marie Rambert, Sally Owen and Susan Salaman. Only Andrée Howard reached a total (16) approximating to the most prolific men: compare with Alston's 25, Ashton's 23, Bruce's 30, Morrice's 23 and Tudor's 15.

In 1989 a history of the first 21 years of London Contemporary Dance Theatre was produced (Clarke and Crisp). From its inception in 1966 to 1983, Robert Cohan was the sole artistic director, joined then by Siobhan Davies and Janet Eager, as choreographer in residence and administrator respectively, in an arrangement that did not last beyond the end of this 21-year period. Of the 108 works performed in this period, approximately 80% were made by men, although the ratio of male to female in terms of the number of choreographers was almost equal. More women were given opportunities, though none but Siobhan Davies (with 15 new works in this period) were successful in a substantial way. Cohan produced 31 for the company, Alston 7, Bergese 9 and North 11.

12 In another book I explore some of the theoretical positions in a more sustained essay on intertextuality (Adshead-Lansdale, 1999).

13 See Adshead ed., 1988, and Adshead-Lansdale, 1994, for a similar argument.

14 This is a paradox to which Keith Watson refers in an article that spans DV8's life (1997).

15 Further, the post-war expectation that the welfare state will provide education, health and social benefits, e.g. in supporting children and single mothers, and in paying allowances for disability etc, has been drastically challenged by economic recession and political change, during a long-standing Thatcherite economy in the UK (and by the Republican agenda in the US) with its emphasis on providing for oneself. The 'me' generation, whose experience of the unlimited consumerism of modern life has been matched by sexual freedom, has now to change its expectations and values and to take literally the need to protect the self, financially, socially and emotionally, as well as physically.

16 A pair of articles published in *Dance Chronicle* illustrates this point well. The struggle for respectability, as determined by scholars in other fields, against the relevance and value for an understanding of dancing and dances, is a debate recently revisited by Ralph (1995) and continued by Adshead-Lansdale (1997).

CHAPTER 4

Men, Myth, Misogyny: Constructions of Masculinity in *Strange Fish*

> It is in ritual – as practices that act upon the actions of others, as the mute interplay of complex strategies within a field structured by engagements of power, as the arena for prescribed sequences of repetitive movements of the body that simultaneously constitute the body, the person, and the macro- and micronetworks of power – that we can see a fundamental strategy of power.
>
> Bell, 1992, p.204

For this chapter it is important that the reader carries forward the uncertainties of an intertextual approach. Traces that are set in motion construct an apparently logical account, but in fact they are only some of the scattered set of dispersed intertexts that might mould both Chapter 4 and Chapter 5.

Greek and Christian intertexts are just the tip of a textual iceberg. Many other texts can be constructed around *Strange Fish* and located in the critical writings about it. Threads are interwoven so that major belief systems are brought into tangential relationship, glancing off each other in a manner typical of the pluralist arts of the 1990s. In this sense, it is a work more in keeping with a postmodernist performative view of the world, where the reader may choose a personal, and in this case intertextual path. The metaphor of a 'path', however, may itself be too linear to accommodate the threads of fabric, or the 'mosaic of quotations' that such an analysis creates in exploring the 'creative ambiguity' of intertextual analysis (Worton, 1986, p.21) and in seeing these texts as the traces of 'otherness' to which Frow refers.

> Texts are not structures of presence but traces and tracings of otherness. They are shaped by the repetition and transformation of other textual structures ... These absent structures at once

> constrain the text and are represented by and within it, they are at once preconditions and moments of the text.
>
> 1990, p.45

Nonetheless, sections must follow each other in this two-dimensional chapter, and inevitably a sense of logical priority emerges. The saving grace is that sections of each chapter subsequently set other logics in play and work with other traces.

Symbol of male or female deity

The title of *Strange Fish* invites comment in itself. Attaching 'strange' to 'fish' immediately evokes a multi-layered image. It is not immediately obvious how this title relates to the work, apart from allusions to things that are 'other', peculiar, or different. The complexities of reading to which the title gives rise can resonate in many ways. In Chapters 4 and 5 I explore these resonances from male- and female-gendered perspectives, while simultaneously questioning each gendered position. In Chapter 6, alternative identities emerge through a number of metaphoric constructs.

The sign of the fish is a prime example of the way in which Christianity appropriated symbols and ceremonies from earlier religious practices. Seymour (1999) suggests that the deeper significance of the fish symbol lay in the pre-Christian anticipation of a new Piscean age. He argues that the Magi would have understood astrology and predicted from esoteric knowledge the coming of a leader, a 'Christ'. The 'fish' symbol may have carried this subversive, pagan history into Christianity.

Douglas (1974) writes a typical history of early Christianity. He refers to the recurrent use of the fish as a common symbol representing Christ in art and literature. Indeed, the Greek term for fish, *ichthus*, came to stand for the phrase 'Jesus Christ, Son of God, Saviour'. Around the second century it served between Christians as a sign of their belief at a time of persecution. After the era of Constantine the cross began to replace the fish as the most commonly used symbol, as the spreading faith acquired more and more 'archaic' themes, many not specifically Christian.

> These mythological themes ... have a long and complex pre-history: from the blood and the body of a sacrificed god or primordial being, wondrous plants grow.
>
> Eliade, 1982, p.402

It is often argued that the Christian message is seen as universal *because* of its successful assimilation of the pre-Christian religious heritage – the Cross as tree of life, the ritual use of wine, and so on – while it simultaneously denies such derivation and claims to be unique.[1]

Burkert (in Bremmer, 1987) acknowledges the conflation of traditions that supported Greek beliefs within the newly evolving early Christianity. For example, there are tales of Hindu and Chinese deities, known as fish-goddesses, who were the precursors of the penis-swallowing Kali, also known as Minaksi (the fish-eyed). So alarming is this myth that it was transformed in Greek mythology to become much less threatening. Kumarbi, now assumed to be male, swallows the 'manhood' (as he politely terms it) of Anu, the god 'Heaven'. He becomes pregnant, swallows his own children and performs other feats, which owe their heritage to several different pre-Christian cultures. The swallowing of genitals and the giving birth to rivers, gods and so on is a significant way not only of expressing the fears of the male (as Freudian commentators suggest) but also of conferring greater power and dignity on him, mainly by appropriating features particular to women.

Bremmer (1989, pp.53–4) finds that similar myths or Freudian fantasies arise in comparable cultural moments in history. He cites the relationships between mothers and sons for upper-class Greeks around 350BC, and locates parallels again at the end of the nineteenth century – evidence of the lasting influence of the Oedipus complex. It is not necessary to refer directly or in detail to Freud to substantiate such ideas. They have been endemic in Christian and other religions. It is generally accepted that male priesthood and patrilineal descent combine with the blood sacrifice of the Eucharist as the liturgical *centre* of ritual in the Christian churches despite the lack of scriptural validation for such a view.[2] Beers, writing on the rites of *The Book of Common Prayer* of the Episcopal Church in America, reveals a contentious relationship between the 'Eucharist as the central liturgical rite of the Episcopal church and women as the origin of sin and defilement' (1992, p.165).[3] It can be seen that these elements are maintained solely in the interest of a male-dominated social order.

Christ's humanity

Steinberg (1996), in a fascinating historical study of Renaissance painting, pursues the question of how Christ's sexuality is dealt with, curious about why these paintings 'attend so insistently to the genitalia of Jesus in infancy, during crucifixion and in death'. He is shown clothed until about 1260 when painters undressed the infant Jesus and 'pictured him naked but without genital emphasis' (Kermode, 1997, p. 11). By the end of the fifteenth century, however, they not only painted his penis but represented it as something to be 'pointed to, garlanded, celebrated, stared at and venerated' (p.11).

In paintings of the 1530s the penis is sometimes depicted erect, and was repeatedly shown thus (under a loincloth) in renderings of the Crucifixion and *pietà*. This is part of a long history of ignoring, then glorifying, destroying and defacing genitalia on the Christ figure. It is interesting in exposing the intertextual threads available to Lloyd Newson. These paintings reveal a male obsession with sex to be a pervading theme, not a recent phenomenon. For the modern reader this revisionary history allows new weight to be given to the significance of placing a woman on the Cross, even in the late twentieth century.

Theologians argue that it was important to demonstrate that the 'Word' was made 'Flesh' in human form – or, in an older language, in the 'inhumanation' of Christ as man. Steinberg argues that this representation was as important as the showing of wounds on the crucified Christ.

> In many hundreds of pious, religious works, from before 1400 to past the mid-16th century, the ostensive unveiling of the Child's sex, or the touching, protecting or presentation of it, is the main action.
>
> 1996, p.3

To sustain a religious hierarchy it was absolutely crucial that Christ should be explicitly sexed as a male. In reinterpreting these images Steinberg argues for a complex response to these and other paintings of the period.[4] Far from being naturalistic representations or prurient self-indulgence, they can be seen to be tokens or symbols that spoke volumes at the time and that functioned to 'confirm the mystery of the Incarnation' (p.6).[5]

In other words, arguments about whether dying and dead men in fact touch their groins, or whether grandmothers usually handle the penis of the child, are irrelevant, since it is only Christ who is ever depicted thus. Similarly, references to ancient or folk customs are equally unconvincing, on the basis that likeness to ordinary experience is not the point. Christ is like no other child – 'he is at all times the Incarnation – very man, very God' (p.10). 'It serves to set Mary's son apart from the run of the sons of Eve' in order, Steinberg suggests, to prove 'nothing less than what the Creed itself puts at the center: God's descent into manhood' (p10). It is therefore entirely appropriate that grandmother St Anne 'guarantees Christ's human lineage' by displaying his penis.

It is also important in the context of continuing challenges to Christianity during the period in which these depictions were made. According to Steinberg,

> in the imagery of earlier Christianity, the claims for Christ's absolute godhood, and for his parity with the Almighty Father, had to be constantly reaffirmed against unbelief – first against Jewish recalcitrance and pagan skepticism, then against the Arian heresy, finally against Islam.
>
> 1996, p.10

Probing further, Steinberg asks why such venial representations became so important, and suggests three theological considerations. Firstly:

> to profess that God once embodies himself in a human nature is to confess that the eternal, there and then, became mortal and sexual. Thus understood, the evidence of Christ's sexual member serves as the pledge of God's humanation.
>
> p.15

This creates a more human, loving concept of God, 'deathbound and sexed' (p.15), dependent on Mary's breast for nourishment. Secondly, in relation to Christ's adult ministry, chastity has to be seen to triumph over lust in Jesus's mortal life in order to claim the virginity and virtue expected of him; hence no representations exist of him that depict sexual activity. Thirdly, in the character of the Redeemer, he is seen as 'without sin' – 'not only without sins committed, but exempt from the genetically transmitted stain of Original Sin' (p.18). And thus, like the stigmata, the portrayal of his genitalia is 'as a nakedness immune to shame' (p.19). This literal 'shame-less', 'aboriginal innocence' as Steinberg terms it (p.24) is a profound return to a time before Eve. Redemption through death balances the Word becoming Flesh, in the womb and on earth.

The Eucharist, offering relief from the taint of Original Sin, is just one of the Christian texts available to Newson. Others referred to directly, by symbols such as the cross, are the Crucifixion and

Resurrection, and renewal through baptism. In *Strange Fish* Lloyd Newson's portrayal of the Christ figure is both subtle (in Scene 1) and brutal (Scene 12). Meanings, layered on each other from a historically accumulated series of traces, offer a range of interpretations. They include dishonour of an icon; the ridiculous, indecorous offence against decency; violation of a woman's honour in the sense of loss of chastity (to which men are not subject); and reproach at the immodest insensibility to disgrace that is exposed. Here the 'wages of sin' are on display; here the movement tells the reader that this person on the cross is sexually experienced, feels the sensuality of flesh against surface, exploits this to draw others closely in – displays in fact the very antithesis of Christ's position. The mythic dimension of the visual image is nowhere more vivid – a single image evokes the whole story (Doniger, 1998).

Theologically, the origin of pain, illness and suffering can be traced to the fall of Adam at the hands of Eve and the serpent, and the origin of each sinful life to the moment of conception in the womb of a woman. Newson, it can be argued, shows how this theology can be exploited and transposed, making the male the victim in Scene 11 and the female the sacrificial Christ in Scene 12. The bread and wine, which symbolise the body and blood of Christ, the sacrificial victim, take on a particular importance in the violence of the final acts of Scene 12.

Traces of myth in *Strange Fish*

This reading of *Strange Fish* offers a challenge to traditional notions of myth, and has profound things to say about how myths and rituals function in the late twentieth century for certain groups in white Western societies. My argument is that Lloyd Newson's work can be read as relying on shared mythic understandings and on the specific codes and characteristics of dance, music and theatre genres, not only to lay out the grounds and terms within which the reader is encouraged to see the work, but also to create some incontrovertible, largely unavoidable trails for the reader to follow. While much may still lie in the eye and ear of the individual reader and depend upon the reader's experience, sympathies and knowledge, much mythic referencing can be seen to reside in the culture of the 'text'. Newson's deliberately ritualising techniques serve to undermine the conventional narrative of religious and social belief.

It is commonly said that myths are much-told stories, or traditional tales, or legends that are in some sense transparent and neutral. They allow many meanings to be constructed and many variants of the story to be told, as well as incorporating many voices (e.g. Bremmer, 1987; Burkert in Bremmer; Blundell and Williamson, 1998). There have been many attempts to draw clear borders around each of the terms 'myth', 'legend', 'fairy story' and 'ritual' and to trace the relationships between them. Whereas Greek and earlier myths from Eastern Mediterranean civilisations have dominated anthropological and archaeological scholarship, an argument can be made that new myths continue to emerge, related in complex and interesting ways to these prior myths. The openness of interpretation that typifies post-structuralist scholarship, however, would raise no difficulty for the idea that myths of many kinds impinge upon the creation of late-twentieth-century theatre works. It is the interplay that is of interest here in the re-workings, re-creations, revivals and reconstructions of the stories told.

References to myth abound in several senses: firstly, historic myths or stories that white Westerners have inherited, largely derived from Greek and early Christian stories; secondly, modern twentieth-century myths or narratives of how we see ourselves, for example in the widespread truisms of psychoanalysis; and thirdly, stories that tell of the recent history of art, dance, theatre and music, as in the story of expressionist arts in Europe and the US during the early twentieth century. As I argue in Chapter 2, each act of narration has many tellers, who approach the telling from potentially different points of view. Myths, on the other hand, were long understood as conveying universal beliefs regardless of culture. Latterly, however, even these supposed universals have been recognised as representative of beliefs that those in power *think* should be held universally (or at least within their own cultures) and that they use for religious, economic and political ends.

Thus, myths become a 'tool in the hands of human beings', not universal constructions; they are defined and used in different ways by different people at different times (Doniger, 1998, p.2). Seen from this position, it is myth that is the overarching concept, covering ritual, ethics and other terms and approaches, functioning as 'the narrative that underlies the whole series of tellings' or versions of a story (p.3). In *Strange Fish* the question 'What is it about?' or 'What does it signify?' can be answered in terms of narratives underlying the various stories from the standpoint of different participants as each makes and creates different sequences of events (see Chapter 2). Nigel's story is different from Wendy's and from Melanie's, yet in a sense they are all part of the same narrative. In each case the story arises from the very act of selection: from the choices of the performer/reader. None emerges as the 'right' or the 'true' version or interpretation.

Yet, Doniger is also right to argue that there are several easily understood and underlying narratives about justice, kindness (or its absence), trust in other human beings or trust in a deity, which seem to sing through the differences and which anyone with a roughly similar heritage will comment upon (as indeed has happened). It may be in this sense that Burkert's theory of the universality of a few known narratives – for example, the quest and the combat, or the sacrifice of the young girl – carries some conviction (in Bremmer, 1989), although the idea that these narratives remain relevant across all cultures must invite scepticism. Doniger's construction is remarkably similar to Lyotard's 'grand narratives', a construct from a philosophical postmodernist position.

If myths invoke and legitimise dominant and divine authority, as Bremmer suggests (1989, p.4), then Lloyd Newson I suggest, tells 'stories' from the Bible and from Greek mythology, re-writing them with new endings and subversive messages. It might be seen as an amusing parody – the jester telling the story – or more seriously as a kind of Satanic re-working, adding to the heritage of perceptions of the Crucifixion and of the belief systems of Christianity. Lloyd Newson is at once occupying the roles of Homeric poet, Christian apostle, satanic cult figure and gay icon.

Given the direct link with Christianity in *Strange Fish*, Wendy Doniger's suggestion that all myths are stories, but not all stories are myths, merits comment. She argues that what distinguishes myths (or, more precisely, comparative mythology within the history of religions) is that they raise *religious* questions subsuming those pertaining to ritual. Bremmer, too, suggest that myths deal with things of collective importance rather than with the light-hearted subjects of, for example, fairy tales. There is a vital connection between the poet, the myth and a general audience, where a story is situated in time and place and is enacted by named heroes as part of a continuing narrative. This differentiates myth from the private, prose fairy-tale, whose characters are abstractions (the wicked stepmother) and whose moralist overtones are added later rather than being integral to it (Bremmer, 1989, p.6). On this basis *Strange Fish* is not just a story: it constructs a myth of its own.

Myths from other people's cultures, Doniger suggests, often provide us with useful metaphors that are more refreshing than our own, a point that I carry forward to the next chapter too. In appreciating the myths of others, the political impact of a theological vision may be highlighted, as may, conversely, the theological impact of a political stance that we hold dear. Myths act as lenses for each other in Doniger's terms. Many of the allusions in *Strange Fish* are to 'other' cultures, those of early Greece and of early Christian times, as well as to the many re-interpretations of those same narratives in the intervening 2000 years. For many young people of the late twentieth century in England, a thoroughgoing Greek myth or Biblical study has been entirely absent both from their education and from their social and family groups. This is not 'their' culture any longer, but truly a species of the 'other'.[6]

It is also possible to posit that the 'other' for Lloyd Newson is not found in groups outside white Western European society, in some colonial sense of African or Asian cultures, but within it. It may be that it is the person who holds the religious perspective who is the 'other' – that Newson is turning the binoculars to focus on received wisdom, but from his own (and his group's) rather different positions. In another variant, *Strange Fish* may be as much a critique of the late twentieth century's uncertain gender identities, and its needy and demanding individualism, promiscuity and violence, as of commonly held beliefs of Christianity. In other words, *Strange Fish* can be construed as an attack on the failure of these much-vaunted systems. Long-standing beliefs can thus be undermined by drawing attention to the violence that seems inevitably to accompany religious conviction, now in Israel/Palestine, Iraq, Indonesia and Northern Ireland as much as in Ancient Greece or early Christian times. Or can Lloyd Newson be constructed as some kind of 'divine' poet, narrating a new myth for our time – not 'other' except in these senses alluded to already, but our 'man for all seasons' for the late twentieth century?

Traces of Ancient Greece

One well-known myth to which Newson is particularly indebted is that of Herakles (or Heracles). This hero can be traced across several cultural strata and appears in several guises (Burkert in Bremmer, 1989). It is the siren figure, and men's inability to resist the sensuality of women, that is traced from these sources through to Lloyd Newson's characterisation of women in *Strange Fish* (this is pursued in greater depth in Chapter 6).

However, it is also reasonable to draw parallels of a more general kind here between late-twentieth-century culture, Lloyd Newson and the tellers of tales in Ancient Greece. Bremmer describes the evolution of Greek myth from the telling of a new story or a development of a known story to a large audience in public places, to a telling of stories that are 'bricolages' of older ones, told to a physically confined audience consisting of 'a small circle of literary friends' (1989, p.5). Lloyd Newson's audience is small (even within the arts spectrum) and limited to the theatre stage. His work is seen in a small part of the world by people from highly particularised age groups and cultural interests. It is, nonetheless, a public sphere, and without doubt he and his collaborators are telling stories that contain just this mixture, threading elements together in a distinctive way. The technique of bricolage is much in evidence.

Because my subject matter is how Lloyd Newson constructs and extends our understanding of material from Greek myth in the late twentieth century, and because I argue that he has (as we have) a strong interest in male/female sexualities and identities in relation to constructs of a god or the divine, it is appropriate to relate the subject matter of *Strange Fish* to gender and the construction of male and female identity in these stories. It can be demonstrated that we share an inheritance of how we should behave that continues to influence constructions and perceptions of works such as *Strange Fish*. Our ideas of woman as virgin, sex symbol, wife and mother are rooted here.

In this section I rely heavily on the recent study from Blundell and Williamson of the sacred and the feminine in Ancient Greece, based on material mainly from the period 750BC to 330BC (1998). Interestingly, as they point out, one area in which women were allowed to participate was that of religious life. Women's contribution was seen as necessary in this sphere; goddesses were respected, a woman could take the role of priestess, and women were an integral part of the rituals of initiation for girls, and of marriage and death. The term 'myth' is used for the narratives or tales that represented the divine, while 'rituals' describe ways of giving respect to the divine: the forms of action undertaken. Gods and goddesses were seen to be like super-humans: that is, in some ways like humans and in some ways transcendent, and therefore different from them. All deities were immortal but, as also with the Virgin Mary,

> the differences are especially significant in the case of goddesses who are seen as wielding great power in a period when real-life women were, in general, socially and politically subordinate to men.
>
> Blundell and Williamson, 1998, p.2

Heroes, on the other hand, whether real or imagined characters, were able to reward and punish individuals. Females were rarer in this category. Blundell, who argues that the Virgin Mary symbolises a later, intensely refined version of the femininity of mortal women, addresses the special characteristics of female divinity, saying that

> at the core of this difference lay the fact that on a temple dedicated to a virgin goddess, marriage was being presented as the paradigm of an ordered civilisation.
>
> Blundell and Williamson, 1998, p.47

Also at the heart of the civilisation of Athens at this time lay the protection of ownership of property. It was (and continues to be) one of the main driving forces for marriage, based on rules introduced in Athens governing the dowry and extent of sexual relations. For instance, adultery became an offence, and obligations were introduced for widows to marry their deceased husband's father's next-of-kin (p.48). Female claims in the human sphere (e.g. of the Amazons, women whom no one would want to emulate – deliberately exaggerated, like the dungaree feminists of the 1970s) were balanced by the victories of virgin goddesses such as Athene. Rejecting the role of wife and mother in order to be loyal to their fathers was not a threat but a highly desirable action. In its turn, therefore, this is the precedent for the glorification of one special supposed superwoman (the Virgin Mary, Margaret Thatcher, Princess Diana), a strategy that only succeeds in elevating the male rather than in empowering all women. Patriarchal power is simply endorsed by these strategies, as Blundell comments.

> The goddess who presided over Athens from her eminence on the Acropolis was nurturing and protective, but at the same time powerful and virginal. Her duality was such that she could honour the male in all things, but at the same time resist the bonds of marriage.
>
> Blundell, in Blundell and Williamson, 1998, p.67

The sexual status of Greek goddesses as unmarried virgins, brides or wives reflected the symbolic representation of other community values. The irony of a virginal female god presiding over the Parthenon, the city and its all-male institution reveals the paradox of the power and powerlessness of the female at this time. Behaviour not permitted of ordinary women could be acceptable in a goddess. For example,

> Hera is not only party to an incestuous marriage ... but she also displays a degree of independence, and vindictiveness towards her husband's paramours, that would not be tolerated in a mortal woman.
>
> Blundell, 1998, p.4

The relevance of these arguments about Greek mythology can be demonstrated in Wendy Houstoun's behaviour in *Strange Fish*. She is a goddess in the sense that her often-appalling behaviour is tolerated by the group (Chapters 5 and 6). She is the only performer allowed this degree of licence, and her role cannot be compatible with the later virgin goddess role since it is taken to such extremes. Melanie Pappenheim occupies a more conventional goddess position (see Chapters 6 and 7).

Cole points to another sense in which women were valued: as liminal, borderline figures who conducted rites at places on the physical margins of a *polis*, to mark a territorial frontier. Female unreliability was seen to threaten the entire community; the act of one woman could threaten the safety of all, particularly in 'the failure to maintain sexual purity' and the 'violation of a ritual requirement' (p.30). The protection of the goddess Artemis was necessary at these dangerous sites to ward off possible invaders. Cole suggests that unprotected ritual 'was in fact part of a larger religious system, one that defined, sustained and protected the entire community' (in Blundell and Williamson, 1998, p.29).

The marginal position that women occupied is also seen in women's involvement in laying out, lamenting and burying the dead, and in grieving in an unrestrained way, crossing the private–public border line into a liminal sphere, so that men were released from this role. But the men also had control of the women (Stears in Blundell and Williamson, 1998). Women were essential to the life of the society despite (or because of) their being subordinate. Polluted and polluting – a view of woman that made its way inexorably into the Christian Church and on some accounts, continues to this day.[7]

In Scene 3 in *Strange Fish* the women are clearly positioned as 'polluters' in being the initiators of uncomfortable tactics that preserve existing group structures. It is reasonable to suggest that they incite the men to act upon their malicious gestures of exclusion, directed largely at Kate Champion. The question that is not answered is: are they doing this for their own benefit or for that of the men, or of the group? The men, almost innocently (boys will be boys), exaggerate these movements and emerge from the scene with rather greater credit. That women, rather than men, should conduct or initiate these boundary/centre rites in the case of *Strange Fish* recalls Foucault's notion that the best way to police potential dissidents is to get them to do it themselves. Similarly, in the scene that follows (Scene 4) Jordi Cortes Molina remains uncorrupted – the victim of predatory women. Throughout this scene Jordi remains relatively protective and gentle, although wary of the women.

The performance anthropologist, Turner, focuses on 'process' or experience in human action (1969).[8] His notion of 'ritual symbol' operates through the idea of *condensation* that unites individual intentions and the social order. The power of 'sacrifice' is found in the way it 'mediates the conflicts of various socially liminal dramas'. Separation from the previous state, experience of ambiguity and, through the representation of death, the emergence of a new state permit both conflict and contradiction to be expressed so that some resolution might occur. There is no resolution in *Strange Fish*, despite some surface accommodations.[9] The significance for an analysis of the work of DV8 lies in Turner's perception that, though weak, those in the liminal condition have power.[10] The insights from feminist and gay theories might challenge this – it is a popular but questionable view: better to be outside the accepted conventions in order to challenge them. The more cynical position says that being outside means one can never change such conventions, since one remains impotent.

Geertz discusses a Javanese funeral ritual that becomes the site of psychological and social tension because of 'a basic ambiguity in the meaning of the rite for those who participated in it' (1973, p. 165). This rite had both religious and political significance: hence its paradox. Many parallels exist with Western societies where Church and State were at one time so intertwined that the religious, the political, the sacred and the profane could barely be separated. It is a parallel that has echoes in *Strange Fish*, since Newson's agenda may indeed be to shape the social order and to create something different but ambiguous. Interview statements clearly reveal his desire to change the world through his work, to alter the position of gays, to address homophobic attitudes, as well as to deal with the loss of a spiritual dimension to life in the late twentieth century. As the autobiographical material presented in Chapter 2 shows, Newson has both psychological and social concerns.

Extrapolation from supposedly simple to complex societies and from one continent to another is obviously dangerous, but the qualities that Turner ascribed to this transitional state are reported widely. They are just as typical of the Christian tradition as of Muslim and Buddhist belief systems, and are institutionalised in ascetic practices of guru, monk and nun. Reference can be made to the court jester of the European courts and, latterly, anti-war protesters of Western societies as symbolic figures who are allowed to intervene, usually on the side of 'humanity' or 'communitas', as Turner referred to it. This, however, may only reflect Turner's pre-disposition to think in terms of his own culture and to interpret the activities of other cultures accordingly. The limitations of Turner's insights when he moved on to grapple with complex post-industrial societies are exposed in his final essay in the posthumous 1985 collection: *Are there universals of performance in myth, ritual and drama?*. He links stage and social drama in a 'continuous "genealogy" of performance' (p.15) and seeks to reverse what he sees as 'the process of fission into sub-disciplines' in order to move toward a 'renewed fusion' among anthropological, biological, ecological, structural, semiotic, semiological, etic and other disciplines.[11] Universals are dangerous territory in dance and music as well as in performance studies. Snarrenberg refers to the 'competing myths' of procreation and natural science that underpin theories of music analysis, saying that 'each image is a source that funds a repertory of analytical fictions' (in Pople, 1994, pp.52–3).

> Myths are stories we tell ourselves, repeatedly and in a wide variety of contexts, in order to preserve ourselves as a community of like-minded music-makers ...
> myths are part of the discourse to which we pay little attention: characterising all discourse within the culture, they remain more or less invisible to those within the culture.
>
> Snarrenberg, in Pople, 1994, p. 54

Returning to the position of women in ritual practices: if, unusually, Artemis was allowed to preside over female biological and social transitions, it was because she was invulnerable to them herself (a precursor of the nun and the female unmarried school teacher as the person most suitable to take responsibility for the education of girls). The dedication of the Parthenon to Athene may then be seen to be a precursor to the cult of the Virgin in Christian mythology. In *Strange Fish* it is Melanie Pappenheim who is given this privilege in watching over the abortive rite of sexual congress by Wendy Houstoun and Dale Tanner. Her affinity with the Virgin Mary is qualified, however, by her sensual portrayal of the Christ figure.

The celebration of marriage has also been an important recurring feature in Ancient Greek myth. However, conflicting messages emerged from such festivals as that celebrating the sacred wedding of Hera and Zeus. They ranged from the validation of incestuous acts, to romantic public ceremonies celebrating love and to sacrificial acts, compounded by less than happy characterisations of marriage itself. Seduction used for political ends, infidelities, marital discord, the goddess who is vindictive towards those (particularly her best friends) whom she perceives as threatening her status as wife to Zeus and other familiar stories continue to fuel twentieth-century marriage myths and are reflected in such works as *Strange Fish*.

Hera, the marriage or wedding goddess, was the model to emulate in the initiation of young females into the only job available – that of wife and mother – and the only one that was valued, since a 'true woman' is one who has borne a child. Rejecting this role makes a woman dangerous (unless she is a goddess), since she must be tamed by marriage, not permitted to roam free and enjoy a 'wild' and unpredictable life (Clark, in Blundell and Williamson, 1998, p.15). Nevertheless, if marriage, childbirth and death were the main threads of female life, then maenadism offered an alternative and more exciting route for those brave or foolhardy enough to take it.

Seaford offers an interpretation of a Dionysiac scene, drawing ideas of initiation, identity and psychoanalysis together. In maenad ritual, girls before marriage, and women even after it, revisited the oppositional conflicts of their transition into marriage. In this ritual they commonly appear to be 'like animals' or 'like males' in their behaviour (in Blundell and Williamson, 1998, p.129). The cult of Dionysus in which wild women worshipped in wild spaces, a state associated with pre-marriage freedoms, emphasised lack of respect for the family and failure to accept responsibility. The latter provides a historical precedent for the behaviour of Wendy Houstoun and Lauren Potter in the bar scenes early on in *Strange Fish*. Neither 'animal' nor 'male' behaviour is inappropriate as an epithet for the Blonde Terrorists in *Strange Fish*. This wildness is evident in Scene 4, a scene of sexual play where the two Blonde Terrorists (as I label them) tease Jordi Molina. It has further validation, since their wildness excites him to sexual involvement and, by implication, to procreation.

The protection and patronage of the male is constructed as vital in order to civilise these women, and indeed Jordi does control the situation and finally get the girl (or at least *a* girl). This itself is an ambiguous layer in the social argument, since *women* have been held responsible for civilising the *male* in some later nineteenth- and twentieth-century moral codes.

On the other hand, Wendy Houstoun is very vulnerable when she subsequently offers herself, half-naked, to Dale Tanner in Scene 9. Her exposure demands that she should be treated with care, protected, respected – but this is of course the last thing she could expect in the 1990s non-Greek world, and she offers herself with more than a touch of disinterested bravado. It is as though her nakedness is yet another challenge to the male, to treat her worse still. Throughout the work, the more her demands and the level of her exposure increase, the less warmth of response she evokes from either friends or potential lovers.

There is a clear moral here somewhere! To be respected by men, women still need to return to a self-effacing charm, revealing their attributes only slowly and giving favours even more slowly. Once the means of controlling fertility became available and women rather than men could exercise this power (the pill rather than the condom), it was not necessary for men to think twice about where they planted their seed.[12] It has often been said that this is the downside of feminism, since women and children are then no longer protected.

The discussion above is an illustration of the centrifugal movement towards *Strange Fish* and away from it, drawing on traces from Ancient Greece and from early Christianity and linking them to twentieth-century psychological insights. I have argued that a further thread or part of the mosaic is found in anthropological writings on myth.

Doniger (1998) argues that myths are narratives of a special kind, which, using the metaphor of the telescope and the microscope, make it possible to see both the cosmic scale and the detailed reference to an individual's life. There is a methodological parallel here with dance analysis, which looks both inward to the micro-picture and outwards to the meta-world. Doniger sees mythic narrative as a form of prose, not poetry, that is capable of cross-cultural translation through dealing with questions that are common to human experience, such as 'Why are we here?', 'What happens when we die?', 'Is there a God'? (p.54). Again, these are grand narratives, linking anthropology to late-twentieth-century philosophy. They are also questions commonly dealt with through art, often with direct reference to specific myths. I suggest that this is in effect what Lloyd Newson does.

Doniger's telescope/microscope analogy focuses at the microscopic end on the detail of bodily experience. It helps us to articulate the physical activity of dance and theatre. Underpinning expression in these arts is everyday physical experience. Linking the physical experience of procreation, pain and death to the telescopic level of major life experiences draws compassion and a level of personal engagement from the observer.

Traces of ritual

An alternative is to take the idea of 'ritual' as the organising concept for this discussion, particularly since it has a focus on the active, changing nature of events, rather than on the handing-on of traditional tales. Of many characterisations of ritual, those having to do with the sacred are most helpful for my purposes. Bell (1992) refers both to sacred events and to the effect of sacralising people and things, where ritual operates to enhance social cohesion and equilibrium through symbolisation and social communication. These are familiar ideas, coinciding with the emergence of 'culture' as a category of analysis, and with the cultural anthropology of writers such as Turner, Geertz and Leach. On this view, rituals are analogous to culturally produced texts. A surprising degree of consistency can be found in descriptions of ritual, summarised here in Bell's words:

> ritual is a type of critical juncture wherein some pair of opposing social or cultural forces comes together. Examples include the ritual integration of belief and behavior, tradition and change, order and chaos, the individual and the group, subjectivity and objectivity, nature and culture, the real and the imaginative ideal ... a mechanistically discrete and paradigmatic means of sociocultural integration, appropriation, or transformation.
>
> p.16

A typical example in *Strange Fish* can be traced in the scenes already described in this chapter where the forces of sociality and of individuality conflict. They are ritually inscribed in this work, tracing the ideal in moments of harmony and exposing the devastating effects of exclusion.[13] On the complex relationship between ritual and performance, Bell argues that ritual

> as a paradigm ... is gravely disadvantaged in several ways. First ... ritual comes to be seen as a performance in the sense of symbolic acts specifically meant to have an impact on an audience. Second, the notion of performance as a theoretical tool for approaching certain activities comes to be used as descriptive of the fundamental nature of those activities; in other words a model of ritual activity provides the criteria for what is or is not ritual. Third, although

> performance may become a criterion for what is or is not ritual ... there is no basis to differentiate among ways of performing.
>
> p.42

As Bell points out, with some of these definitions it becomes impossible to make any distinctions between ritual performance and theatre. In extremes, sport and street events are also included, with the result that the term has no specificity. Ritual, in performance-theory terms, simply 'communicates'; but what it communicates, and to whom, remain questions to be addressed. Nor does it bear close examination that ritual is the cultural medium by which thoughts and acts are re-integrated, since this claim has been made of many activities and not yet demonstrated – what would a re-integrated thought and act look like? How would we recognise it?

Bell breaks free of circularity by undermining this category of ritual, to see it not so much as a set of special practices as a set of 'common strategies of ritualization, a way of acting that differentiates some acts from others' (p.ix). It is this view that informs my analysis of *Strange Fish* as ritual. Again, in dance theorising, distinctions of this kind tend to lead to ritual/dance being formulated in terms of the rational and irrational, both clearly identified with emotional and cathartic poles in consequence. A pervasive explanation from social and individual catharsis is shared between performance arts and ritual forms, and becomes powerful in justifications and explanations of their powers. At the other end of the argument, where ritual overlaps with everyday activity, it is interpreted as routinisation, regularisation and repetition, and is reduced to being a form of language (Bell, 1992, p.72). It is not the particular set of features but the formal ones that indicate the ritual character in this case – the ritualisation of everything is inevitably the ritualisation of nothing. If everything is dance, nothing in particular is dance. All dance is movement (*pace* stories and myths), but not all movement is dance. Movement is global, dance is local.

Nonetheless, with these cautions, it is suggested here that seeing *Strange Fish* as a 'rite', and exposing its strategies of ritualisation, explains something of its effectiveness and power in an art context. It commands more forcefully than a physical display of army or police power alone might. Rather than being dependent on external violence, it operates persuasively through its own effects, generating laughter, seducing the emotions, provoking the reconsideration of ideas, and swallowing the audience in sensuality, movement, music, light and colour.

Rather than affirming 'clear and dogmatic values ... ritual actually constructs an argument, a set of tensions' (Bell, 1992, p.195) and it does it on its own terms, in its own language, not pretending to be something else. It is a perspective that resonates with *Strange Fish*. This characterisation makes 'ritual' a useful dynamic category alongside Doniger's 'myth', to avoid what Bell refers to as the static nature of myth. As she says:

> the dynamic interaction of texts and rites, reading and chanting, the word fixed and the word preached are practices, not social developments of a fixed nature and significance. As practices, they continually play off each other to renegotiate tradition, authority and the hegemonic order. As practices, they invite and expect the strategic counterplay.
>
> Bell, 1992 p.140

It could be said that ritual, in common with many of the theoretical systems referred to so far, functions 'to resolve the complex problems posed by an initial bifurcation of thought and action' (p.6). Further, the success of ritual might be the result of its 'replac[ing value-laden] terms such as "liturgy"' which relied on an opposition to 'magic', and 'which were used to distinguish high religion from primitive superstition or our ritual from theirs' (p.6). Whether ritual is any less open to value-laden (mis)use is not clear. Newson can be configured as a choreographer/theatre-maker who 'ritualises' psychological and mythic events in a late-twentieth-century mode, capturing these events and reworking them to generate exactly the same commitment and excitement formerly generated by Greek and Christian myths, but using political and consumerist strategies of the present to reinforce the message.

Bearing these differences of perspective in mind, I find it more profitable to approach the issues of myth in *Strange Fish* firstly through psychological and then through theological traces. This is bound to be problematic, and the division is in some sense false. Theologies can be regarded as mythic structures, while myths can be part of theology. Similarly, psychological interpretations align themselves readily with both theological and mythic characterisations. Doniger's conception is particularly helpful, since it addresses directly the relationship of myth with theology and politics. Myths as 'political lenses' enable the outsider to move easily between the political implications and the theological implications of actions and views embedded in a particular mythic perspective (1998, p.19).[14] It is this conflation of gender issues with religious issues and the dilemmas of modern political life that make *Strange Fish* worth investigating further. These intertwining threads are followed separately through the next two sections in order to make the cultural heritage of each clear. Ritual, too, is created in this piece as the means by which DV8 embeds these ideas in our imaginations.

Echoes of instability and disintegration

Part of the purpose of all myth, it has been widely agreed by comparative religionists and by anthropologists, is to allow societies and their individual members to deal with such difficult emotions as anxiety, aggression and eroticism, by removing them to an abstracted, symbolic sphere. It is argued that by so doing these feelings are made safe. The value of myth and ritual practice lies in providing a shared social response to psychological needs, in helping individuals to deal with traumatic occurrences, while promoting the stability of the group. This is as true of our Jungian or Freudian psychological frames as of other myths. Indeed, to take a different, contemporary example referred to earlier, Walser argues that the form of music known as heavy metal, while invoking madness, struggle and disorientation, also 'mediates social tensions. It works to provide its fans with a sense of spiritual depth and social integration' (1993, p. xvi), although, like Newson, into an alternative rather than a mainstream community.

Plainly the insights of Freud and Jung are hard to avoid in contemporary theorising, or even 'psychologising', in a colloquial sense, over a cup of coffee or a glass of wine. They have become our own twentieth-century myths, which, like the Greek myths of old, have become the currency of everyday talk.[15] Caldwell (1989) traces psychological threads that have accreted to anthropological notions of myth, including the idea of the expression of unconscious, usually repressed material. This understanding then also allows the manipulation of the emotional content of myth for social ends. It is incontrovertible that these are also psychological concerns. Their relevance here lies in the psychological narrative crucial in this analysis. *Strange Fish* is a work that deals explicitly with the interaction of individuals as they create and change small social groups, through highly ritualised strategies. In constructing its own ritual practices it draws on myths of many kinds – Greek, Christian and modern psychological myths – and in re-telling them, asks questions of them and invites them to deconstruct themselves.

Lloyd Newson is not alone in dealing with psychological and Greek material. They both have an honourable history in modern dance and there are many examples, of which Martha Graham's *Night Journey* might be the most easily recalled, taking as it does subject matter that is directly Greek. While *Strange Fish* is more allusory in its treatment than is Graham's interpretation, there is a parallel with more recent expressionist pieces of modern dance. As with Martha Graham's work, there is an overlap between an individual making sense of his or her own life and that individual's choreographic work that results in themes of death, eroticism and the maternal body (Burt, 1998). It might be suggested, equally stereotypically, that for the archetypically self-obsessed and narcissistic gay male choreographer, the maternal body is of little *erotic* significance. However, more to the point for Newson is the male fear of avenging angels, as in Nigel Charnock's fear of Wendy Houstoun. In turn this draws on an 'almost universal, deeply seated aversion to the female body' (p.49), which Burt attributes to the 'violence and horror of separation' from the mother – truly a psychoanalytic interpretation but one that resonates neatly with Greek obsessions. Ramsay Burt concludes that, as revealed in many recent works of physical theatre, 'men in many ways hate and fear women' (1995, p. 196-197).[16]

Another parallel in the history of modern dance can be seen in the endless re-writings of works with archaic ritual themes, notably *The Rite of Spring* to Stravinsky's music, re-worked some 100 times since Nijinsky's version in 1912. Beers's (1992) demonstration that public rituals of the *current time* continue to be rituals of sacrifice seems to be justified. To support this he constructs a dynamic psychological and anthropological model[17] of the relationship between self, symbol and culture.[18] He argues that where the 'sacred' is not only socially constructed but also subject to change, the threat of instability is always present.[19] This threat can take the form of a challenge from a number of places, either inside or outside the system, or from the ambiguities of the boundaries themselves, or from tension within elements that are within these boundaries. According to Douglas, in these very marginal positions lies power (1966).

There is an episode embodying this idea in the stage version of *Strange Fish*, which is not repeated on the video version. Diana Payne-Myers, the older dancer who appears first of all as a frail, nun-like figure, is tossed around by a group of young men, like a doll or a ball. This sadistic entertainment for immature men on a night out is a means of establishing their difference, thus assuaging their needs. It is not just in *Strange Fish* that Newson explores rage and aggression towards women – they are common features of Newson's work, as the more recent *Enter Achilles* (1995) exemplifies.

Beers discusses the almost universal occurrence of ritual blood sacrifice among patrilineal societies, arguing, in brief, that far from being a stage through which men pass, narcissism is the 'energy and form of ... the self' (1992, p.127). The intrusion of archaic forms of narcissism, of intense forms of narcissistic hunger or fear of fragmentation, it is believed, is the source of the anxiety in the modern world's disorders. Rage and aggression are common outcomes where the individual perceives the activity of others as 'wounds to the self', not as independent of the self.[20]

It is not unreasonable to suggest that *Strange Fish* can be seen as a ritual of blood sacrifice, a *male-identified rite that is gender-specific, an expression of male narcissistic anxiety*, applying Beers's terms (1992). Blood sacrifice embodies complex metaphors of women's difference from men, while offering men expiation and relief from their fears. 'Hunger for merger and the desire for rigid ego boundaries reflect the ambivalent tension' involved (p.144). Sacrifice is understood as an ancient male-bonding ritual: an act of separation from women by means of which they can both bond with each other and appropriate women's power. This seems a more than adequate characterisation of Scene 3 in *Strange Fish* (described earlier in this chapter). Beers attributes this need for appropriation to a 'male psychological constellation involving the envy, desire and fear of women' (p.11), a theory that would find a sympathetic audience in feminist anthropology as well as in some branches of psychology. Bremmer (1989) makes a direct link between Greek male homosexuality and tribal rituals of initiation, arguing that the function was similar: for adult males to initiate younger males.[21]

Strange Fish, however, shows relatively little bonding overall. Rather, it *exposes* trauma and suggests that the outcomes of our society's rituals are not comfortable for many. Characters are presented as real individuals, not as representations of some named character, nor as archetypes. This extends to Wendy Houstoun's use of Nigel Charnock's real name in moments of extremis, just as Nigel addresses individuals by their own names in the party scene. These scenes of social interaction are treated here as modern rituals, which perversely cause distress and discomfort for the performers, and do not 'make safe' dangerous feelings as myth is supposed to. Occasionally, Wendy and Nigel glimpse the possibility of belonging to a duo or a group, but this sense does not last; the fleeting moment of comfort serves only to point up its continuing absence. What it does 'make safe' is another layer that says that it is all right at the end of the twentieth century to expose our wildest and bitterest moments (as television chat shows and confessional series demonstrate). Perhaps anything less would be trivial.

Thus while it may be said that the ritualisation of behaviour serves 'to maintain psychic health and stability' of the group (Caldwell, 1989, p.7), Newson demonstrates quite pointedly the obverse of this position: the destructive and alienating function of social rituals for certain groups – their potential to isolate individuals who do not 'fit' and to promote change and political action, either through the individual or against existing societies. Indeed, a crucial function of rituals, if Geertz (1973) is correct, is that they do not merely inscribe, or reflect social structure, 'nor do they merely express or create conflicts symbolically ... [but] ... *shape* the social order; shape the conflicts of society' (Beers, 1992, p.53).

Newson's concern with loss of faith finds resonance in this theoretical explanation, just as his work demonstrates the restlessness and foreboding to which Giddens refers. The 'narrative of self-identity [is] inherently fragile' (1991, p.185), requiring continual re-ordering of experience in the light of its fragmenting character. If a pure relationship offers 'intensified intimacy', it also 'allows for and demands organised and continuous self-understanding'; yet this intimacy 'creates enormous burdens for the integrity of the self' (p.186). If there are no agreed external referents, the sense of self has to be even stronger, 'shorn of external moral criteria ... vulnerable to life transitions' at fateful moments (p.186). Nigel Charnock has an obvious and appealing vulnerability; he twitches heartstrings, and yet there is the suspicion that he is merely manipulating these responses quite deliberately. Since his end is tragic and unsought, it seems to be explained neither by parody nor by a critique of supposedly gendered qualities. This surface-level representation may do nothing more than reinforce stereotypes of male dominance, since the result in the case of *Strange Fish* is that we laugh at him. He isn't a real man – and this is why we laugh. We learn nothing of female behaviour that isn't derogatory.

Giddens's sociological account says in another way something similar to Beers's psychoanalytic position, and illustrates the intertextuality of theory that is part of the method and point of this essay. Giddens continues, 'It is not surprising that rage, anger and depressive feelings swirl through the contexts of pure relationships and, in concrete circumstances, intimacy may be psychically more troubling than it is rewarding' (1991, p.187).[22] In Scene 2 (Corridor

Scene 1), Nigel Charnock conspires with Wendy and Lauren to make a threesome, in which he is successful until the appearance of other males (Scene 3), when the male/female split seems to counteract any more general human sympathies or anxieties.

In Scene 6 (*The party, the isolate and the group*) Charnock's extreme and increasingly hilarious physical manoeuvrings culminate in his standing on the shoulders of one of a closely entwined pair of lovers with his hands on the shoulders of the other, literally pushing them apart. Desperation indeed; we, women as well as men, laugh as we feel for him, and in this sense Charnock taps an anxiety of all human beings. Whether it is more narcissistic in the male, as Beers proposes, is debatable and may depend upon the position taken up by the reader! For all of us it may trigger recognition of the pathetic scramblings that people engage in to find a place in social groups; recognition of the painful fact of exclusion that we all experience at times, emphasising the need to belong. But belong to what, and to which groups? Is it always clear, even to ourselves, which groups we want to join? Newson points out that it is actually no easier for men than for women in this respect.

Returning momentarily to Greece: Dionysiac scenes for men can suggest an inversion of identity, a mystic initiation through male transvestism. Drawing on Lacan, Seaford argues that the liminal stage of a rite of passage involves a regression to infancy – a pre-condition for a new identity (in Blundell and Williamson, 1998, p.139). Inversion of gender serves a similar purpose in rites of passage, producing liminal confusion through fragmentation, driving the male to seek merger again with the mother. The contemporary equivalent can perhaps be found in re-birthing courses. Nigel Charnock's desperate cries for attention seem to state this in a perfectly obvious manner.

This depressing picture of narcissistic anxiety or 'dread' (a more diffused term in which there is both desire and disgust) is predicated on the uncertainty of boundaries. These fears wound. They lead to a sense of incompleteness, fear of women, and the subsequent attempt to control and degrade them. From Freud, however, Beers (1992) links this 'pre-oedipal devouring' directly to the male fear of being castrated or devoured by women.[23] Hence the need for men to protect themselves against women, and an explanation for positioning women as 'monstrous' and themselves as victims in this strange transposition of cultural characterisations of the male and female.[24]

A contrasting example can easily be found in which the female displays aggressive tendencies. In Scene 8 the lovers sit on a bench, intensely focused on each other, stroking and kissing. Wendy Houstoun tries to intervene by sitting close. She moves nearer, peers at them, pushes her head between them and lies alongside Lauren Potter. Finally she uses her feet to remove the couple forcefully from the bench, turning the incident not only into a fight for its possession but also into an attempt at the ruthless destruction of a new relationship.

The tussle between the couple and Wendy Houstoun has its amusing moments and some clever manipulation of the bench, but it gradually takes on a more ominous character, that of predation. Houstoun attempts to squash Potter underneath the bench as if she were an insect. Molina lifts the bench clear, balances it across his back and, with Potter perched on top, menaces Houstoun. In this they resemble the carapace of a particularly large and sinister beetle, which in turn suggests intertexts from the insect world, and instinctual fights to the death, rather than the supposedly rational nature of human interaction. This farcical exaggeration of human behaviour carries echoes of Nigel in the party scene.

There is a contrast between attempts to construct gentle, caring relationships within a private, coupled world and the cavalier destruction of others' lives. This connects with our own time – with a loss of spirituality and of humanity, in the face of excessive consumerism and the commodification of emotional life as well as literal goods. One aspect is a lack of commitment in the heterosexual world, where the freedom of the 1960s has had well-documented and disturbing consequences in England as well as in North America, the backlash to which can be seen in conservative views on the 'family'. This is mirrored by tabloid newspaper reports of lack of commitment among gays. In both cases (the freedom of women and the choice of gay and lesbian people) the negotiation with the political rhetoric of the day challenges accepted conventions and is itself a political act.

The intertextual layers that collide in this section are drawn from interpretative positions that make it possible to see both the male and female as victims *and* as perpetrators of violence and evil. It is like flipping a coin to reveal its reverse – they are still sides of the same thing, the one entailed in the other. Both female and male are victims of a capitalist, consumerist society in economic turmoil.

Models of sacrificial rituals point to disintegration anxiety, a form of anxiety associated with differentiation and separation. Sacrifice is not Oedipal, but is based on 'anticipation of the break-up of the self, not the fear of the drive' (Kohut, in Beers, 1992, p.104).[25] There are a number of incidents in *Strange Fish* that chime well with this idea.

Fear and the expectation of disintegration are emotions that are most visible in the party scene (Scene 6). Charnock vividly displays this fear, not only in relation to the large group but also more widely in his interactions with other individuals from the beginning to the end of the work.[26] His incessant babbling and his desperate attempts to connect with another human being offer the reader a clear example of what Caldwell calls the anxiety associated with an emerging sense of the self and the simultaneous threat attendant upon that anxiety – the threat that the anxiety may turn out to be justified after all. When Charnock fails to meet with success, he resorts to trying to divide existing groups, placing himself in between their members, addressing individuals directly – physically and psychologically forcing himself on them. But still he fails – either to fit in, or to register their distaste for his all-too-obvious needs.

The paradoxical character of their actions reveals other similarities between Charnock and Houstoun: for example, their fascination with sadomasochism. On the one hand the characters they represent are apparently impervious to the reactions and feelings of others, and on the other, deeply dependent on each other, and still capable of being hurt by others. Charnock makes this evident in the conversational scene (Scene 2) where he 'shadows' the movements and postures of others, trying to ingratiate himself, and in the bar scene (Scene 3) where he competes in a frenzy, but inadequately, for female attention. Even though they are exaggerations, these sections draw very obviously on ordinary behaviour, highlighting conventional movement and gestures as used in ritualised social situations. However, by elaborating them and distorting them almost out of recognition through parody, by bringing the reader to a point of incredulity, the ludicrous nature of such social engagement is exposed. Thus by the construction and simultaneous deconstruction of images and conventions Newson aligns himself with postmodernist practices, installing a convention in order that it can be subverted. By doing this he exposes his own subversive agenda, at least in some areas of gender politics. For this purpose the paradoxical character of myth helps him. Its two sides incorporate on the one hand the 'orgiastic' elements, leading to comedy, harmony and the dissolution of hierarchy; and on the other hand, the conflict generated from the reversal of roles, permitted simultaneously (Versnel in Bremmer, 1987), both of which are evident in *Strange Fish*.

Hierarchies and schemes of binary oppositions are visible in many ritual contexts. Christian ritual, for instance, emphasises the raised altar, the elevated host, the contrast of standing and kneeling or prostrating oneself before the ultimate resolution in that central moment of receiving the body and blood of Christ, in the bread and wine. Ultimately the higher reality is internalised through the food shared by participants. In the first scene of *Strange Fish* the camera angle emphasises the distance between the kneeling supplicant, head bowed, and the Christ figure, high and looming on the cross.

In the final scene the reality is of Wendy forcing wine down the throat of the Christ figure, not of Christ generously sharing the benefits of his sacrifice with his adoring apostles. The idea is heavily deconstructed of a hierarchical god sharing food and wine, able to create goodness in the form of food as well as other aspects of spiritual well-being, and as being the one in control of its distribution to those who deserve it.

In ritual, contrasts are generally agreed to be very important, particularly between the sacred and profane. Contrast is a means of asserting difference – yet it is often asymmetrical, not balanced, to create dominance, hierarchical relationships and eventually integration. Ritualisation techniques may include (but are not defined totally by) certain features – often formality, fixity, and repetition (Bell, 1992) – and examples of these motifs abound. As part of its undermining technique, *Strange Fish* quite deliberately disrupts these links, which are normally taken for granted.

One example is the fact that the final scene matches the first in its location. It generates a sense of a ritualised return, a rite undergone, and a return to the first place. Such scenes are themselves repetitions (although not exact) of ancient traditions combined with radical innovation, in the way Bell describes. Ritualisation might involve

> the exact repetition of a centuries-old tradition or deliberately radical innovation and improvisation, as in certain forms of liturgical experimentation or performance art.
>
> p.91

The recurring motifs of Scenes 3 and 4, where group relationships are established and destroyed, convey an obsessive reiteration of ideas. Scene 6 and 7 use the exaggeration of contrasts and the repetition of phrases so often that the ritualistic nature of the exchange lies on the surface. The speed of incident in which others are manipulated, both literally and emotionally, increases in pace to grip the stomach of the watcher until cathartic release is obtained in the silence and solitude of Nigel's isolation. In Scene 5 the same technique is used to a different end, where the lovers seem to tighten the screw on their closeness by the impossible physical intertwining of bodies, until the repetition becomes almost unbearable. Neither scene resolves in the sense of a happy (or climactic) ending, but activity ceases, bringing some relief. These rituals are clearly moulded through the shaping of the movement, through the emphasis on different spatial distances and through the timing of action, just as much as by the environment in which they are located. Long narrow corridors create, invite and respond to certain kinds of movement and behaviour towards others, as do large open rooms, or small, contained spaces, or water tanks.

These internal–external strategies of ritualisation have no resolution, but act by 'maintaining and multiplying oppositions' (Bell, 1992, p.104). Here the link between ritual and the post-structuralist free play of Derrida is apparent. What it is supposed to 'mean' is endlessly deferred. Derrida's deferral into the wider world collects up these experiences, conventional conflicts and oppositions – yet never yields a final answer, a single meaning, a coherent act. Instead this process results in a sense at best of 'a loosely knit and loosely coherent totality, the full potential of which is never fully grasped and thus never fully subject to challenge or denial' (p.106).

This negotiation of power relations and the outcomes of the interactions in *Strange Fish* provide a fruitful stepping-stone to the next chapter, via an analogy with another of Lloyd Newson's works. But first, I must reflect on the power relationships within homosexual constructions in the context of the Western Christian Church, since it may be relevant to ask why Newson chose such an obviously oppositional context. Given Newson's choice of gender identity, is he making a point about gay men – do they adopt the same mechanisms within their own groups as heterosexual males and females do, and as lesbian women do? Lloyd Newson cannot 'speak' for the whole of DV8 in gender terms, and indeed each of their gender positions carries implications for the ritualisation of movement behaviour. Do the performers therefore speak from experience, or are they making a point about heterosexual and/or homosexual relationships that is both dismissive and ironic?

Bailey (1955) wrote one of the earliest studies of homosexual men and the Christian Church in an effort to construct an objective and impartial account of the history of the Church. Despite his intentions, this text has to be understood in the light of then-prevailing debates about removing homosexual acts from the criminal category and the furore that this movement created. He medicalises homosexuality as a 'condition', which the individual cannot help, and seeks its causes in a maladjusted childhood while allowing for innate or inherited tendencies. He holds out little hope for a 'cure' for this condition, although advocating relief through psychiatric or other medical treatment.

Interestingly, what underlies his argument is the association of the control of sexuality by religious groups with a wide range of actual practices over the years. It emerges clearly that no one specific practice is universally condemned, and that any practice can be made to signify wickedness or saintliness, given the appropriate gloss. Practices that are condemned change over time, and this in itself exposes the importance of the power and control over people's lives that the early Christians needed in order to counter paganism. Controlling people's sexuality was one way of ensuring adherence to the new dogma and separateness from previous traditions. Modern governments continue in the same way.

Bailey's account reinforces Bremmer's anthropological/archaeological view that before the twentieth century the notion of homosexuality as a matter of choice for adult males rarely existed. Sex with widows, virgins and boys was treated as one category of forbidden territory (Bailey, 1955, p. 69). Action of this kind was held to be responsible for earthquakes, famines and other calamities – in other words, strange sexual practices were blamed for natural disasters, a tendency now seen again with AIDS. The increasingly refined categories of proscription that Bailey describes show either an obsession with sexual practices or simply a need for control and a cynical manipulation of ordinary people (pp.102–105).

Although Bailey may be right to emphasise that homosexuality was not a possibility as a named and respected way of life, literature throughout history illustrates a tradition that is more or less hidden but nonetheless clear and continuous. As Mitchell and Leavitt (1998) show in their collection of extracts from literature written between the middle of the eighteenth and the early twentieth century, the authorities to whom writers appealed included the most revered of the Greeks (such as Plato and Plutarch) and later Christians (such as St Augustine). The Biblical love of David and Jonathan that was 'wondrous, passing the love of women' is an oft-quoted example. It is not only in Greek thinking that these ideas are prominent; they dominate other religious systems, but for the purposes of this text it is the Judaeo-Christian interpretations and re-interpretations that are of greatest significance.

Under these constructions of relationships there emerged 'a high-minded, even exalted ideal of same-sex love' (p.xv) in which 'friendship' between men was elevated above male–female or female–

female love. Although often allied with celibacy, a romantic or spiritual form of love also frequently sheltered explicit male–male sexual practices. Exclusion of women from the ranks of priesthood (common in many religions) was based on a logic of inherent male superiority; on the sex chosen by God; on the uncleanness of women arising from menstruation and childbearing; and on women's 'lack' of spirituality. This exclusion ensured that 'spiritual love' remained a male–male form while the female equivalent was more deeply hidden and more easily dismissed.[27] The knowledge systems and practices of worship embodied in the Church guaranteed that women remained ignorant and illiterate while men built an intellectual and spiritual tradition in which they dominated.

At this point I draw on a review of *Enter Achilles* by Judith Mackrell to illustrate a number of theoretical points, as well as to provide evidence for my statement that much of *Strange Fish*, not untypical of Newson's work, can be read as showing a lack of awareness, and often hostility, to the position and views of women, whether heterosexual or homosexual. The views that Mackrell expresses are not uncommon from female critics, although rare from male critics. Provoking and disturbing as they are, they serve to open up questions of misogyny and to challenge them. There is no intention here to impute misogynistic positions or any other set of characteristics to any of the individuals involved. I am outlining a potential intertextual reading here.[28]

Judith Mackrell (1995) picks up a text of a popular television show of the 1990s, *Men Behaving Badly*, which, as a cultural reference, has served many purposes in attacking supposedly 'new' men. The language that she uses to describe the action is as explicit as the action itself. I include virtually the whole of this review because her own response to the work is of interest and because it is a reference to a different work, demonstrating some similarities with *Strange Fish* and some differences from it in that the behaviour of the men is more obviously challenged. I also include it because it chimes with my own experience of the work and expresses responses succinctly. Newson's justification for its polemic is also interesting.

Truly, badly, but terribly manly

LLOYD NEWSON'S latest piece *Enter Achilles* is about men behaving badly. That's not just badly as in getting very pissed and arseing around. It's badly as in beating up any male who's remotely effeminate; badly as in slashing the breasts of a plastic sex doll and badly as in repressing emotion. Eight dancers, confined in a claustrophobic pub interior, share a 75 minute drinking session that becomes more angry, defensive and explosive by the pint. The group's body language is brilliantly and often hilariously observed. Several of the men are raw with tension, their chins thrusting like turkey cocks, their legs as stiff as a group of drilling squaddies. They take up too much air space, they jab their fingers to ram a point home.

Periodically the beer turns them into puppies so that they sprawl into rugby scrums, beam blearily, sing sentimental songs and snicker. But it also turns them nasty. One man at least is covertly gay but he tries to be one of the lads. The first time they turn against him he fulfils every boy's dream by whirling around and trouncing his attackers, his clothes falling off to reveal his Superman suit. But the next time is for real, with ugly fighting and even uglier mimed rape. The same violence is unleashed against a plastic doll which gets beaten up in brutal pantomime sex and mutilated with a broken bottle. The hatred of women, of bodies, of physical affection is wound to a terrifying pitch. These, says the show, are the feelings and fantasies men store up to take home after a night at the pub. As we watch these scenes, though, it's not actually the anger and repression that most shocks – we know it all too well. What's really startling is the fact that a group of men could have produced such an unloving and unforgiving portrait of themselves. Lloyd Newson has made a brilliant career out of anatomising the politics of sex – from male alienation to female masochism – and by instinct and circumstance he's a polemicist ... His new work, *Enter Achilles*, however, originated from Newson's own feelings of discomfort with his sex. He was working in Glasgow with some male dancers who happened to be straight and, spending time with them, he found himself in an unfamiliar 'hard man' culture of pubs, pints and anti-gay attitudes. He watched himself, fascinated, as he tried to fit in. 'Men have been criticised for oppressing women,' he says, 'but we also have to realise how much we oppress ourselves.' Newson observed how most men are afraid to dress as they want ('we all go around in camouflage'), how they don't drink what they want ('guys will order beer even if they don't really like it'), how they don't express their emotions ('we're only meant to show anger or humour'). How they are in denial – 'so much of our masculinity is defined by negatives'. To explore these attitudes he developed a broad scenario which he then spent weeks improvising with his eight dancers. The latter contributed many of the final words and actions and some of the show's most worrying moments, Newson insists, are theirs – the violence with the doll, the filthiest jokes. This is important, because Newson feels that what he learnt about his dancers – their aggressive defences and their unwillingness to share their secrets – bore out the rest of his research and proved that the viciousness and inhibition portrayed in *Enter Achilles* 'represent the vast majority of heterosexual men'. He can cite countless episodes to support this, of strangers baiting gay men in the street and of physical intimidation of outsiders. He can talk about how his cast of largely straight dancers turned out to be much more buttoned up than any comparable group of gay men he's worked with (although he's anxious to stress that gay men recognise aspects of themselves in the show). But however true the anecdotes are and however vivid the work's imagery, *Enter Achilles* deliberately presents only the damning evidence against men. The extreme discomfort I and many other women felt with Newson's grim portrayal of victimised women in his earlier work (is that really how he saw us?) I now find myself feeling on behalf of men (are they really so vile?)

Certainly I'd expected *Enter Achilles* to make me laugh and to make me angry, but I'd also expected a work that claims to ask 'fundamental questions of what constitutes masculinity' to take me into some hidden areas of the male psyche (what do guys do when women aren't there?); I'd hoped to be surprised and what I got instead was a series of stereotypes, expertly and wittily manipulated, but routinely familiar all the same. Apart from a few snatched moments of camaraderie, a guilty bit of sensitivity, and of course the token vulnerable gay man, there was no glimpse of the way individuals operate within the social mould, of the tension between men's eccentricities and decencies and their horrible gang behaviour. It was funny and deadly but it was too bad to be true.

Newson defends himself by back pedalling a little. 'Well of course it's not meant to be all men ... it's fantastical, a parody ... There is always a problem with representation in dance. If you watch a play like Arnold Wesker's *The Kitchen* you just think this is a bunch of men in a kitchen, you're not thinking this is every man.' The difficulty is partly that 'people aren't used to seeing characterisation through movement' but it's also that choreography can have a generalising effect on its material. Newson discovered this when

> making his last work, *MSM*, a piece about cottaging in which he'd intended to use movement as well as text. Because he found that the words (which he'd gathered from extensive interviews) carried the truth of the piece so precisely he couldn't use dance at all – 'the movement didn't fit, it was too abstracting'. ... It's the movement that carries the bulk of characterisation and makes the larger statements.
>
> But even if *Enter Achilles* feels as if it was made to prove a point and even if its aim seems skewed it does manage to splatter a lot of targets en route. The humour and the horror of it will touch nerves, cause arguments and revisit the debate about nineties man. It may not be a credible human document but it does effectively and entertainingly what all polemic should do – which is divide its audience into angry support or dissent.[29]
>
>

In an interview with Meisner (1995), Newson associated the responses of male friends to an injury to his Achilles heel with his perception of macho man and the 'posturing' that stifles the expression of feelings in men. Newson argues that the piece is about masculinity, since these behaviours characterise both hetero- and homosexual men, and is not about being gay; but his representations of masculinity are extraordinarily crude. He seems to 'play' with different emphases on sexuality, presumably in an attempt to steer a course between speaking honestly from his own situation (which would at least be in line with his outspoken views on the integrity of artists) and chasing audiences, who of course may be of many persuasions.[30] Links could be made to the early Greeks as well as to Freud and ideas of desire, guilt and murder; to the role of ritual sacrifice as the central act of a cultural system; and to sacrifice as the ritualised killing of substitutes which itself substitutes for violence, and which can be released through the controlled displacement of chaotic and aggressive impulses.

Conclusion

A mosaic begins to emerge in which the ostensible focus of this chapter, on men and the construction of masculinity, is constantly moved aside to consider the reciprocal position of women. This is hardly surprising, since the binary of male/female makes sense only in this way. Already, however, even within the Ancient Greek and early

Christian traces, there is evidence of ambiguous characterisation and an ambivalent position between male and female. A study of myth shows us that our supposedly distinct cultures share many value positions and differ in interesting ways – they slide into and across each other. The ritualisation of anxiety and fear is another thread that can be traced through and across time and space, manifesting itself in diverse ways. In *Strange Fish*, male anxiety is dominant and threatens to destabilise the world it presents, offering no consolation or resolution. In Chapter 5 the tables are turned to view similar issues from the position of the construction of an equally ambiguous femininity.

1 The essentially intertextual nature of religious practice was brought home to me on a visit in 1997 to New Mexico, to the Pueblo of the Santo Domingo tribe, whose Native American origins can be traced to 1000BC. Within a small, apparently 'Christian' church are the signs of many religious traditions – Native American, Spanish Catholic, etc. – alongside modern artefacts of consumerism. In their official leaflet, the Governor of the tribe says of their religion that while they have 'adopted Catholicism ... they also maintain their native ancient religious beliefs. The two religions exist side by side'. Their own religion revolves around nature, and views all living things and inanimate objects as having their place in the spiritual life. Man is no more or less important. The contradictions are not uncomfortable for the Santo Domingo tribe.

2 Not just of episcopalianism, of course, but of other versions of Christianity too.

3 Beers extends Kohut's work in a case study of *The Episcopal Eucharist: Women, Sin and Christ in the US* (1992, Chapter 14); hence its particular relevance for an analysis that draws on these Christian rituals.

4 Steinberg refers also to the 'chin chuck', not just as a playful childlike gesture but as an erotic token by which the artist shows Christ choosing Mary as his 'eternal consort in heaven' (1996, p.5).

5 Steinberg argues that the better naturalism gets in painting, the more self-defeating it becomes, since the images lose their mythic significance.

6 For people of my generation and kind of upbringing, they were central if not very specific in their re-telling. They were both the

folklore and the substance of education and religious practice, at home and at school.

7 Stears, however, suggests that both death and childbirth resulted in the household rather than women in particular being 'polluted' by virtue of their closeness. Nonetheless she recognises that the emotional involvement of women in lamentation underpinned the idea that women were illogical and in need of control. Although the interpretation of the original sources is interesting, it is the versions adopted by Christianity that are more to the point in the 1990s (in Blundell and Williamson, 1998).

8 The three rites to which Turner refers are those of separation, limen or margin, and reaggregation (1969). The liminal state is seen as being between identities or states, and unstructured – likened to death, to bisexuality, to the wilderness and to eclipses of the Sun and Moon. Re-integration into the larger society occurs through 'communitas' (pp.94–5).

9 One of Turner's research projects dealt with the Ndembu of NW Zambia and the passage of adolescents from lower to higher status through a limbo of having no status at all (1969, pp.99–100).

10 In the rite of the Kumukindyila group, despite being sexless and anonymous, submissive and silent (or because of it), these are the people on whom new knowledge is inscribed, a view that Turner shares with Douglas.

11 His work has become seminal in Schechner's influential development of performance studies (Turner in Schechner and Appel, 1990). While Schechner recognises a multiplicity of performance modes and thus opens up the discipline to many new activities, its basis is still the search for universals of process.

12 Who cares? Re-enter triumphant biologism: 'He can't help it', 'It's only natural to spread your genes', 'It's in the interest of the quality of the human race'. It is another calamity of post-1960s claims to equality for women, the message of feminism, that the more equal woman is economically, and asks to be politically and sexually, the more violent is the dashing of her hopes of establishing an equal relationship with man.

13 Bell also argues that after tracing connections that make discourse on ritual useful for analysis of cultural activity, 'few if any of the current theories of ritual avoid a rather predetermined circularity. This circularity functions to constitute ritual as an object of analysis in such a way as to mandate a particular method, expertise, and way of knowing' (1992, p. ix).

14 Doniger (1998) uses an example of the conflation of racism and sexism in assumptions made about groups of 'others' being 'all the same' or indistinguishable (the examples she cites are women in the dark, and the Japanese).

15 In fact our twentieth-century myths can be seen to be closely derived from them. See Blundell and Williamson, 1998, and Bremmer, 1987.

16 Popalisky (1998) argues that Burt in his own book reveals a particular linking of innovative practices that should be challenged. He suggests that Burt's preferred representations of masculinity 'are tied to sexual preference, specifically homosexual' (p.79). Whether one agrees with Popalisky or thinks Burt has homosexual preferences or not, it is a view that yet again underscores the double twist of applying gender ideas; they can always be turned around to undermine the writer.

17 He sketches the work of theorists from Durkheim to Levi-Strauss, Geertz and Turner, arguing that a psychological dimension is necessary to explain experiences of anger, fear, ecstasy etc. within anthropological constructs, and seeking to entwine the two. Troublesome as this endeavour has been in the history of both psychological and anthropological thought systems, a concern with the structure of the mind can be said to be common (see Beers, 1992, p.31, on parallels between Levi-Strauss and Freud).

18 On the symbolic in culture, Beers uses the work of Mary Douglas and Victor Turner, and in particular the articulation of 'structural conflicts and contradictions, which symbols initiate, conceal and transform' (1992, p.40), while criticising the absence of a psychodynamic position in work of this kind.

19 As Mary Douglas argues (1996, p. 140), all social systems can be seen to be 'at war with themselves'.

20 Kohut's adherence to observation and empathy as methods in psychoanalysis leads to the proposition that boys, as reared by women, are treated less as extensions of the rearers than are girls. Boys are therefore seen as less fluid in their modes of identification with others. They are regarded more as 'objects', and allowed to become more self-centred and thus to need the admiration of others (in Beers, 1992).

21 A useful method of analysis can be derived from Beers's application of Geertz's anthropological insights (1973). He sets up a methodology to examine individual human action and motivation in the context of particular social structures and cultures. *Psychoanalysis in search of a theory of culture* is the title he uses (Beers, 1992), but these ideas could just as easily be transposed to become 'Culture in search of a theory of psychoanalysis'. In other words it is just as important for cultural theorists to recognise the importance of individual agency as for psychoanalysts to recognise the importance of culture.

22 For Nigel and Wendy this is surely the case, as is demonstrated by the rise of counselling and couple guidance in contemporary society, along with the continuing ambivalence to it.

23 That this is a male fantasy is well established. What women want, as Beers states, is 'the social liberty that comes with the possession of the organ' (1992, p.76) rather than the organ itself, disappointing as this may be to male vanity.

24 Beers (1992) sees Jung's theory of sacrifice as not fully appreciated. The notion of archetypes is clearly a fruitful one in dealing with shared images within a culture and their power in symbol formation, even if his theory does not amount to a psychodynamic, culturally related account.

25 Although Beers finds Freud's view of sacrifice chimerical and unpsychoanalytic, he uses other aspects of his work, less developed, but potentially useful, in the relationship between narcissism and sublimation, within the context of a theory of symbolisation and symbol formation (p.71).

26 If this 'self' to which Kohut refers (in Beers, 1992) emerges satisfactorily, it leads to 'individuation', a self that is recognised as separate from others, but that in turn gives rise to feelings of dependence, aloneness and loss. The attempt at re-integration arising from this loss of symbiosis produces a mutually contradictory set of wishes and fears, which last through life. To become 'whole', and yet maintain a separate identity, are aims in conflict. In an attempt to counter this fear of the loss of identity, the need for symbiosis emerges. The 'fear of alienation and estrangement, of losing the ability or opportunity to have emotional bonds or meaningful relationships with other people' (Caldwell, 1989, pp.24–5) is in tension with the aim of establishing a separate self.

27 It is common still for men to think that a homosexual woman simply needs a good man and then she will be instantly converted to heterosexuality, and by the same token of arrogance to think that if she does not desire a particular man she must be a lesbian.

28 Other critics have expressed similar concerns: e.g. Daines (1987).

29 DV8's *Enter Achilles* was performed at the Royal Northern College of Music, September 27–30; Oxford Playhouse, October 9–10; Edinburgh Festival Theatre, October 13–14; West Yorkshire Playhouse, October 18–21; and London QEH, October 26–30.

30 Watson (1995), writing on *Enter Achilles*, captures the same sense of Newson's dilemma as does Meisner, but in a different context: that his female and gay friends could offer nurturing when he was injured but his straight male friends could not, feeling 'paranoia, insecurity that only found an outlet in violence'. Watson is, however, more sympathetic than Mackrell, in claiming that 'you might kick against Newson's inflated vision of straight sexual inadequacy – a blow-up doll is the only female the men can relate to – but there are unsettling truths being exposed here, emotions welling to the surface like a slow-burning bruise'.

CHAPTER 5

Faith, Fish, Feminism: Constructions of Femininity in *Strange Fish*

> Dance is trace and its writing a theatre of memory and meaning ... the sexuality and the expressivity of the body in action are fertile breeding grounds for revolutions.
>
> Lepecki, 1995, p.70

Christianity, in order to establish male superiority, had to carry forward pre-existing notions of female wickedness and make them distinctively Christian, so that women's subsequent salvation by men could be effective. The Fall from Grace (Eve's fault); the necessity for women to be 'cleansed' and kept separate from men; men's control of access to God; the denial of the physical and sensual process of procreation and birth – these are all part of this myth. 'Fantasies of origin are cultural myths that have a powerful hold in subjectivity', according to de Lauretis (1994, p.xv); but they are not valid for all time, instead being historically structured and changing. One of these fantasies,

> the seduction of the homosexual-maternal metaphor derives from the erotic charge of a desire for women which, unlike masculine desire, affirms and enhances the female-sexed subject and represents her possibility of access to sexuality autonomous from males.
>
> de Lauretis, 1994, p.xvii

Even in marriage, women's sexual magnetism is seen as highly dangerous. All women are thus held guilty for Eve's supposed sins, and the male is absolved of responsibility. In Walker's view, the

> practical goal was not to prevent women from hurting men, but to prevent women from acting independently of men: from owning their own property, earning their own money, making their own sexual choices, or raising their own children without interference.
>
> 1983, p.viii

In other words the debate is already about power, not spirituality, except insofar as spiritual control is a powerful tool for other kinds of social control. Walker is less charitable than Beers, who, by constructing an explanation of male narcissism as buried in the masculine unconscious, suggests that men cannot help it, and therefore cannot be held responsible for their actions – a familiar but unconvincing story.

Greek and Christian histories carry forward into the constructions of femininity as well as masculinity in *Strange Fish*. In this chapter, interlinking traces are found in the way in which woman's position is constructed as Virgin Mary and as Eve, in the contexts both of early Christianity and of the late twentieth century. Fixing gendered identities is seen to be problematic, and alternative readings are offered from an empowered female position. A lesbian reading draws this out, balancing the masculine perspective explored in Chapter 4.

Goddesses, witches and sirens are not far apart in our thinking. All three are dangerous to the male in their capacity to 'bewitch' or even to castrate. Madness, women and dance/music are easily associated, augmented here by the danger that gay men pose to heterosexual men – Newson regularly portrays this in other works. In his *Dead Dreams of Monochrome Men*, the threat of the gay male hovers over the scene.

Newson's work is contentious because of the potential ambiguity in reading its gender politics. A number of different critical positions can be adopted from the standpoints both of feminism and of queer studies. The strategies that each suggests can be seen both as supportive of each other and as deeply antagonistic, just as they can be constructed to be critical of Lloyd Newson, or enthusiastic about him. The temptation is to think of them as being 'either/or' strategies, depending on the political stance taken by the critic; but I suggest that their relationships are more complex and interwoven, and that it is helpful to see *Strange Fish* through many such inter-related lenses in order to explain why male and female, heterosexual and homosexual, find his work significant.

In creationist theory, the male God creates without sex or female presence and indeed creates woman *from* man, thus audaciously reversing biological understanding. Simultaneously it is necessary to maintain that she is the source of sin, and thus 'the narcissistic dimension of creationism may seem a bit clearer', as Beers rather mildly states (1992, p.169). Casting aside the ancient world's view that the supreme deity was a Goddess, the creator or Mother of the Gods, Christian men re-wrote themselves into this role. The denial of man's need of woman and of the physicalities and realities of being born of her and being unable to procreate without her was a necessary part of claiming superiority.

Lloyd Newson's statement that the sex of the Siren/Christ figure in *Strange Fish* is not important is very questionable in terms of gender politics. The tension lies in the very ambiguity of the changes of character this female Christ personifies. Newson's work challenges a view of the priesthood that argues that only men, as models of the human personification of Christ, can be priests. When asked about the choice of a female singer for the 'Christ' role, he says that he simply took the best voice: 'it happened to be a woman; it could easily have been a man' (Meisner, 1992, p.12). This is either mischievous, or naïve, since our shared codes tell us that to choose a woman is to challenge convention in a way that a male 'Christ' would never do, just as to choose a stereotypically gay male would challenge other beliefs.

However, this role reversal, which dominates the work from the moment of Newson's choice of Melanie Pappenheim as the 'Christ' figure and Wendy Houstoun as the 'Judas' figure, may be simply misleading. The fact that we see women enacting male roles of the most extreme and embedded type in Western society seems on the surface, and to those of an optimistic nature, to suggest a shift in gender politics. But in the roles that they play, nothing changes – Jesus and Judas enact their roles with humility and abstinence, and violence and vigour, respectively, doing nothing to challenge the characterisations of good and evil enshrined in these (male-constructed) roles. These are women behaving like men. They add little, perhaps, that is thoughtful or positive to constructions of women; rather, they overload a Marian virginity onto an already serpent-like evil.

Most readers are more conscious of this complex coding than of anything else in the work, as many reviews and discussions reveal.[1] Perhaps in order to give the work wider appeal, a white, heterosexual surface was seen to be necessary. Although the homoerotic subtext is never far below the surface, such devices serve simply to reinforce social values of heterosexuality, of brute males and of evil, conniving females. That these practices can rebound on the originator is a point that Solie makes (1993). She reflects on the problem that arises from denial of the binary difference between male and female in the interests of an anti-essentialist position, arguing that through elision it can also obscure cultural and historical differences of many kinds.

It is not difficult to interpret Lloyd Newson's *Strange Fish* in the light of the discussion in Chapter 4 and of these preliminary points in

Chapter 5. Newson's chosen social rituals are frequently threatening, often physically so, and invite an unsettling myriad of intertextual traces. They unsettle by challenging highly valued belief systems within the Western world, including those of the Christian religions. While in the Western world we are accustomed to seeing a half-naked male body as the representation of Christ, in *Strange Fish* the threat of its inversion is palpable, since traces of other religious traditions intrude – traditions dominated by women. We are forced (given awareness of feminist issues in the late twentieth century) to reflect that neither the female nor the male body is ever neutral, that both are romanticised and sexualised.

Faith and Fish

As in the previous chapter, I start from Greek ideas and move on to early Christian thinking, focused directly from a female perspective. I pick up the myth of Kronos, to illustrate the long-standing complexity of sexual placing and gender positioning. These are not ideas common only to our own times. Versnal relates this myth to the transfer from the old year to the new (in Bremmer, 1987). To revenge his mother for his father's banishment of their children, Kronos chops off Uranos's genitalia. Giants and nymphs spring from the ensuing blood, while Aphrodite is born from the semen. After marrying his sister Rhea and producing children, fear of their power leads him to eat them. Rhea, however, shelters one son, Zeus, who in turn wreaks revenge on his father. Earlier oriental versions are more violent still, and tell of Kronos biting off genitalia and becoming pregnant himself, eating and then regurgitating his children. Male dominance is everything in these stories.

Less violent but still common in many Western households is the practice of eating fish on Fridays. Unbeknownst to many, doing so recalls the orgiastic fish-eating goddess, the Greek Aphrodite, Salacia. Her day, Friday, is also the day of Venus, or of lovemaking (Walker, 1983, p.314). Davidson (1998) argues that the Greeks were passionately fond of fish to the extent that it amounted to a dominant obsession in fourth-century discourses. A twist to this story is that the fish involved in this literal or metaphorical seduction may have been a source of occult power as well as being as 'mouth-watering' as women (pp.8–9). Nothing is so simple, however. Interpretations of fish madness also suggest that writers were being ironic or bathetic, since fish, in contrast to the heroic sacrificial position of animals, were part of a private and modern discourse of connoisseurship. Comedy at that time included shopping lists, fish menus and recipes. Davidson's conclusion takes account of post-structuralist thinking and is worth quoting in full:

> the ancient passion for fish, then, can be explained largely in terms of what it was not, in terms of its positioning within a series of intersecting contrasts that set it against other types of food. Eating fish was free of a prehistory commemorated in festival banquets, or Homer's epics, or Platonic recollections of the primitive condition. It was not a serious or venerable activity. Fish were not slaughtered or distributed in a ritualized symbolic context. Fish stood outside the theatre of sacrifice and outside official banquets. It had no public role or responsibilities, free to play itself, the quintessential modern commodity fully fetishized for the private consumer, a good whose value could be gauged only according to desirability and demand, the object of constant assessment according to species and specimen, and the subject of an exquisite discourse, argued over and haggled for in comedies and dinner-parties, in markets and treatises.
>
> Davidson, 1998, p. 20

To clinch this connectivity of texts, 'fish' and 'womb' are synonymous (*delphos*) in the Greek language. The fish symbol was so prevalent, and this goddess so revered, that the 'Christian authorities insisted on taking it over, with extensive revision of associated myths to deny its earlier female-genital meanings' (Walker, 1983, p.314). Indeed, it is clear even from a cursory reading of mythological texts that the fish is a potent symbol in many traditions. It encompasses both spirit and phallus, and links both sea and sky in bird–fish forms; by the number of its eggs it represents fecundity – not solely a human or physical fecundity, but on a cosmic scale. The cosmic fish enshrines the whole universe and has two complementary parts, which serve to distinguish higher from lower beings.[2]

The female fish imagery was also then adopted by men. The fish, rich in allusion as Davidson describes, was readily available as a symbol of membership of a newly emerging Christian society to minimise the threat of discovery, persecution, torture and the torment of punishment by association. Membership of such secret societies has always required initiation rites in which water commonly plays a role. Sects or secret male societies draw forth ideas of tribal rituals modified through Christianity in priestly communities, and in recent centuries through such organisations as Freemasonry. This has remained a common literary and operatic theme ever since Mozart's *The Magic Flute* (1791). In the time and place to which *Strange Fish* refers, the 1980s and 1990s in Western Europe, signs that allow members of the gay community to recognise each other may be seen as a modern equivalent, using a ribbon in the shape of the fish symbol. These traces coincide in Newson's work, with the persecution of sufferers from HIV and from AIDS, as well as with the wider exclusion of homosexuals from some professional fields and from certain social programmes (Cranitch, 1992; Parry, 1992a).

Indeed, Pisces, the Zodiac symbol, denotes the moment of dissolution, which contains within itself the beginning of a new cycle of life. It embodies a rather different view of woman as goddess. She is seen as the source of life, rather than of Original Sin – as the means by which intimations of mortality can be assuaged through giving birth to another life. She was one of the most powerful symbols of many earlier religions. She was known by the same sign of the fish, the pointed oval sign known as *vesica piscis*, or vessel of the fish, in celebration (not denial) of women's genital odour and as an analogy for the womb (Walker, 1983, p.313). The Great Hindu Mother Goddess is also associated with the fish and has been rediscovered in recent anthropological and feminist texts. No reference to these traditions can be found in earlier histories such as those written by Douglas (1974). This should raise a suspicion that the 'fish' symbol, too, might have the potential to resonate in a different way from that proposed in the received wisdom of patriarchal Christianity. An equally contentious idea was to position Mary as the Mother of God. Pelikan argues that it did not relate to any previous goddess worship cults, as some have argued, but emerged

> in the language of Christian devotion to her as the mother of the divine Savior and ... eventually received its theological justification from the church's clarification of what was implied by the orthodox witness to him.
>
> 1996, p.58

Thus Mary became transcendent, the highest of the saints, the image of perfection for human creatures. Warner, like many others, does see a link between pagan belief in virgin goddesses and the later Marian constructions (1990). Although both male and female gods were worshipped and written about within mainstream literature of the pre-Christian era, it was always female goddesses who defined the category of 'female'. Woman was literally embodied as vagina, and

Illustration 1: Virgin Mary. C.XV, Moissac Abbey, France

her role was that of sex partner. Frymer-Kensky (1992) argues, however, that this was a celebratory reference to the female organs, not an insulting expression of male anxiety, as our twentieth century Freudian heritage might have it.

Among a number of commentators on the reworking of myth, Frymer-Kensky is more sceptical than polemic in her analysis of the recent flowering of books on goddesses designed to counter the misogyny of religion. She speaks from a scholarly perspective on Assyrian and Sumerian writings, and argues that the monotheism currently under attack 'has little to do with monotheism as it first appeared in biblical Israel' (1992, p.1). Basing her argument on recent archaeological discoveries of ancient tablets, she counters some of these stereotypes, finding that

> instead of capricious gods acting only in pursuit of their own desires, we meet deities concerned with the proper ordering of the universe and the regulation of history. Instead of divine cruelty and arrogance, we find deliberation and understanding. Instead of lawlessness and violence, we see a developed legal system and a long tradition of reflective jurisprudence. Instead of immoral attitudes and behaviour, we find moral deliberation, philosophical speculation, and penitential prayer. Instead of wild orgiastic rites, we read of hymns, processions, sacrifices, and prayers. Instead of the benighted paganism of the Western imagination, cuneiform literature reveals to us an ethical polytheism that commands serious attention and respect.
>
> pp.2–3

Frymer-Kensky's thesis of Christianity's later misreading of earlier myths can be aligned with Walker's view that Christianity was responsible for a quite deliberate transition from female-oriented to male-oriented religions in Western civilisations. We are encouraged to believe that man, not woman, is created in the image of God, despite the existence of an older and widely prevalent concept of a *female* Holy Trinity ruling 'all cycles of creation, birth, and death' (1983, p.viii). This concept was common across Asia before the time of Christ. As Walker ironically states, the female Goddess, the original Holy Trinity, is the one generally 'viewed as "mythical", having been replaced by a God (equally mythical but more acceptable to a male-dominated culture), who took over most of her attributes' (p.xi). One of the first acts of the Christian Church was to declare that the Asian Goddess was to be despised, cast aside – in an attempt, Walker surmises, 'to hide the fact that Christianity itself was an offshoot of Middle-eastern Goddess worship, skewed by the asceticism of Persia and India' (p.viii).

In a sense this is a false conflict – it barely matters whether the ideas we inherit reflect some 'real' fact, or were perceived in the same way some 2000 years ago. What is significant is that we can now see changes which, over a period of time prior to Christianity, gradually reduced the significance of women. It created a climate in which they could be conceived as 'radically other', while the balance of power moved toward the male – a view subsequently reinforced by Christianity (Frymer-Kensky, 1992, p.31) to the extent that the female Christ in *Strange Fish* can still shock.

Pelikan (1996) argues that if Jesus represented 'humanity' in its inclusive sense, as distinct from representing man as male, even to the extent that some have characterised him as androgynous, the same cannot be said of Mary, quintessence of the female and of femininity, arguably a greater inspiration than any other woman through the centuries in the construction of 'womanhood'.[3] Although quintessential, this Mary is in fact a compound of many figures of 'Mary'. The historical conflation of various 'Mary' figures, including Mary Magdalene, with several 'Miriams' reveals the lack of interest in Mary initially in the early Christian faith. She is absent in the Bible, and the growth of the myth or cult can be seen to have happened long after the first century.

Mariolatry was indeed a quite extraordinary later development (Warner, 1990). The idea that a human female could give birth to a divine Jesus while being a virgin has spawned much contentious debate through the centuries, from which a number of different, if related, accounts have emerged (Pelikan, 1996; Warner, 1990). Mary shapes the paradox of Christianity in its ambivalence to women. She is the epitome of 'the glorification of virginity over matrimony' (Pelikan, 1996, p.113). The imprecation *Ave Maria* ('Ave' itself a palindrome for Eve/Eva) captures the Mary who is full of grace, both in being privileged by God to take the role of mother of Jesus, and in dispensing grace to others. As Pelikan states of the later development of this model,

> the *Ave Maria* epitomized not only the irony of Mary's having become a major point of division among believers and between churches but the dichotomy between the sole authority of Scripture and the development of doctrine through tradition.
>
> 1996, p.14

Illustration 2: Mary at the Annunciation. C.XIII, Reims Cathedral, France

The challenge of a fully transcendent Mary for the Christian Church is apparent in the split between the Protestant and Catholic faiths on the subject of Marian doctrine. It is important for theology that she should be seen as directly in the line of David, as a link to Israel, and as human in every respect; but her explicit Jewish ancestry creates difficulties of acceptance, just as characterisations of her as black (in the black Madonna) compete with white histories, though simultaneously make her acceptable to (other) millions. As leader of a heavenly choir she has been celebrated in the endless *Ave Marias* of Western music tradition while maintaining the role of 'bridge builder to other traditions, other cultures, and other religions' (Pelikan, 1996, p.67). Material relating to Mary is shared between the Koran, the Gospel of Luke and a number of other texts, although their differences are clear, too, particularly in the incompatibility of the Christian belief in a Trinity with the strictly monotheistic position of Islam (Pelikan, 1996). In *Strange Fish* the resonances are not exclusively Christian, even if the symbol of the Cross is.

The Second Eve is a model of Mary that parallels that of Christ as the second Adam. She is the means through which Eve's disobedience could be ameliorated. Her strength in resisting the temptations of Eve is matched by her virtue. She is always and forever a virgin, bearing no children other than Jesus. In this sense she matched Christ more closely than any other human being.

As Pelikan says:

> once it was introduced into the vocabulary, this dialectic of Eve and Mary took on a life of its own ... elaborations upon the disobedience of Eve and the obedience of Mary produced extensive psychological comparisons between the two women – [Eve] vulnerable, irrational, emotional, erotic ... an easy prey for the wily tempter.
>
> 1996, p.44

In order to lay the ground for an application of these arguments to specific characterisations in *Strange Fish*, several types of 'Mary' are each briefly described before being used to draw out traces that remain, or that can be summoned or attributed, in considering the role of the Angel/Mary/Siren figure in *Strange Fish* – i.e. the roles taken by Melanie Pappenheim and her alter ego Eve, in the person of Wendy Houstoun.

Illustration 3: Mary Magdalene. C.XV, Moissac Abbey, France

Eve: alive and well in the late twentieth century

The counterpart of Mary the Virgin is Mary Magdalene, positioned as the wicked contrast, the warning to all young women of the dangers of straying from the path of enlightenment and purity.

The controversy over Dan Brown's book *The Da Vinci Code* (2003) rests not solely on the case of plagiarism brought against him in 2006, but on the contention that Christ was married to Mary Magdalene. Both the reinterpretation of the figure on the left of Christ as a female, and a notorious one, Mary Magdalene, is compounded by the contention that they had a child or children. Plainly these issues remain contentious both in scholarly and wider worlds.[4]

Jusek (in Bremmer, 1989) suggests that the pseudo-scientific theorising on sexuality of the late nineteenth century picked up where Christianity left off, positing a ferocious male drive that must be satisfied at all costs. Concomitant with this were two classes of women: those who will and those who won't (outside marriage) – Eve and Mary. He cites Otto Weininger, whose 'scientific' research supposedly 'proved' that women were polygamous, irrational and chaotic, and lacked logic, ethics or morality. These traces clearly emerge from earlier thinking and were readily absorbed into Christianity.

The rhetorical virtuosity much prized in Greek and early Christian times was differentiated. For men it was an act of will directed to control in the public realm, while for women it was part of the art of seduction (McClary, 1991). In this arena, issues of gender, power and speech intersect. Applied to *Strange Fish*, this is a productive line of argument in which power structures can be seen operating. Which gender acts/sings/moves and which controls? Melanie Pappenheim uses the rhetoric of seduction in the first scene of *Strange Fish*, arousing expectations and channelling desire, teasing the spectator both through virtuoso movement (exposing her breasts) and through languorous song. But she can hardly be said to be in control at this point; rather, she represents the opposite – excess – in the dangerous conflation of sensuality with religious practice.

It is still her '*feminine* sensuality and suffering' that is exhibited for the 'pleasure of the patriarchal gaze and ear' (McClary, 1991, p.50). Insubordinate and threatening women need to be controlled, and 'critiques are safer, after all, when displaced onto marginalized Others' (p.51). The control of woman as the Other is very evident in the dance and music of *Strange Fish*, where 'the organization of sexuality, the construction of gender, the arousal and channeling of desire' are central (p.53). McClary, writing about *Carmen*, focuses on Carmen's sexuality but also on her '*discursive* promiscuity' – meaning that her mimicry of dominant discourse and her use of vernacular, as well as high-art, forms make her a 'victimiser'. In some sense this can be used to justify José's self-defence through violence. But it is not as simple as this, since José has contradictory impulses – 'someone actually has to die as a result of José's mind/body crisis' is how McClary puts it (1991, p.66). The analogy with Wendy Houstoun's role is striking – 'Christ' has to die to satisfy Wendy.

There is another kind of narrative about gender roles in which women take up membership of an all-female sorority, united only in trivial concerns of appearance and dress and in their scorn of men, while being always ready to compete for men's attention. An extension of this vision is the lesbian-feminist man-hater, eager only to castrate the male. Wendy Houstoun justifies both these Eve-like portrayals in the second and fourth scenes, where, first with Nigel Charnock, she creates an exclusive twosome, which Lauren Potter is allowed to join. The three then connive in creating discomfort among the other performers (Scene 3). In the next scene it is the two women who tease the ardent male, although one of them captures him (or is won over by him). This theme of exclusivity, of denying others the privilege of belonging, partly so that one can feel better oneself, is a major intertext of *Strange Fish*. It captures not only a psychological agenda but a consumerist one, too, in the rise of the 'me' society compounded by commercially driven pressure. Anything is permissible, including 'owning' other people, if it serves one's own psychological ends or profits the purposes of commodification.

The world of couples is itself a complex secret society from which single people feel excluded, but which paradoxically many may not wish to join. Western society deliberately seeks to perpetuate this model of relationships for both religious and political reasons. The intervention of the State in this context is often the basis of the objection of those who, in an act of political resistance to its institutionalisation, refuse to marry. This coupled world of the romantic novel, *Strange Fish* tells us, is part myth, part deception, part convenience, but still a powerful force. There are gays who marry to obscure their sexuality, or who wish to marry to celebrate it. Heterosexual partnerships may simply hide the emptiness of living together and prevent escape. These practices can be seen to be representative of larger social structures. Recent legislation for same-sex partnership benefits of the kind given presently to married couples reveals the extent of the link between government, 'morality' and power (the pink pound).

Dale Tanner's sexy arrogance, his position as the narcissistic centre of the universe in both the candle dance and the sex scenes (Scenes 4 and 9), place him apparently in control of himself and his own pleasure. But it is the two blonde terrorists (female) in Scene 4 who insidiously take control, paradoxically through being out of control, subject to the excess that is dangerous in women's sensuality. It is evident that Dale 'can't help himself' or stop his sexual urges: as the sex scenes dissolves into his fatal illness, he is duly punished. This scene evokes Mary Daly's description of phallic lust, as 'unable to be whole, those driven by phallic lust attempt to find holes everywhere, to penetrate, to pierce into an inner reality which they yearn to destroy but cannot even find' (1984, p.49). But the judgement in *Strange Fish* is on something that is (essentially) the woman's fault – sex.

Wendy Houstoun's casual and pointless sexual encounter with Dale Tanner in the ninth scene evolves when he accepts the offer of opportunistic sexual gratification and, absorbed in his own ritualised seeking after pleasure, he grinds away, oblivious of the fact that Wendy Houstoun has slipped out from underneath him. She reverts to being the observer that she has always been up to that point, and her actions demonstrate that there is nothing sexually satisfying for her. Female loneliness and detachment at the moment of male climax is well documented in sex research, and this textual trace may be nothing more than another metaphor for male egocentricity.

The immediate retribution is, however, against Wendy only, not Dale, since in the Christian myth it is not the fault of the male. In early Christian times the penalty for adultery was that the woman should be stoned – as it is to this day under Islam – not much of a celebration of sexuality, it would seem, despite rhetoric to the contrary. Small pebbles are dropped on to Houstoun's bare stomach by the singer, who now depicts an avenging angel or, at the other extreme, a saddened mother who has observed this scene. As Houstoun lies spent on the floor, these single pebbles become an avalanche and she rolls and writhes in pain as they overwhelm her in an act of public exposure and ritual purification.

Embarrassment at being caught in the act, and gossiped about, by a group of 'friends' is more than Houstoun's character can bear. For the first time she seems nervous, grabs her shirt to cover herself and effaces herself against a wall. Although intertexts about disapproval of random lust might provide some reason for this behaviour, it seems unlikely in the amoral world she is creating. An alternative explanation might lie in her dislike of exposing any weakness or vulnerability. It is not insignificant, then, that Houstoun is subsequently the cause of the downfall of the Christ figure – another form of retribution, perhaps.

Beside these cultural traces others can be found, which also echo conflicting attitudes to the female body. On the one hand the eroticism and sexual power of the female is evident, tracing a particular kind of stereotype, but one directly juxtaposed with another stereotype: that of female vulnerability, *naïveté* and purity. Whore and virgin – the ever-present tension for women. The sexual identity crisis that *Strange Fish* recalls is one where male, female and trans-sexual biological identities are compounded by choices in terms of gender identity. Add to this the woman as temptress and Wendy Houstoun as an inverted satanic Christ, and the dominance of the male in God's grace can comfortably be assumed, at least within this reading.

Wendy Houstoun's capacity to re-emerge from the waters of death is awesome, and evokes references in the Bible to the indestructible spirit and supernatural powers of Jesus, calming the tempest's waves and walking on water. He declares himself Christ – an analogy for the all-powerful, indestructible life force. Are we to see Wendy in this light, as the all-powerful life force; or as a fatal disease? By implication *Strange Fish* leaves woman, as a modern Eve, still responsible for the evils of the world. Scene 10, in particular, which can be read as Wendy's 'infecting' of Nigel, brings the idea right up to date with the 1990s. Although it is Dale Tanner who suffers and apparently dies as a result of the infection, the responsibility does not seem to lie with him. It is Wendy Houstoun who swipes the back of her hand across Nigel's face, who terrorises others, who 'infects' them. It is Wendy's sexual encounter with Dale that spells disaster for him.

The metaphor upon which Lloyd Newson draws is both powerful and poignant, and unsurprising at a time when knowledge of such extreme behaviour was being made public: i.e. that someone infected with HIV might deliberately seek to infect other people. Compounded by the ease with which partners can escape their responsibilities for children or for each other, and when HIV raises the fear that entering into a new relationship could damage more than one's psychological equilibrium or bank balance, perhaps taking away life itself – the detachment and wariness that Wendy Houstoun portrays resonates for all of us. But holding woman responsible for this largely male-inflicted disease (as perceived in Western representations) is to demonstrate the ultimate in violence against women, once more held responsible for the pain and suffering of men – Eve, the source of original sin, flourishes in the late twentieth century. Mary, the second

Eve, who takes away the sins of the previous Eve, seems not to have been successful.

The final insult, in a sense, is to lay the analogy or metaphor of HIV/AIDS on Wendy Houstoun, the female, even though she uses movement previously given to Nigel in earlier scenes. Social infection and disintegration turn into life-threatening disintegration as the textual layers of this piece emerge.

As many have argued,

> sexuality is a fertile source of moral panic, arousing intimate questions about personal identity, and touching on crucial social boundaries. The erotic acts as a crossover point for a number of tensions whose origins are elsewhere; of class, gender, and racial location, of intergenerational conflict, moral acceptability and medical definition. This is what makes sex a particular site of ethical and political concern – and of fear and loathing.
>
> Weeks, 1985, p.44

As he notes, following Sontag, the moral panic around AIDS 'condenses a number of social stresses with its victims often being blamed for the illness', particularly in Western industrialised countries where most of the victims have been male homosexuals. In Africa the real victims are uneducated and oppressed women and the children they bear.

> In the fear and loathing that AIDS evokes there is a resulting conflation between two plausible, if unproven theories – that there is an elective affinity between disease and certain sexual practices, and that sexual practices cause disease – and a third, that certain types of sex *are* diseases.
>
> Weeks, 1985, p.46

The argument that the existence of AIDS proves the 'unnatural' character of homosexual practices was rife in the early days of the appearance of the disease. If homosexuals deliberately flouted 'nature' both in their practices and in their 'promiscuity', disease would inevitably result (according to leaders of the moral Right and many Church leaders). Add to this the moral retribution of flouting God's sexual order, and the medico-religious construction of this belief is clear.

The Hutcheons (1996) refer to the 'apocalyptic rhetoric' of the 'gay plague', and its more recent extension of metaphor to the 'mass death' of the bubonic plague in its manifestations in Asia and Africa. I suggest that the dominant view of the occurrence of AIDS in the West has not been seriously challenged other than by evidence of AIDS in drug users (equally culpable, of course, in this logic) and by those unfortunate people contaminated through blood transfusions. This type of argument is still used to control sexual behaviour, to limit what are perceived as 'excesses' of sexual freedom outside the moral Right's 'family' life.[5]

To some extent the construction of Wendy Houstoun's relationship with Nigel Charnock in *Strange Fish* is a vignette of this time-capsuled moment. In Scene 10 Wendy's excessive demands and continuous advance–retreat behaviour towards Nigel is highly disturbing. Some of her actions seem wildly disorientated, directed at no one. She is entirely indiscriminate in her endless repetition of the gesture most associated with an AIDS interpretation. As the café music of their first acquaintance is heard again, Nigel attempts once more to make a connection; Wendy grinds his hand into her breast, but as soon as he holds her tightly, she fights her way out. He is violently hurled aside. His own nightmares recur as she uses his gestures to swipe the back of her arm across his face with great force. Finally he is jumped on by Wendy, and, in a heart-stopping attack, bundled through the door backwards into the tank of water.

But there is a moral of a kind. Although Wendy flourishes, and is the sole survivor of this drama, there is a price to pay. Her relationships deteriorate inexorably and insidiously, as every attempt to make contact is matched by withdrawal or physical violence. Brief moments of tenderness with Nigel Charnock become frantic swipes, and when she leaps around him he seems impotent, as Scene 10 describes. Miming of conversation in bodily form, and music from the second scene, which accompanied their initial, friendlier contact, returns to haunt their relationship in the tenth scene. Here she pursues him fiercely, chasing him relentlessly along and across the corridor towards a violent end, where she pushes him into a deep tank of water, never to be seen again. Earlier moments from the work thus become intertexts themselves, able to comment upon the new events.

Recent film theory makes it clear that such images of women still underpin the modern cinema, and by extension the modern video and performance arts more widely. Creed argues that the construction of woman as the 'monstrous-feminine' 'speak[s] to us more about male fears than about female desire or feminine subjectivity' (1993, p.7) – a view that ties in well with Beers's analysis referred to in Chapter 4. Even in the music of our own time, gender construction in heavy metal serves the interests of the male musicians and fans who, as in other cultural practices, have dominated.

> Women are more often offered heavy metal empowerment through adaptations of the ideology of romance, the ambiguous implications of androgyny and their increasing ability to identify with constructions of power that had previously been understood as inherently male.
>
> Walser, 1993 p.xvi

'Women who identify with male constructions of power' might be a phrase specially written for Wendy Houstoun in *Strange Fish* – her expectations of being in control, her ability to use menace and violence to manipulate others, both male and female, represent a strong thread of her character that aligns her more with the male characters than with the other women. In Scenes 2, 3, 4, 10 and 12 this is very evident.

If all this masculinity becomes too much for the modern woman, one answer lies, as ever, in madness. In Mats Ek's re-visiting of *Giselle* this modern woman retreats to a twentieth-century asylum. As McClary (1991, p.48) asks of Monteverdi's hero, Orpheus: is he a hero or a transgressor? Is he virile or effeminate; rational or mad? In any event, one reason why this particular opera is regarded as less than successful is simply because only women can be mad, not male heroes. Only women are manipulative, as Salome's character demonstrates – just as Wendy does in *Strange Fish*, making 'pathetic victims' of male humanist discourse (p.49). Melanie's ultimate death is in line with the historical Poppea's at the hand (or more accurately the foot) of Nero.[6] That the initiator is another woman in *Strange Fish* only reinforces the subsequent Foucaultian insight that women, too, are then thoroughly indoctrinated into patriarchal values.

Susan McClary's seminal text, much quoted by male music theorists, shows how a semiotics of musical madness was created by Monteverdi in the seventeenth century. She relates this to the attitudes of contemporary societies, demonstrating how desire, longing, frustration and fulfilment occur in the music (1991, p.36). In a telling description, she shows that one of the reasons for Shakespearean erotic dialogue was that contemporary theories suggested that a woman's arousal was a necessary condition of conception. When science showed that this was not so, 'not only the *necessity* but finally even the *possibility* of desire' in women was silenced (p.37). Not until the mid-twentieth century was female desire revived (or re-invented).

Divas, and demented hysterical women, are the dominant stereotypes of opera, ballet and modern dance. The history of madness, re-written by Foucault and later by feminists such as Showalter (1998), reveals a progressive closeness between madness and an excess of feminine sexuality. Long before Freud clinched it in the construction of the female hysteric, these assumptions were prevalent. How dementia is delineated in terms of dance and music is a question worth addressing, as the analysis of the Blonde Terrorist scene from *Strange Fish* illustrates (Chapter 6). It is one of the contradictions of history that such a paradox should be found in dance, which shares with music 'its compulsion for theoretical control and yet its craving for strategies that violate and exceed that control' (McClary, 1991, p.82). Given that musical metaphor is in line with social assumptions of an extramusical kind, the emergence of musical and dancing madwomen was inevitable.

Mary: the Virgin

This Second Coming of Eve, in the form of Mary, is regarded as evidence of the steady progression of the world to goodness and virtue under Christianity. The Nativity, like the Crucifixion, becomes a defining moment.

> Salvation depended on the true and complete humanity of Christ in his life and death; that true and complete humanity depended in turn on his having been truly born; and his true birth in its turn depended on his having had a mother who was truly and completely human. And if ... it was the voluntary and virginal obedience of Mary by which the voluntary and virginal *dis*obedience of Eve was undone and set aright, Mary became, by that voluntary obedience, both the Second Eve and the principal guarantee of Christ's humanity.
>
> Pelikan, 1996, p.50

The Blessed Virgin is this chaste Mary of the Annunciation, 'in paradoxical combination with her maternity' (p.16). The theological, not to say cultural and medical problems of this immaculate conception and virgin birth have long vexed Christianity, leading to increasingly transcendent valuations of Mary and culminating in Pope Pius XII's dogma in 1950, concerning her Assumption into heaven. Mary's obedience to God and to her faith, captured in the phrase 'be it unto me according to thy word' (Luke 1:38), is a model for all female mortals. Warner positions Mary's willingness to remain virginal as an odd occurrence, unlikely of itself to be valued, given the biblical and Jewish enthusiasm for procreation, although she also cites concurrent evidence of virgin births as being widespread in classical mythology (1990).

What is retained in common is the idea of virginity as 'powerful magic ... [which] conveyed strength and ritual purity', resulting in an overwhelming value being attached to it as part of an ascetic philosophy (Warner, 1990, p.48). Marriage is tolerable only because more virgins are born thereby. As Warner says:

> it is almost impossible to overestimate the effect that the characteristic association of sex and sin and death has had on the attitudes of our civilisation.
>
> p.50

Having said that, women have not been above exploiting this virtuous state in order to achieve independence from men and to develop projects such as the education of women, sanctioned by the Church but still controlled by it. Only by denying their sex might they attain the sublime state of the Virgin Mary – or the secular equivalent, of freedom of action. Updated as these ideas have been, they rest, as always, on the doctrine of Original Sin; when Adam and Eve sinned, sex and death entered the world. That Mary should be free from such taint is important, as only thus could Jesus be free of sin. 'The Word made flesh' is the miracle of the Annunciation, into which the passive and submissive Mary, the model of patience, was cast, 'by a deadly combination of nature and creation and fall' (Pelikan, 1996, p.83).

Asceticism, the denial of the self and the practice of abstinence in order to achieve some greater end, as embodied in the 'ascetic life', relies on positioning the body and physical matters as lower than things of the spirit, so as to distinguish man from animal. Historically it may also be a reaction to periods of excessive self-indulgence. It was common among sects pre-dating Christianity in the Middle East, and provided a ready model of self-sacrifice for this new cult (Pelikan, 1996, p.115). The hermit, monk and nun emerge as the holiest members of a community, as 'professional' ascetics.

If a connection could be made between Original Sin and sexual union, and between the sinlessness of Christ and his virginal conception, then marriage and 'normal' sexual relations were always going to be problematic in themselves. In the hands of power-hungry homosexual or heterosexual men, this translates into the misogyny of dominant males. They need only refer to Mary as Virgin and as Mother to justify their position. Or, as Warner argues, 'Christ the God-Man and Mary the Virgin-Mother ... manifest that the impossible is possible with God' (1990, p.336).

> In this battle of the flesh and the spirit, the female sex was firmly placed on the side of the flesh. For as childbirth was woman's special function, and its pangs the special penalty decreed by God after the Fall, and as the child she bore in her womb was stained by sin from the moment of its conception, the evils of sex were particularly identified with the female. Woman was womb and womb was evil.
>
> Warner, 1990, p.57

As de Beauvoir had already said of Mary (and this is repeated by both Pelikan and Warner),

> for the first time in history, the mother kneels before her son; she freely accepts her inferiority. This is the supreme masculine victory, consummated in the cult of the Virgin – it is the rehabilitation of woman through the accomplishment of her defeat.
>
> de Beauvoir, 1971, p.171

Di Leonardo explores a number of ethnographic examples of institutionalised non-marital alternatives for women, spanning China, Africa, North America and Europe (in Comstock and Henking, 1997). She finds positive views of 'spinsters' in situations where choices made against marriage resulted in greater freedom for women. From the middle of the nineteenth century through to the middle of the twentieth century in both Europe and North America, the single woman – never married, often intellectually active and able to work (a privilege sometimes denied women once married) – contracted a relationship with another woman, and through such a partnership created the equivalent of a 'family' structure. 'Boston marriages' find their equivalent in the governess, nurse and later the schoolteacher in Europe. The perceived uncleanness of women, once married, led some in the Kwangtung districts of China to refuse marriage and to remain active in rituals (unlike their married sisters), enjoying a literate and employed life in self-managed co-operatives.

A number of Albanian women in the same era swore virginity in order to enjoy exclusively male privileges of tobacco, coffee, alcohol and money and in order to escape the low status of women and avoid marriages planned for them before birth. In this case they retained the negative status of spinsters; they were assumed celibate, though heterosexual, and lived apart from the blood family.

In the Sudan region of Africa until the 1930s, a Nuer woman might become the 'husband' in marriage to another woman and might take on children as a legal father. The crucial explanation lies in the 'context of universal desire for cattle and children, a formal model that accords women low status, and an informal model which admits their considerable power and autonomy' (di Leonardo, in Comstock and Henking, 1997, p.149). In the upper class of Benin at the time, woman-marriage was a viable alternative, although almost exclusively for the upper class. It was seen as 'an independent route to power and autonomy for women. It is thought to have been at that time a vehicle for lesbian expression' (p.149).

The inclusion of this material is not for prurient display of the 'other' but to illustrate the limited and controlled models of womanhood available in the late nineteenth and the twentieth centuries in North America and Western Europe – the lack of flexible gender identities. The features that these disparate examples share are that they remove women from economic dependence on a male partner or on kin, and allow them to refuse heterosexual activity (a position in the west of Europe we seem only now to be understanding as a possibility). Alternatives to marriage have conventionally been constructed through Christianity as 'second best', whether in the single state or in the female embrace of a religious vocation. They are both seen as failure, rather than as a genuine preference. But there is no way to win this game, since heterosexual acts have also been construed as polluting. The positive aspect of the conflation of single status with sexual purity is that it allows women to 'fulfil ambitions, to escape domestic drudgery and male oppression through marriage avoidance' (p.153).

In the late twentieth century, fasting for purification and to match an ideal is associated rather more with anorexia nervosa than with religious practice, but the underlying theme is very similar. In this case it accompanies the fashion industry's control of the female image and of an aesthetic ideal of the late twentieth century that dominates both advertising and dance training. In both sectors the alarming frequency of eating disorders has been observed. And so another link can be made between the ascetic self-denial encouraged by a religious cult and the training of a professional 'body', whether as a model or as a dancer – each is equally wedded to her ordinance of physical submission to a greater moral or aesthetic ideal, made manifest in a physical model of androgyny.

The reason and the effect are much the same: to remove as far as possible any sign of womanliness – to serve the goddess of Dance or Fashion. Both goddesses are constructed by male impresarios, company directors, choreographers, fashion designers or publicists of the twentieth century who, in many cases, have been just as antagonistic to women as ascetic religious men were in the previous two thousand years. In patriarchal fashion, the female dancer epitomises the same old Christian dilemma. She is seen as a modern Virgin Mary compounded by continuing traces of Mary Magdalene, the pure and the passionate, the virginal and the sexual being. *Strange Fish* exposes this in the Wendy Houstoun/Melanie Pappenheim dialogues. The only (sane) resolution of these intolerable conflicts may be found in the construct of the mad woman, of which Eve is a species and Wendy the instance.

Mary, Mother of God: intercessor

There are alternative positions on Mary as virgin, which claim that her receptivity to the future was embodied in her willingness to be part of this scenario, as an active state of free will, an unconstrained response, a risk that God operates by, 'respecting human freedom and integrity' (Pelikan, 1996, p.87). In this mode she becomes a champion – a leader of the Church, guiding the ship of faith. Thus there are scenes in *Strange Fish* where Melanie is the compassionate observer, comforter and wise commentator, although always outside the main events. In Christian stories this role of women can be traced in the tears of women weeping at the well, at the foot of the Cross – the mother (Mary); Mary, the mother of John; and Mary Magdalene – the three Marys of popular folk song, evoked in the melancholic wail of the singer in *Strange Fish*. Another trinity.

The Pisces fish-goddess, the watery mother figure, is evoked by the 'Angel' comforter in the penultimate scene (11), where she tries to soothe the distraught and desperately ill male, who shivers, faints and cannot be revived. Her singing and her gestures evoke the absolution of sins through the 'holy water' of baptism – a few drops onto his forehead, although her black leather jacket speaks of other times. She cradles him, rests his head on her shoulder and sinks to the ground with him, supporting him as she moves. Dipping the head three times while standing in water was universal in early Christian times. Interestingly, and not coincidentally, a symbolic fish was given as a pledge, or as a token of the rights conferred in the full immersion of baptism.

Illustration 4: The Angel of the Smile. C.XIII, Reims Cathedral, France

Baptism and the absolution of sin is an attempt to lodge knowledge and spirituality where it rightfully belongs, in the male. Little has changed from the account of immersion in water that Smith and Cheetham gave in 1880. Complex forms and associations were refined over time. They describe how the scene would be set, with scented balsams and burning gleaming lights, illuminating the deep vessels filled with water, let into the ground. An exact parallel might be made here with Newson's concept in *Strange Fish* by referring to the candlelit scene at the beginning of the work, soothing and warming, evoking the Church as Mother. Although there is no water in this scene, the other elements are present. Newson's typically destructive water scenes show the waters of baptism and death mixed together. The presence of a tank full of water on stage into which people jump, are thrown, slide and in Scene 10 ultimately disappear evokes other texts, of the waters of suicide and death rather than total immersion at baptism, which speaks of faith.

Mary at the moment of Christ's death, the *Mater Dolorosa*, inspired paintings and music through the centuries: the mother, wounded and sickened by her son's death. But it is a sweet pain, translated through later stories of Francis of Assisi and reaching the height of ecstatic expression in the poem of Jacopone da Todi (c.1230–1306) and in musical renderings of the *Stabat Mater* ever since.[7] Warner (1990) argues that the arrival of the plague, the Black Death of the fourteenth century, itself seen as retribution for evil, encouraged extreme versions of faith, whether in flagellation or in identification with the sufferings of Christ in other ways. The Virgin's sufferings as mother provided a model that epitomised the terror of the time. It was she, however, to whom people turned in their pleas for mercy, as intercessor with God as well as one who understood their suffering.

Whether Mary herself responded to Christ's death with stoic calm or with frenzied hysteria is a paradox that allows the two sides of Eve/Mary to remain vivid in popular imagination. Warner also finds a continuing reference to fertility goddesses of antiquity in

> propitiating those same forces of sterility and death that the sacrifice of her son is attempting to appease ... the tears she sheds ... have the power to give life and make whole.
>
> 1990, p.221

Tears – the only acceptable bodily fluid, symbol of grief and motherliness, pure as the waters of baptism, engendering renewal and hope, predominant in subsequent visions of Mary – are never seen in *Strange Fish*. Here there is no recourse to what Warner calls 'the universal language of cleansing and rebirth' (p.223) – this is an altogether more sinister world in which nobody cries.

Gendered Identities

Even young audiences who accept a largely secular world, and who profess strong feminist views, continue to be shocked by *Strange Fish*. In approaching this problem I have drawn on various histories of religions and on feminist studies that re-interpret mythical figures but that also reveal them to be deeply paradoxical. Walker's study (1983) of woman-centred myths reveals a picture that is strikingly different from male-constructed histories of Christianity, and by the same token reveals how vigorously these alternatives have been suppressed. It should not be surprising if even today such images are difficult to confront.

As de Lauretis (1984) argues, the female body is constructed first and foremost as an object, a site of desire, for male pleasure. Only through the acceptance of this binarism are women allowed access to speech, language and power. Wendy Houstoun, the Director, and you and I, the viewers, are watching intimate relationships, for example in Scene 5 – scenes normally reserved for the private sphere. This viewing becomes an obviously voyeuristic activity when pointed up in *Strange Fish*, inviting debate about whether any relationship can withstand such scrutiny, such weight of the gaze.

Under this pressure, however, it might be expected that more fluid relationships might emerge where narrative, meaning and pleasure can be challenged. But fluid gender identities depend upon freedom from secrecy and paranoia; in *Strange Fish* individuals are free to approach each other, to make the move towards friendship, but they are also unconstrained in rejecting each other, in giving pain. In other societies and at other times, some greater responsibility might be felt for those who find difficulty in surviving. Protective mechanisms are often set in place, so that individuals are kept within the 'bosom of the family' – both the family of the Church and the family of other institutions, and the physiological birth family. Social constraints operate to prevent the inflicting of pain, to forgive failings, or not to punish failings too severely. In conflict with this view, frequently giving the lie to Christian charity, were the Poor Houses, and the 'lunatic' institutions in which women who sinned were incarcerated out of sight for years, along with the 'feeble-minded'.[8] The religious environment of *Strange Fish* evokes these traces, too, where in the name of purity and chastity, in the name of the Christian religion, evil can be committed.

Mary Jacobus (in Jacobus *et al.*, eds, 1990) leads on from the feminist historical views of Marina Warner to give political and theological point to current views of feminine desire. She suggests that modern relationships between 'feminine desire and conception, and between conception and maternal desire' can be seen to construct a 'disordering figure'. This figure is disordering in the sense that 'it disorders our sense of a unified, coherent subject' (p.11). Thus the shifts that have separated religious (Christian) views from daily experience in the twentieth century can be clearly seen. By reading three different stories, culminating with Kristeva on the Holy Family, she makes the case that the 'Church's mission to safeguard this notion of personhood, indivisibly corporal and spiritual' continues to underlie official rhetoric and remains dominant in the cultural history of the Western world. Even late-twentieth-century debates on contraception, abortion and surrogacy turn on the legitimacy and sanctity of the rupture between physiological, psychological and moral life. Sexuality remains 'inseparably joined to procreation in a shatterproof subject rather than a petri dish' as Jacobus says, commenting on Pope Paul VI's famous 1968 Encyclical *Humanae Vitae* (p.23). In explanation, Jacobus argues that

> to admit the possibility of intervention at the level of conception is to threaten – to shatter or disorder – a theory of the subject founded on a traditional unity-in-duality (body and soul as two-in-one).
>
> p.23

While these arguments, as Jacobus reflects, 'are unlikely to cut much ice either with post-structuralists or with contemporary feminists' (p.24), an exception can be seen in attitudes to surrogacy. She argues that the father in such an arrangement 'occupies the traditional position of God' and the mother becomes 'a mere uterus on legs' (p. 25). Kristeva attributes the lack of a 'satisfactory discourse on motherhood' to the decline of religion that 'has left nothing to put in its place' (Moi, ed., 1986, p.160). Drawing on Kristeva's articulation of the relation of subjectivity to language, Jacobus argues that the Virgin (in the first artificial family known) becomes 'the sublime incubator for the Word' or 'provider of the material or bodily element necessary for the Incarnation'. Both feminism and psychoanalysis 'consecrated femininity under the sign of a sacred Mother – firmly subordinated, however, to God the Father' (1990, p.21).

> The fulfilment, under the name of Mary, of a totality made of woman and God is finally accomplished through the avoidance of death. The Virgin Mary experiences a fate more radiant that her son's: she undergoes no Calvary, she has no tomb, she doesn't die and hence has no need to rise from the dead. Mary doesn't die but, as if to echo oriental beliefs...according to which human bodies pass from one place to another in an eternal flow that constitutes a carbon copy of the maternal receptacle – she is transported.
>
> Jacobus, 1990, p.168

Kristeva argues that the 'gathering of the three feminine functions (daughter-wife-mother) within a totality where they vanish as specific corporealities while regaining their psychological functions serves to define eternity, to condense powerful emotions into a single universal image'. In her essay *Stabat Mater,* she asks if Christianity's reduction of the feminine to the maternal is, in fact, no more than 'a masculine appropriation of the Maternal, which ... is only a fantasy masking primary narcissism?' (Moi, ed., 1986, p.163). She asks what ends this fantasy still serves for both men and women, and argues that the virginal cult enshrines powerful notions of death, sexuality and the nature of love, 'thus fitting an entire range that goes from sublimation to asceticism and masochism' (p.165).

Lesbian Readings

The sexual ambivalence of Wendy Houstoun's character, and the threat that this poses, can be understood by reference to the everyday, performative nature of gender and its representation. Case describes *Lesbians who kill*, by Lois Weaver and Peggy Shaw, as revealing 'the way lesbian is marked semiotically as violence and is also the site of potential violence' (in Case *et al.*, 1995, p.viii).[9] There are times in *Strange Fish* when Wendy Houstoun is clearly positioned in this way, particularly in relation to Nigel Charnock.

Throughout the work, Houstoun is the character who observes and manipulates, and in this way might be said not to be involved with anyone. She represents 'the gaze' beloved of psychoanalytic film criticism, a theory that is relevant to this argument, being itself both about psychological insights and about a film.[10] In Scene 5 the camera positions itself as if behind Wendy as she watches the love scene, setting up a position for the viewer as well as for the Director. She reflects the cynicism and detachment of the postmodern world in taking up this position, and by so doing alienates the observer of the video as well as herself. Because of her stance it is not possible for the reader to identify entirely with the couple, despite their apparently loving commitment. In effect she questions their (our?) involvement, asking if it is ever possible to 'lose oneself', in the best romantic tradition, or if the 'lover' is always keeping one eye open – aware of the humour, the cliché of making love or the danger of giving too much. There are echoes of the first scene, where Wendy observes the religious ritual; here she observes the expression of love, equally unconvinced, equally uncommitted and still potentially subversive.

She reinforces the voyeuristic position that gaze theory identifies, but, as Manning argues of the early modern dance, it is not just a subversion of the male gaze (given that Wendy is female) but also simultaneously a projection of 'essentialized notions of identity' (Manning in Desmond, 1997, p.155). There is more irony and self-awareness in *Strange Fish* than in the work Manning refers to, but this only multiplies the layers of gaze, and the result is perpetual uncertainty about how the reader is placed.

It is ironic, given the sexual orientation of Lloyd Newson and Nigel Charnock, that the play with political issues of sexuality lies within heterosexual groupings in this work. The result is a fairly obvious attack on both women and men for shallowness and lack of sincerity in their relationships with each other. Or perhaps it is not ironic at all, but only to be expected given social norms, that his critique is not matched by similarly trenchant comment on same-sex relationships, which might be said to be just as vulnerable to the charge of narcissism and egocentricity as heterosexual ones are. The 'rutting' of Dale Tanner when he has a chance of sex with Wendy Houstoun captures both homosexual and heterosexual stereotypes.[11] Is this reinforcing long-standing views, or disrupting them by the extremity of the performance?

Manning might have been writing on *Strange Fish* when she suggests that powerful expressivity of movement creates a tension with the representation of gendered relationships, which, like that of the early modern dance, 'grounded the paradoxical social function of the form ... [and introduced] a new image of the female body in motion' (Manning in Desmond, 1997, p.164).

Newson may simply be responding to widespread taboos on representing same-sex male relationships in mainstream dance/ theatre, taboos that in turn reflect deeply-held positions. In the Jewish view, the sexes are defined in relation to each other and fierce prohibitions have long existed, based on the authority of Leviticus (Davies in Comstock and Henking, 1997, p.40). It is argued that such clear moral guidelines served to balance the Jews' threatened political identity, first as wandering people, then in exile. Clear and separate categories of behaviour that distinguish a group from another, it is argued, serve to unite and to hold together a particular community.

Davies explains the difference from the Greeks' relaxed views of sexual morality in terms of the Greeks' 'inchoate religion' and their 'ambiguous borders', giving an emphasis on the local character of beliefs. For the Greeks the categories of male and female 'were not holy categories reflecting the essential holiness of the society as was the case with the Jews' (p.41). Protection of the family is seen to be responsible for the few sanctions that did prevail against homosexuality in Greek culture. As with other minorities, the choice becomes one of whether to maintain an exclusive identity or to face oblivion within a dominant ethnic, social and sexual group through intermarriage and strange sexual practices. This is as clearly relevant for the 1990s as for the Ancient Greeks. The persecution of 'deviants' of any kind is a common response to pressure arising from economic or political challenges.[12]

Celibacy, not originally a requirement of the priesthood, became a means of creating a clear distinction between clergy and laity. It also secured land ownership and acquired its own moral and spiritual values. It further served to prevent overt liaisons between (male) clergy, which might shatter the hierarchical structure of the Church. In this Church/State interaction, the increasingly powerful nationalist monarchies of Western Europe in turn required a tightening of the boundaries around acceptable practices – whether imposed through the Inquisition against heresy or in its later manifestations against non-Christians, Jews, Templars and lepers (Davies in Comstock and Henking, 1997).

The changing understanding of conceptual categories of sexuality in the construct of what was expected within the religious life for women around the early 1600s can be seen in several articles in the anthology from Comstock and Henking (1997). Women were allowed, and even encouraged, to identify love of Jesus with love of another nun, through metaphors of angelic visitations. The relationship between a spiritual marriage with Christ and the love of another human being is an interesting but always problematic one in theological writings, and not just with reference to nuns. Erotic devotion becomes part of any believer's relationship with Christ. A sacred marriage, a state of rapture, enjoyed through religious devotion, might automatically connect to human sexuality as seen from the position of the 1990s, but it is not clear that it carried the same meanings in 1600, much as we may interpret the art and sculpture of the time (e.g. the work of Bernini) in this way. Contemporary codes of behaviour and the relationship between the body, the spiritual and the sensual would need to be understood as indubitably discourses of desire (as Matter claims in Comstock and Henking).

The relationship between Wendy Houstoun and Lauren Potter makes an interesting suggestion of bi-sexuality. In Scene 3, Houstoun and Potter are especially provocative in the use of eye-movement to express amused denigration of the men and their irritation with a female intruder. In gesture they mimic the self-importance of the male, and with fast, small steps, sharp focus and impatient dynamic they intimidate the intruder while simultaneously demonstrating the closeness of their own relationship. Meanwhile the camera mimics them and plays with the reader, the voyeur in all these variations of human affection and affectation. Their collusion in the early scenes of teasing the male (Scene 4) becomes threatened by Lauren's subsequent involvement in two love scenes with Jordi Cortes Molina (Scenes 5 and 8). Wendy's observation of Lauren's growing familiarity with Jordi is puzzling. She is intensely focused on this developing scene – the first duet, and the first statement of closeness and intimacy between two people. She seems to be part curious, part dismissive, part envious, but whether in desire for Jordi or Lauren, or neither, is unclear. Certainly, her own later attempts at sexual activity with Dale

Tanner and intimacy with Nigel Charnock prove totally unsatisfactory (Scene 9).

As the work moves on, the role of the spectator, like the role of the Siren, is passed from one character to another: for example, to Molina, standing in the doorway in the corridor conversation scene (Scene 2), and later to the Siren/Christ (Scene 9). In the shifting kaleidoscope of postmodern living, as we slide from one role to another, from one identity to another, the trace that it taps is that nothing engages us for long, or deeply. The fleeting sexual relationships that supposedly characterised the post-1960s period, whether homosexual or heterosexual, perhaps reinforce this suggestion that we are no longer able to love seriously, or to make a wholehearted commitment to another person. We slide and slither around each other like fish on the Great Barrier Reef, ever in motion, in search of tastier fare among the myriad corals. Strange fish, indeed.

A lesbian reading of Wendy Houstoun's character might be sustained, but also a parallel made between performed, theatrical relationships and gay relationships, both of which suffer from under- and over-exposure, denied and ignored on the one hand while made the subject of red-necked prejudice, police action and intrusive curiosity on the other. In this there is finally a parallel with Greek all-male societies in which homosexuality was constructed publicly and allied to initiation rituals with less disapproval.

A powerful analogy can be made with Elizabeth Wood's study of the composer Ethel Smyth, whose operas deal with conventional heterosexual romance but whose own story of lesbian experience may nonetheless be decoded in the music (in Solie, 1993). The music can be read contrapuntally, which, metaphorically as well as practically, is a useful strategy for reading Wendy Houstoun's role in *Strange Fish*. It is contrapuntal also in the sense that to ask how social life and culture construct the differences that all of us understand and enact in everyday life is to recognise the intersection of gender with political power and musical and danced expression.

The fact that the female occupants of Lesbos had musical abilities ties in neatly with the Siren figure and her danger to men. Reputedly, Orpheus was a singer whose skill was vitally necessary to overcome the seductive attractions of the Sirens' song. This story antedates the *Odyssey* and tells of the journey of Jason and the Argonauts, a group of aristocratic adolescents (Graf, in Bremmer, 1987, p.97). Older males accompanied them, as initiators into male ritual, on a journey comparable with days spent in the wilderness, but by sea. Orpheus, author of powerful songs and spells, poetry and sorcery is one of a number of mythological singers whose origins may well pre-date Greek mythology. The poet's special relationship with the Muses sets him apart from ordinary men. Lloyd Newson clearly saw the homosexual possibilities in this story, a story which, I would argue, can also be seen in terms of the misogynist possibilities (see Chapter 5).

Translated to contemporary views, a feminist vision of God's realm 'has at its center resistance to relations of domination, whether they be in the form of heterosexism or misogyny' (Mary McClintock Fulkerson in Comstock and Henking, 1997, p.188). But attractive as pleas or arguments for inclusion are, she suggests that a more complex picture is revealed by looking at what opposing positions share: namely, the framing of the conversation around notions of identity.

> Both those who refuse gay and lesbian persons and those who insist upon their inclusion in the life of the church share the idea that persons have sexual identity and sexual preference and that this identity ... is fundamental.
>
> p.189

Such inclusion in the life of the Church rests on a shared belief that nature or nurture accounts for homosexuality, drawn from biblical sources and adapting Freudian insights, since there are plainly two distinct gender identities, not just biological sexes on this argument. The height of generosity is to 'allow' the homosexual 'other' to join a community that nonetheless knows that the only way to be is heterosexual. McClintock Fulkerson's challenge to this is to destabilise the relationship between specific cultural codes affecting the view of homosexuality (differently applied in different eras) and those Christian tenets that are unchanging. She does so in order to move beyond the outcomes that she sees – a denial of difference, or the acceptance of a normal/deviant binary. In a classic text of oft-cited articles, Fuss articulates the difficulty. The homosexual position, as from the inside, becomes the 'other' and is placed against the heterosexual masculine –

> the homo ... operates as an indispensable interior exclusion – an outside which is inside interiority making the articulation of the latter possible, a transgression of the border which is necessary to constitute the border as such.
>
> Fuss, 1991, p.3

Only by excluding the feminine altogether can the masculine split in this way, given the binary nature of the system.

In *Strange Fish*, just as Brinks argues about the film *Single White Female* (1992), the lesbian is the legacy – she is all that remains at the end, and is therefore far from being invisible: she is marked publicly. But her desire is generalised to a commodified capitalism, and is not specific to a person. Any and all of the performers in *Strange Fish*, both men and women, are subject to her persuasiveness and violence. None can quite deliver what she wants, and thus they are destroyed by her. Finally, and crucially, it is the Christ/Angel/Siren/Mary figure who meets her end through Wendy's passions. It is lesbianism as 'contamination' (Brinks, in Case *et al.*, 1995, p.10). It is pornography as the 'right of inspection' over the bodies of others (Ortiz in Case *et al.*, 1995).

Some accounts of female homosexuality turn back to the mother figure and/or locate female–female desire in a regression 'to a pre-Oedipal phase of infantile sexuality' (de Lauretis, 1994, p.58). Where some feminists

> construe a blissful relation of fusion and undifferentiation [others describe it] as one marked by strong sadistic impulses, guilt feelings, fear, and intense masochistic excitement.
>
> p.58

De Lauretis argues that linking homosexuality to the maternal, while drawing all women closer together, often in the name of feminism, 'erases the actual sexual difference between lesbians and heterosexual women' (1994, p.xvii).[13] Recognising sexual and social difference between men and women can result in *in*difference to women; and, in any event, all constructions of the feminine occur only within models and laws devised by male subjects. That a woman should desire a woman is simply incomprehensible in the phallic regime of sexual difference. The problem therefore is of there being no way of

> thinking lesbianism cleanly outside the discursive–conceptual categories of heterosexuality, with its foundation in a structural difference (masculine–feminine or male–female) that for all intents and purposes sustains a social indifference to women's subjectivities.
>
> de Lauretis, 1994, p.6

Typically and crudely, female homosexuality is simply a 'masculinity complex' where the girl wishes to be a boy and is envious of the male organ, sometimes accompanied by the view that the complex arises from defiance and resistance in women against the father. This is not a position that leaves open the possibility of fluid or flexible relations to either masculinity or femininity, but is at best an oscillation between the two positions of male and female object choice (p.32). Bi-sexuality or hysteria is the result. There are no choices in the underlying philosophy that supports this binary division, termed by Adrienne Rich 'compulsory heterosexuality': a mechanism for ordering thinking on the basis of a male–female and hetero–homosexual divide (1983).

The extraordinary arrogance of this commonly held view simply illustrates the inability to think outside a male-dominated heterosexuality. The importance of discourses that are able to construct a lesbian sexuality cannot be overestimated. As de Lauretis says:

> the major public discourses on lesbian sexuality available in this century are discourses of sexual indifference – of inversion, of masculinity complex, of lesbianism as pre-Oedipal fusion, psychosis, hysteria, bisexuality, or oscillation between masculinity and femininity – and they are all inadequate to the task.
>
> de Lauretis, 1994, p.75

Psychosis and hysteria is what Wendy Houstoun presents to us in her sadistic impulses towards Melanie, mother and angel.

If this is finally a problem of representation, or of the lack of it, does *Strange Fish* in any way change this position? Is it clear that lesbianism is represented? Is it a positive view of lesbianism? In fact, I would argue that it is not: it reinforces the masculinity complex, through Houstoun's aggressive, insistent, 'one of the boys' behaviour. Her relationships with the other women do not get to a stage of warmth that could remotely be classed as pre-Oedipal fusion; rather, she is like a manipulative, jealous male as she observes others' affairs – a caricature of the unattractive woman.[14] In Wendy's early scene with Lauren, the Blond Terrorists scene where they tease Jordi Molina, we see Wendy's jealousy, her anger at the claim that Jordi has above her own for Lauren's attention simply by being male, her lesbian difference, her pain and her defiance (adapted from de Lauretis, 1994, p.89).[15] We do not see an autonomous sexuality for women.

The problem is 'how to represent lesbian desire through cinematic codes imbued with heterosexual presumption', as de Lauretis puts it (p.xvi). In discussion of *She must be seeing things* (McLaughlin, 1987), she points out that few fiction films about lesbians exist, and that even fewer deal with sexuality. The relevance of this film to *Strange Fish* is that similar devices can be seen to be in play. Whereas the film is about two women, one who makes movies in real life and both of whom make them 'in their heads', *Strange Fish* is not about women at all; but the device of a film within a film is crucial to both, as is the representation of female sexualities. McLaughlin's film

> construct[s] for both spectator and filmmaker a new position of seeing in the movies, a new place of the look – the place of a woman who desires another woman, the place from where each one looks at the other with desire; and more important still, a place from where I, spectator, *see* their look and their desire
>
> de Lauretis, 1994, p.88

In Scene 5, at the moment that Wendy Houstoun observes the lovers, she is at her most elegant, dressed in silver, hair brushed in glossy femininity, lipsticked and quiet, for once perfectly still. We do not see Lauren Potter look at her with desire, and in this I read Lloyd Newson's refusal of this possibility, as de Lauretis suggests is common. Here, Wendy is a 'feminine invert' rather than a 'masculine lesbian', or even the lipstick lesbian of the 1990s – glamorous rather than invisible, but still destined to be marginalised. More positively, it can be argued that through Wendy's attitude of scepticism and detachment in observing the loving ritual, she deconstructs the heterosexual subject position to create a lesbian subject position (Dolan, 1993, p.160). It is not clear what this might be, however, since nothing of significance follows for Wendy from this stance.

Not only does desire enter the discussion, but so too does power. Boswell points to the inevitable connection between questions of who penetrates whom, and how, with issues of power and dominance (in Comstock and Henking, 1997). Submission in any form to a more powerful individual carries messages wider than the act itself and is not innocently, or simply, a matter of gender or personal preference. Dworkin's infamous text *Intercourse* (1987) is a series of readings of sexual intercourse in literature – from Tolstoy, Proust and Isaac Singer to Edna O'Brien – and is relevant because it is the literary representation of this act as repulsive, possessive, a matter of occupation, that she analyses.[16] To bypass male desire is to attract opprobrium – she uses the story of Joan of Arc as an example of the insistence of men that women conform and the lengths to which they have been prepared to go to ensure that women do not rebel. The public and legally enshrined ownership of women by men, she points out, has been replaced by woman's willingness to maintain that placing, committing herself to

> her own continuing inferiority: she polices her own body; she internalizes the demands of the dominant class ... it is the best system of colonialization on earth: she takes on the burden, the responsibility, of her own submission.
>
> Dworkin, 1987, p.169

Daly interprets the male ambivalence towards desire and men's denial of the physical attractiveness of women as 'an enormous draining of women's energies into the phallocentric cesspool' (1984, p.41) – a vivid if charmless metaphor. But the relevance of her writing for an understanding of the exclusivity of Scene 2 in *Strange Fish* and the girls-against-the-boys mood of Scene 3 is seen in the competitive and manipulative sado-masochistic play between the women. Lloyd Newson makes a huge investment in getting women to 'buy' this version of reality in the later 'love' scenes, too.

Conclusion

The control of women and of both male and female eroticism is undoubtedly a dominant political theme in Christian thinking. The distinction between sex for procreation and sex for pleasure becomes a troubling motif by the Middle Ages. From saving the soul, it is a short step to saving the body, as in our twentieth-century preoccupations arising from the scientific and medical appropriation of the person, and a focus on the part such attention can deal with – physical health. In turn, heterosexuality becomes the 'healthy' norm, and homosexuality, in oppositional contrast, a disease. At this point another distinction enters into religious thinking: to be homosexual (male) in preference, *but to refrain from acting on these preferences*, is to achieve greater spirituality, on the same rationale as that used for heterosexuals. Boswell argues that

> the conceptual distance between 'homosexual' and 'heterosexual' is vastly greater in modern understandings of sexuality than its nearest correlates in ancient or medieval systems. 'Homosexual/

> heterosexual' is the major dialectical foundation of all modern discourse about sexuality – scientific, social, and ethical – and it seems urgent, intuitive, and profoundly important to most Americans
>
> Boswell in Comstock and Henking, 1997, p.125

and, I suspect, almost equally to Europeans. The dichotomy between so-called 'natural' inclination and socially constructed 'choice' becomes the issue and can be seen to have long been the issue, from the start of writings on the subject, although it may not always have carried the same level of approbation or disapproval.

But, in an interesting insight, Davidson links the work of Adrienne Rich with that of Eve Sedwick, in order

> to suggest that ... obligatory heterosexuality is reinforced even when those [literary or artistic] communities contain a large number of homosexual males ... the structure of homosocial relations, genitalized or not, often undergirds the production of new art forms and practices.
>
> in Case *et al.*, 1995, p.198

In studying literary circles in San Francisco in the 1950s, he concludes that

> women were often absent from the centres of artistic and intellectual life in general during the 1950s, their absence in these groups was a structural necessity for the liberation of a new, male subject.
>
> p.198

This new, male misogynist subject is typified in Allen Ginsberg's work, where women exist only as 'sex toys or castrating viragos' (p.200) in order to create a 'compulsory homosociality' in defiance of Rich's 'compulsory heterosexuality'.

A reminder is apposite, too, of the metaphoric tendency of theorists (e.g. Barthes and Kristeva) to idealise music (one might say dance, too) and to place it in an autonomous space outside the symbolic sphere, widening further the split between physical and spiritual bodies, as also does the account of *Akhnaten* cited earlier (Richardson, 1999). If music is the one art most dedicated to denial of the body and the erotic, then *Strange Fish* provides interesting reading. If music is then identified with the feminine as in Kristeva's writings, with the maternal as distinct from the symbolic realm of the father, music simply perpetuates the 'female irrational, male rational' mode of thought and achieves no shift of perspective. De Lauretis challenges such positions by insisting on actual subjects (not just linguistically-situated perspectives) and therefore on the dimension of individual experience (1984, p.171).

McClary suggests that if these issues were taken more seriously

> they might even contribute to the creation of new models of gender and desire: models that do not pit mind against body, that do not demand shame – or death – as the price for sexual pleasure.
>
> 1991, p.79

Recognising that the very idea of a fixed identity based on sex or gender has become increasingly problematic, Boswell makes a link between Galatians 3:28 (that there is 'neither male nor female ... in Christ') and post-structuralist discussions of fluid categories of gender identity. She points out that theories of this kind *depend* upon a binary divide for their meaning. The categories are 'left intact' (in Comstock and Henking, 1997, p.190) by the strategy of inclusion. Many such arguments rest on an interpretation of Butler's studies of gender. Butler refuses to unify the person as a sexual subject by tying sex to gender, since this would be to accept a normalizing of heterosexual power structures. In Chapter 6 I work on these themes, particularly exploring 'the metaphysical threesome, sex, gender, desire – that keeps the man–woman binary in place' (Mary McClintock Fulkerson in Comstock and Henking, p.192).

1 As Douglas points out, citing New Guinea, such views of women, as polluting the male, occur in other societies (1966, p. 147).

2 There are twentieth-century echoes of this theme in Elaine Morgan's popular reversal of theory, which suggests a marine evolution for man rather than an evolution from apes (1972), and which would be in line with sea-goddess theory.

3 Lest the reader think this excursion into theology, and Mariolatry in particular, is a small byway in the late twentieth century, Pelikan

(1996) cites more than 2000 on-line references at Yale University Library of predominantly twentieth-century texts solely on Mary, and not including thousands more on Christianity.

4 The court case brought a challenge from two of the authors of a previously published book, by Michael Baigent and Richard Leigh *The Holy Grail* (1982) which made the same claims although in a scholarly manner.

5 The British Labour Government's attempts to overturn the infamous Section 28 legislation forbidding the representation of homosexuality as a viable life style were thwarted in 2000 by this resurgence of conventional morality underpinned by fear of disease.

6 The events depicted in Monteverdi's *The Coronation of Poppea* occur long before this sad pass was reached.

7 This poem still resonates, as in Robert Cohan's *Stabat Mater* for London Contemporary Dance Theatre, created in 1975.

8 'Secret societies' also recall the communist incarceration of non-believers as recorded in Solzhenitsyn's *Arkhipelag Gulag 1918–1956* (1978). Orphanages in Romania, in the former Soviet Union and in the former Yugoslavia, a secret society of unwanted children, are the most obvious equivalents in the 1990s.

9 Lesbian identity is a subject of much recent discussion, and in psychoanalytic terms can be and has been reduced to a 'compulsive, parasitic tendency to make her subjectivity into a reversion to sameness – precluding difference ... the *lesbian* immediately drops out of sight ... she produces her [own] invisibility' (Brinks in Case *et al.*, 1995, p.7).

10 Seminal essays by Annette Kuhn (1985) and Laura Mulvey (1989) have impinged to a considerable degree on dance analysis in recent years.

11 It is interesting that gods were not defined in terms of their sexual status in the same way that goddesses were, and could find sexual partners in men or women. Their inter-sex character extended to giving birth themselves. Equally fluid, it is often thought, were Greek views on homosexuality, overt in Greek writings and records of practice – carrying explanations and justifications springing from initiation rites.

12 Davies draws on another example from the period 1150 to 1350 in Christian Europe, where a shift can be seen from viewing homosexual behaviour as a matter of preference, to a dangerous, anti-social and sinful aberration (Boswell, in Comstock and Henking, 1977, p.51). Linking homosexuality with bestiality, and with sex with non-Christians, created a powerful impetus for disapproval. Indeed, institutional rigidity, as well as the rigidity of geographical boundaries, can be seen to reinforce the need for clear moral boundaries.

13 She reworks Freud's castration theory, but to conclude that castration 'rewrites in the symbolic as lack of a penis what is a

primary narcissistic loss of body-image, a lack of being that threatens the imaginary matrix of the body-ego' (p.xviii). It is 'disavowal' of this lack, a refusal of it, that gives substance to de Lauretis's version of perverse desire.

14 If all women suffer from penis envy, lesbians 'have it more' in de Lauretis's delightful phrase (1994, p.66). She argues that the idea of 'castration' cannot be ignored but must be re-worked, otherwise there is no means to symbolise lesbian desire and therefore to theorise it.

15 A cautionary note is relevant here. There is no attempt on my part to maintain that Wendy Houstoun is in fact a lesbian – I am simply illustrating the spectator's view of the construction of subject positions and the filmic and other devices that make it possible.

16 Dworkin describes intercourse as an act of possession in which 'a man inhabits a woman, physically covering her and overwhelming her and at the same time penetrating her: and this physical relation to her – over her and inside her – is his possession of her' (1987, p.73).

CHAPTER 6

Sacred and Profane: Evocations of the Siren

> Barthes uses the Siren metaphor in his discussion of intertextuality and characterises it 'as a music of figures, metaphor, thought-worlds; it is the signifier as Siren' (1977, p.145).

In this chapter on the Siren I elaborate the consequences of a loss of fixed gender identities and fixed sexual orientations. The subject is twofold: the construction of subjectivities, and the manipulation of shifting subjectivities in constantly fluid power relations. It is an act of re-appropriation, re-reading *Strange Fish* in my own terms but reflecting on the power structures that the event sets up. Readings of the working of the narrative and its effects reflect, self-consciously, the engagement of the individual.

Continuing the line of argument in Chapter 5, I take de Lauretis's view as a starting point. She argues that the subject is a complex construction made of many different types of traces or threads. The subject, she says, is

> constituted in gender ... though not by sexual difference alone, but rather across languages and cultural representations; a subject engendered in the experiencing of race and class, as well as sexual, relations; a subject, therefore, not unified but rather multiple, and not so much divided as contradicted.
>
> 1987, p.2

Gender analysis alone produces an incomplete or partial picture, hence the necessity of interrelating modes of analysis, combined as a form of political commentary. De Lauretis suggests that since 'language means more than one wants it to mean' (1984, p.3) we do not have to accept a given set of answers. We can intervene politically as feminists (or as some other group) if we recognise that it is through such personal action that political realities exist. This becomes a 'confrontation with theoretical discourses and expressive practices which construct and effect a certain representation of "woman"' (p.5).

In tension are a rather 'pure' series of musical traces and the dramatic events of *Strange Fish*. The prior discourse that is obviously relevant in Newson's descriptions of the work as well as in the reactions of most readers is the Greek myth of the Siren. It tells of a sea nymph, part bird and part woman, who entices sailors to their deaths on the rocks by her enchanting singing. She is alluring but deadly. She sits among her headless victims' bones. Typically, as Hathorn (1977) describes it, the sweet song that the Siren sings hides the reality of her addiction to rotting flesh, skin shrivelling on the bones of headless bodies after she has consumed their flesh. Men do not survive giving in to her attractions, a notion underlined by another sense of the meaning of the name – that of 'binder' or 'strangler'. To escape from the Siren is to escape from worldly temptation. By further extension, to escape from worldly temptation is to escape from women. Nigel's failure to escape from Wendy is rewarded with death.

Sirens appear in many guises, as bird-women or fish-women. Women turned into birds of the air or fish of the water (mermaids) are ideas that are omnipresent in marine communities across many cultures (see Chapters 4 and 5). Eliade (1982), for example, finds similar fish images tied to sexual symbolism and yearly cycles in prehistoric China. Further, belief that souls could take the form of birds is well established in many Indo-European theologies. Such birds may appear in several forms, including the Egyptian Horus (hawk) who represents the Pharaoh's spirit, and the phoenix (or firebird) that rises from its own cremated body. Birds are free to travel, and 'were everywhere regarded as angelic messengers, givers of omens, possessors of occult secrets, as well as soul-carriers' (Walker, 1983, p.101).

Bremmer makes a direct link between the Sirens and Orpheus, a Greek god-like figure who charmed animals and nature with his music making. Bremmer does this through the notion of secret societies (as described earlier). Orpheus has a special relationship to the Muses, in some societies re-interpreted as a shamanistic role (1987, p.97). When he sailed on the *Argo* with Jason he was responsible for getting the ship safely past the Isle of the Sirens by countering their ravishing songs with the music of his own lyre (Graves, 1992, p.154). Other characterisations refer more widely to initiation rites prevalent in many societies in which young men perform dangerous and difficult tasks. Here the idea of an ordeal to be undergone to claim membership of a special society can be traced through to present times.[1]

The Siren in *Strange Fish* is constructed through theatrical gesture, dance and music, creating an androgynous character through the shadowing of moving and melodic lines and through the striving for movement and melodic independence. It achieves this position of androgyny by crossing the realms of vocal register, and by extending ranges of movement, tonality and dynamic expressivity far from those most usually associated with one gender. It is perpetually ambivalent, establishing one voice only in order to change it. Methodologically, an example of this process can be found in Foster's analysis of the 'self' and the 'body' that are produced in selected training systems for dance. My interest is not in training systems, but the detail of events within *Strange Fish* can readily be analysed in the same way. This analysis makes it possible to see both how a bodily consciousness is formed, and how it is situated 'in a cultural and aesthetic moment' (in Desmond, ed., 1997, p.236). My own contribution in analysis is to elaborate a non-dualistic moment, to deny this split, and to reveal how the cultural moment exists *in* the movement.

The pleasure we derive from telling ourselves stories – of our own lives, of society, past and present – is reflected in the genres of cultural performance that are part of our lives. I respond finally to the movement and driving character of narrative, which holds disparate events together and generates an intensity that we crave. However, in defiance of Freud, and of the male narrative that requires woman to be constructed to suit his desire, I reverse the narrative to re-read the Siren figure as the empowered female in this story.

Firstly, picking up from the final sections of Chapter 5 on shifting gendered identities, I deal with the parody of gender that *Strange Fish* sets up, perhaps at a greater extreme than Lloyd Newson or the participants intended. How satisfactorily I can do this depends in part on whether I can establish that *Strange Fish* is to some extent at least a parody, a witting and understandable challenge to conventional gender relations, which is what I would like to be able to sustain in this chapter. As a reminder of how parody in performance might be conceived, I refer here to Butler's position, that a

> set of parodic practices based in a performance theory of gender acts to disrupt the categories of the body, sex, gender, and sexuality and occasion their subversive resignification and proliferation beyond the binary frame.
>
> 1990, p.x[2]

I argue that it is reasonable to see the relations in *Strange Fish* as a parody of gender constructs, and that this in itself is good reason to value the work (in my terms). As its characters come into being, we can ask how they are 'regulated' – what codes of sexual and gender practice do they observe, and how are they visible in gesture, movement, dynamic and use of space? This idea of regulatory practices originates with Foucault and is a useful one when analysing these characters, since they can be seen to operate within what Butler terms a 'unity' of gender construct that drives towards compulsory heterosexuality (p.31).

There are historical precedents for gender-specific parody conducted through music and movement, for example in Lully's erotic parodies of the seventeenth century. Both men and women were caught in this trap. In a commentary on Louis XIV's court, nobles were attacked through depictions of their supposed sexual inadequacy, clearly used to undermine, by allusion, their political efficacy. Widows were portrayed in both opera and parody as witches, while women of 'any age were thought of as having voracious sexual appetites' (Gordon-Seifert, 2002, p.141).

The repetition of significations, such as are evident in the Blonde Terrorist section, provides the material for a further discussion of whether gender norms are displaced or reinforced by this ritualisation. The collision and collusion of sensual traces and fragments encourages the construction of the Siren as a metaphor of musical seduction, as mythic dancing woman, entirely in control.

A parody of gender: the Blonde Terrorists

In Scene 4, which I titled 'Sexual play, two against one (female–male)', Molina enters the now-empty bar where, with lighted candles placed one on each shoulder, he performs slow, curving and sinking movements, arms held outstretched. His movement is reminiscent both of a very elegant Spanish bullfighter and of a Balinese dancer, in a complex mixture of masculine and feminine sensuality and skill. The soundscape includes a whining cry, almost like a cat. A *pssst* to call attention announces footsteps that reinforce the rhythm of voices. Rapid movement of the feet and small, quick hand gestures construct a chattering of movement 'voices' in a fashion similar to the vocal chattering, which is punctuated by short repeated chords and periods of stillness.

Before long Wendy Houstoun and Lauren Potter enter, dressed in blonde wigs – shoulder-length and fluffy for Lauren, straighter and shorter for Wendy. Wearing short shiny dresses, black tights and shoes, they adjust their clothes, play with their hair and admire each other before targeting Jordi Molina, circling him and drawing him into their game. It is a teasing game in which the women's repetition of unison movement and their canon-like phrases are much enhanced by the close-up camera action, which conveys extremes of distraction and motion as the women swirl around him, beckon, insinuate, seduce.

The movement, like the small high-pitched shrieks emitted almost as squeaks, starts quietly at first, and is interspersed with sighs and silences. These pauses between events (they can hardly be called phrases) are themselves interrupted by an abrupt repeated keyboard chord. The two blondes – identical in every respect except for the length of their hair – mimic this vocal madness. The bewigged sirens create their own version of 'shrieks' in subtle and small shifts of parts of the body, often moving a small part out of alignment with the rest, as though commenting on the sound and reflecting the counter-tensions and paradoxes within it. Their hair-twisting, astute movement observations and commentary as they circle Jordi, drawing nearer and nearer to him, is predatory. He cannot escape. This is the stuff of nightmares or satanic ritual practice.

This virtuosic Blonde Terrorists' duet combines voices, movement and filmic extremes in perfect illustration of a peculiarly female form of madness (see Chapter 5). It is based on a mastery of the body and the repetition of highly skilled, complex, fast movements, often arrested at unlikely moments by pauses that stop the whirl and create vertigo for the observer.[3] The duet effects its message through vocal screams and shrieks; through quirky and often threatening movement, splitting the body into parts and transgressing any idea of a known technique or style; and through high-speed changes of level and direction, leaping high and rolling to the ground, creating unbearable tensions. The filming choices made by the director combine to fragment any phrase of movement, just as the voices are fragmented by silence and intermittent, unrelated shrieks.

Martin, talking generally about video, suggests that

> the more the video pursues the kinaesthetic content of dancing through its own visual form, the more it disrupts the appearance of continuity in the standard documentary shot that purportedly places the camera in the seat of the audience ... video relies on a displacement of activity that occurs within a three-dimensional space into some virtual equivalent.
>
> 1998, p.35

There is no attempt in this scene to shoot it as though it were a documentary. Instead, it challenges those conventions of accurate representation and distorts the viewer's perception. The shooting of this scene is an extreme version of 'the active looking that editing shots from different angles allows, [showing] an awareness of how history is written' (p.35).

The singing voices that at first mock with brief and varied phrases based on vocalising *ooh* and *aah*, shrieks and *psst* sounds develop into a series of repeated nasal chants in repetitions of *na*. Cells are added and subtracted from rhythmic patterns, illuminated by changes in pitch, but across a huge vocal range, and not 'placed' in a particular melodic form as might normally be expected. These fragments of rhythm are given compelling force by a syncopated, pulsating beat. Changes in the density and complexity of the polyrhythmic fabric, from a thin texture of a single call to a multitude of voices and sounds in overlapping cycles, are echoed in the bodies, from a single gesture to a whirl of complex movement rippling through the entire body and across two, and then all three, bodies.

These rhythmic cells alternate between patterns of threes and twos, giving an emphasis as though in triple time and then in duple time, using the repeated exclamation:

na na na/ **na** na na/ **na** na/ **na** na/ **na** na na/ **na** na na/ **naaaaaa**

These are overlain with whoops, shrieks and footsteps. The pattern changes to an *ooh ahh* construction, equally wordless but inviting surprise and excitement, as distinct from the more aggressive, nasally produced *na na* sounds:

oee ... oee ... oee ... **a** ... oee ... oee ... **a**..**a**

A bemused Jordi follows the women as though they were animals on heat, until the scene reaches a climax when Wendy spitefully pulls off Lauren's wig, with the clear intention of revealing Lauren as an impostor and not really a blonde. Lauren and Jordi, however, have made a different kind of contact, and Lauren follows Jordi down the corridor, Wendy bringing up the rear petulantly, no longer the prime mover. The volume fades and increases in illogical fashion, creating further tension – layering dynamic texture on this shifting ground. Finally the sound fades away into single voices. It unpicks its own density, revealing its bare structures, and ends on a sighing *ooh*ing thread that includes occasional light keyboard chords.

For the Blonde Terrorists, unlike the case with the Christ/Mary plainsong-based duets earlier, this madness is not the excessive ecstasy of the diva as in lyric opera. Because of its staccato nature and its discontinuities, it is reinscribed under language and associated with animal emotion and hence with demonic pleasures. Poizat's comment (1992, p.37) that language disappears and is 'superseded by the cry' should not be seen as a complaint that one cannot hear the words (as is often said in opera), but be understood as a fully intentional progression from speech, through speech sung as language, to the detachment of the sound from language as it reaches the highest notes. It culminates in the extreme upper ranges – it is at its most ecstatic when it is least intelligible. In this way I position the singing in Scene 4 a long way from the highly controlled declamation and enunciation of theatre. It is also a long way from the sacred elements in *Strange Fish* but still refers to them, since fragments of the angelic melodies heard earlier recur, just as fragments of the movement behaviour of the women in Scenes 2 and 3 reappear.

The women try to take control in Scene 4, although their intentions are subtly subverted by the very evident contribution of David Hinton, the director. Distortion is critical to the filming. As Houstoun and Potter tease Molina, darting around him with light playful movements, the camera in close focus directs the reader's attention very specifically to faces and parts of bodies, to whirling hair and complicit smiles between the women. The singing voices contain faint echoes of the Siren song, perhaps in ironic commentary, before high-pitched female chattering, giggling and laughter take over. The viewer's sense of location in space, like Molina's in the middle of the action, is utterly lost as the dancers whirl across the screen unpredictably, sometimes appearing from behind the camera as well as from the sides. Molina's evident confusion about what is real and what is illusion poignantly reinforces the message of the movement text. The apparently harmless, teasing message is made menacing by being filmed so close up. The camera forces the reader to see these events through particular eyes, both by its perspective and by bringing faces and movement in and out of focus. Dislocation, rather than rootedness, is a direct consequence of these video techniques.[4] The result is wildness rather than serious challenge.

What starts as an amusing diversion ends as a cynical observation: that the male does not much mind who this female is, as long as she is available and preferably blonde and sexy (one feels that either of these two women will serve the purpose, and he is easily turned from one to the other). In any event, the female is only out to tease and to cause trouble – the bitch. The women's enjoyment of his discomfort and their remorseless detachment only emphasise the point. This extreme stereotyping of female and male behaviour can either be taken seriously (in expressionist or social-realist mode) or be seen as a spoof, a parody of mating behaviour much as Mackrell (1992) describes it in the phrase 'the intense gang rituals shared by young girls' and Parry

(1992a) as 'the mating games of over-sexed adolescents'. Evident, too, are the Siren texts of Greek myth, as well as the Lorelei (the Rhinemaiden equivalent) and even more blatant twentieth-century Hollywood examples, from Marilyn Monroe onwards. Obvious as this stereotyping is, it also creates amusing entertainment.

Beside these cultural traces others can be found that echo conflicting attitudes to the female body. The eroticism and sexual power of the female is evident, tracing a particular kind of stereotype; but it is directly juxtaposed with another, that of female vulnerability, naïvety and purity. Whore and virgin – the ever-present tension for women. The sexual identity crisis that *Strange Fish* recalls is one where male, female and trans-sexual biological identities are compounded by choices in terms of gender identity. The challenge of a feminist theology is to force into the open the power arrangements underlying gender categories that assume a fixed 'sex', since sex, and the desire to procreate, is held to be coincident with a notion of 'self'. The parody of gender represented here can be seen to be directly in line with the ideas of fluid-gendered identities and the problems they present for religious control.

An evocative trace lies in an essay on the Barbie doll in which the authors comment on the relationship between Barbie's almost anorectic body and 'her seemingly endless desire for consumption and self-transformation'. They argue that hyper-thin bodies and hyper-consumption 'are very much linked in the advanced capitalist economies that depend upon commodity excess' (Urla and Swedlund, in Schiebinger, 2000, p.418).[5] The conflict between repression of the desire to consume and the simultaneous incitement of the same desire through the marketing of products produces an intense self-monitoring that perfectly fits Bartky's notion of the self-policing subject (1988).

Just as Renaissance anatomical drawings were done from classical statues and not from life, the distortion of bodily dimensions continues in Barbie, reflecting the social construction of bodies. The pleasure of control and mastery offers the chance to be powerfully sexual without the danger of reproduction (Urla and Swedlund, in Schiebinger, 2000). It is these complex and contradictory meanings that are contained in the one image with which Wendy Houstoun and Lauren Potter 'play'.

The construction of a queer aesthetic

In opposition to these stereotypes it can be argued that in *Strange Fish* Pook and Pappenheim have created something closer to the 'audacious and rebellious subversion of musical convention' that Elizabeth Wood refers to. Subversion can be seen in both the sacred and the profane traces referred to here, although it is more obvious in the profane and parody sections than in the plainsong references. Wood describes the composer Ethel Smyth summoning the multiple and conflicting themes and dramas of her life and works (in Solie, ed., 1993). Not only does her music contain a coded lesbian message – the craft of fugue speaks to this, she suggests[6] – but it also, combined with her writings, 'replicate[s] the horizontal and vertical lines of musical counterpoint' respectively.[7]

As in *Strange Fish*, when two voices on horizontal narrative lines 'sound together or coincide, vertical chords or harmonies are produced' that reconstruct 'erotic relationships with women and ... shape lesbian experience' (Wood in Solie, 1993, p.166). In addition, these voices work with and against Melanie Pappenheim's actions – her movement, her bodily positioning within the action. By analogy, the vertical chords of harmonies accompany these narrative lines. This use of counterpoint creates a crossing of borders that Wood calls 'Sapphonic'. She uses the term to describe

> a space of a lesbian possibility, for a range of erotic and emotional relationships among women who sing and women who listen ... it is characteristically powerful and problematic, defiant and defective.
>
> [It is based on] an exceptional range of registers [which] cross boundaries among different voice types and their representations to challenge polarities of both gender and sexuality as these are socially – and vocally – constructed. Its refusal of categories and the transgressive risks it takes act seductively on a lesbian listener for whom the singer serves as messenger, her voice as vessel, of desire.
>
> Wood, in Brett *et al.*, 1994, pp.27–8

The Sapphonic voice, according to Wood, challenges

> stable, unchallengeable binary symmetry, for it suggests that both gender and sexuality are transferable ... its combination of different registers refuses vocal categories and natural/unnatural polarities, and confounds simplistic messages about female desire ... in music's texts.

> For listeners, the Sapphonic voice is a destabilizing agent of fantasy and desire. The woman with this voice, this capacity to embody and traverse a range of sonic possibilities and overflow sonic boundaries, may vocalize inadmissible sexualities and a thrilling readiness to go beyond so-called natural limits, an erotics of risk and defiance, a desire for desire itself.
>
> pp.32–3

For Wood, this 'integration of sameness and difference in one solo and undivided voice' (p.36) is hugely seductive. Melanie Pappenheim accomplishes this in the solo melodic lines, while the two soprano voices (self against self in Melanie Pappenheim's singing) also serve to deny the dominant male/female pairing we have come to expect in representations of love, ecstasy and conflict between human beings. In a situation where two *equal* voices work at the extremes – whether two castrati voices or those of two women – such pairings evoke the terror of gay/lesbian difference, and thus are doubly subversive (p.37).

The historical examples that Wood adduces reveal the disturbing effects not only of big, strong voices of unusual range, but also of voices that have unusual flexibility – a chest sound or baritone quality in the female voice that speaks of masculinity in a female body; and in contrast a falsetto voice in a male, the high 'uncannily queer lost sound of a castrato or male falsetto ... [or] a "sexless" boy chorister' (p.31) which seems to be outside the body.[8] The voice draws attention to the body that produces such a sound which, in lacking the physical attributes normally associated with the sound, questions both maleness and femaleness while also appropriating any remaining credibility from the female – women can only stand aside and wonder in the latter case.[9] Unusually, the voices in *Strange Fish* are the subversive voices of women.

The voice is a complex mechanism, and its various tones have been hijacked to underpin cultural responses to sound. To some extent, and using a psychoanalytic interpretation, all voices can be read in this way, not just singing voices of a particular era. As Poizat argues, voices can signify the transgression that is found in the 'cry', where the voice expresses 'a paroxysmal vocal emission beyond the range of music and out of the reach of the word' (1992, p.76). Cries are not notated, neither are they exclamations of a particular word.

The gender parody in *Strange Fish* is in every sense a potent and dangerous 'cry'. Scene 4 follows scenes of pure and lyrical singing and adopts traces of it, but like heavy metal, as Walser says, it bears the significance of "runnin' with the Devil" – the idea that we have the freedom to respect 'no love, no law, no responsibility' (1993, p.52) – all the things our puritan ancestors fought against. In physical theatre, as in opera, 'the masquerade of gender, and aural delusion come together in an intricate web ... challenged by perceptions of multiple voices, a dispersal of authority ... [that lies] at the heart of transvestism' (Abbate in Solie, ed., 1993, p.229). Following psychoanalytic theory, it might be said that Melanie's singing with herself is both schizophrenic and erotic – and thus can be construed as a form of erotic madness.

If it is possible to parody gender, then gender is itself a kind of performance, under the witting control of the participant. It is a style with particular gestures, positions and modes of speaking in which known codes are traded against new contexts where they would not normally appear. But what Lloyd Newson's setting tells the reader is that this is disastrous, not something to be celebrated and not an opening of false strictures to greater flexibility, since the outcome is Christ's death and Wendy's utter isolation. In other words, women still cannot be shown taking control of their own lives and surviving without men. This view can be aligned with the Bakhtinian view of carnival as flirting with the possibilities of freedom, while these freedoms are always contained within the restoration of the status quo.[10] Here we see women who are free from social constraints mocking Molina with exaggerated versions of normal behaviour. Their acts are gross exaggerations of 'femininity'. They also evoke Kristeva's female grotesque – there is nothing maternal about these women (as interpreted in Creed, 1993). As Wolff argues, these are women and men already constructed differently through 'linguistic practices and language itself' (1990, p.74). In this analysis of *Strange Fish* we can see *how* they are constructed as shifting sexual and gendered people.

I take Case's view that 'lesbian' can be separated from 'queer' as a specific sign and can serve to challenge it, as I showed in Chapter 5. Here I focus on 'queer' in order to emphasise the absence of women from this construct (or the assumption of their inclusion within it), and its close association with commodification and capitalism. It is a multi-cultural and transgendered construct that includes all 'anti-normal' practices. Case refers to it as 'unhinged by multiple sexual identities' (1996, p.167), 'embedded in ads, shopping strategies, mall demonstrations, and logos' (p.170), asking as a result if 'queer' then becomes the traditional liberal melting of differences or the multinationals' new capitalism.

The emergence of 'homosexual' and 'queer' as categories is relatively recent. As Weeks suggests that while

> erotic activity between men and men and between women and women has existed in all times and all cultures, only in a few societies does a distinctive homosexual categorisation and sense of self develop.
>
> 1985, p.92

Weeks presents Freud as saying simultaneously that

> gender and sexual identity are precarious, provisional and constantly undermined by the play of desires, and that [a heterosexual adjustment is] necessary and essential, the guarantee of mental and social health
>
> p.148

Freud's ambivalence was never resolved, but he was driven by a reproductive definition of sexuality and the belief that a 'heterosexual genital organisation of sexuality was a cultural necessity' (p.155). Weeks suggests that an alternative is to construct an 'original bisexuality of which both heterosexuality and homosexuality are, in complex ways, derivatives' (p.150). 'Both heterosexuality and homosexuality are peculiar compromises, partial organisations of the flux of sexual desires which are shaped, in complex ways, by the cultural organisation of sexual difference, and the centrality assigned to heterosexuality' (p.154).

Weeks's criticism of Freud is that although he posits an 'unstructured and polymorphous' infantile sexuality, he also argues that it is necessary to abandon this in 'the accession to heterosexual masculinity and femininity' (p.148). Psychoanalytic institutions can be seen as contributing to the construction of homosexuality as an illness, making Freud's work seem conservative, where it might have been seen more radically as disruptive of current insights and as contributing to a theory of desire. If sexuality is polymorphous, there can be no sense of degeneracy or a need to 'cure' homosexuals. Homosexuality emerges as more a question of object choice than of fixed instinct.

Lloyd Newson ventures only part of the way towards challenging constructions of Christ (and the law, it has to be said; he is, after all, an artist in the public arts world). In Rambuss's description of the video *More of a Man* (1990), directed by Jerry Douglas, more extreme challenges can be seen. As two naked males, one on his knees, offer each other sex, the setting can be seen to be an empty church with an effigy of Christ.

> This staging of a porno film in church, to a backdrop of votive candles and cathedral bells [is more than] simply a gay male recasting
>
> Rambuss in Case *et al.*, 1995, p.71

and can be attributed to Christianity's 'own libidinal structures' (p.71). Kokofsky Sedgwick comments on the examples of Catholicism, of 'adults who don't marry, of men in dresses, of passionate theatre, of introspective investment ... and presiding over all are images of Jesus' (1990, p.140). While Newson does not present rosary beads juxtaposed with a spent condom, as Jerry Douglas does, his images parallel this in their profanity (p. 72). In fact Rambuss is making a claim for a continuing tradition of homo-devotional pleasure, as seen in the poetry of seventeenth-century male poets such as John Donne, where divine and sensual love are condensed into a single image of insistent fleshliness. In his account of poetry by Crashaw, 'the penetrated male body thus turns liquescent, a site of utter ejaculatory excess' in consequence of 'texturing the body of Jesus as a surface of multiple, sentimentally rendered openings' (Rambuss in Case *et al.*, 1995, p.76).

Rambuss's argument is that

> any mapping of an erotics of Christianity, whether early modern or modern, needs to consider as well the vagaries of homoerotic desire elicited in devotional expression. Stimulated by a spectacularized denuded male form – the ravished, the ravishing body of Jesus – the performances of the prayer closet, the site of a variety of homodevotional excitations to pleasure, desire, and devotion, require as much.
>
> p.86

The current obsession of the gay male with body culture, with hours spent in the gym, finds its echo in the near-naked bodies exposed in *Strange Fish*. Dale Tanner and Jordi Cortes Molina are the prime cases of 'hunks of flesh'. Bouldrey's collection of essays written by gay men, *Wrestling with the Angel*, is relevant not just for its shared allusions to biblical sources, but because it addresses the needs of the 1990s to connect eroticism and spirituality to the established Churches that carry our sensual as well as religious histories. For example, the allusion to subversive angels is shared across many performance pieces, from *Angels in America* to *Strange Fish*. As many have found, angels have become a kind of 'postmodern commonplace', re-constructed in different eras to serve the needs of the time.

Connor R.P. *et al.* (1997) collect evidence spanning Africa, the Near and Far East, Europe and North and South America from a variety of spiritual traditions relating to queer myth, symbol and spirit, subtitled *Gay, Lesbian, Bisexual and Transgender Lore*. To locate their own experience of the 1990s, the authors examine the relationships between postcolonial living in a postmodern world and a spirituality of an equally mixed and fluid nature. Weaving together beliefs and practices of many cultures (as Anzaldua describes in Connor *et al.*, 1997, p.vii) is no more unlikely or untenable than fusion cooking. On a cautionary note, however, O'Flaherty (1980) argues that androgynes, the mythical mixtures of the human and divine, function as symbols of conflict, not of fusion, as is often presented. The tendency to be labile and open to re-interpretation is clearly significant both in encouraging openness and in threatening the status quo and creating *con*fusion.

Connor explicitly focuses on 'mythic and spiritual aspects of erotic and gendered experience' (1997, p.vii), challenging taboos of tying sensuality to religion – the *(con)*fusion in *Strange Fish* of threads that are inextricably intertwined. What are the varieties of things that *Strange Fish* represents? Are they Lloyd Newson's fantasies of men and women? Does he speak for men and/or women in any generic sense? How does his speaking from a gendered identity position affect us?

This flows into my own argument that the increasing appearance of well-muscled but sensitive men in advertisements (not just for male cosmetics) is but one strand of a gay male aesthetic and rhetoric. Matthew Bourne's phenomenal success with his company *Adventures in Motion Pictures* could only be possible at the present moment. He parodies the classics of dance, *Swan Lake* being the most famous example; he inverts male and female roles; he casts women as stock pantomime characters and men as narcissistic introverts. And it draws huge crowds to a theatre in London's West End, a feat not achieved by anyone in the dance world since Diaghilev in the 1920s. In Bourne's work we can see how our own society is changing. Certainly it chimes with the experiences of a large number of theatregoers, not the small numbers conventionally attending performances at the Drill Hall or the Place Theatre. In its popularity can be read its wider applicability. Most of Bourne's work clearly is focused on challenging gender assumptions in a light-hearted way and with some splendid dancing.

Foster extends this idea to an argument about the closeting of homosexuality in modern dance during the twentieth century, in its creation of 'a nonsexualised corporeality' (2001, p.149), partly to deny the common associations of dancing with female immorality and prostitution in the heterosexual world.

With head shaved, dressed in a skirt and sporting an earring, the gay male dominates – there is clearly no need for women in this world. If men can be both male and female, can move fluidly between nuanced sexual identities, which seem to be neither one nor the other, this is a powerful and dominant position. In contrast, it is a freedom denied to women, since the negativity attached to images of strong, powerful women remains – our cultural constructions might have changed for gay males but they have not changed for women, heterosexual or homosexual, other than to narrow further the possibilities of expression.

In the classical music world, the counter-tenor, chosen in preference to a female alto in musical interpretation, was not long ago dismissed as a castrated or effeminate (assumed homosexual) male. He is now in great demand. The new voices that have overtaken the limpid English–Oxbridge sound are bigger, fruitier, 'toned like bodies from the gym' – a not irrelevant comparison (White, 2000, p.34). The quality of the sound as produced by a male is quite different from that of the female voice, offering the 'purity' of the singing of choirboys without the vibrato and fullness of a developed female voice.[11] Nevertheless the yearning sounds in *Strange Fish* (produced by a woman here, not by a counter-tenor) and the equally yearning movement that accompanies it are both ambiguous and ambivalent. Melanie Pappenheim's and Jocelyn Pook's constructions for *Strange Fish* stand literally and metaphorically for the shift in views of sexuality from fixed essences to fluid practices.

A parody of gender in sound and movement

As I move towards a final reading of *Strange Fish*, the specific physical texts and embodied readers whose voices have accumulated through the preceding pages converge in the immediacy of the theatrical moment and become part of my own voice. They are real, not 'virtual', although constructed and not permanently fixed. All are alive and well, becoming part of this final act. Building on earlier theory I also recognise that myth and narrative operate towards psychic unity by enabling us to account for similarities, while allowing diffusion or difference, through borrowing and re-interpreting.

Saved to the end is the most important and complex construction of the Siren, itself/herself doubly ambiguous and offering multiple versions of the self. 'Haunted by meaning and culture', as Derrida argues (1978, p.5), the Siren is both present and absent. She evokes in one character traces of angels, avenging and comforting; 'Mary' and all our mothers; Christ and every saintly figure; Eve and passionately wicked women – all rolled into one, constructing traces of the competing positions and anxieties of all these figures.

The music from Pook and Pappenheim for the fourth scene bears much less on plainsong than does the music for the scenes discussed earlier. This is the ecstatic and wild end of music, which speaks both 'with and across the text' in layered narrations (Abbate, 1991, p.xiv). Excessive high soprano voices that also transmute to resemble deeper contralto sounds challenge the way the dominant gender order is normally manifest in musical melody. The overload and repetition of frantic calls, apparently arbitrary but with a strong enough structure in the vocal line to create a vibrant and threatening rhythmic pattern, compel the listener into the drama.

For many centuries music has been the driving force of much danced expression, although it has become less clearly the case in the late-twentieth-century forms of physical theatre and pedestrian dance practices. This is one reason why *Strange Fish* is something of a cultural enigma and why it invites such a strong reaction: it reaches deep into the Western history of melodic significance while tapping effectively into late-twentieth-century moods and anxieties. The very idea of musical narration – that it can connect with life in some significant way – is both seductive and problematic.

Indeed, the traditional approach to music analysis is based on an assumption that music lies *beyond* the body, that it is transcendent, that it refers to the soul, the essence of the divine or some such configuration – but for Barthes its referent *is* the body. Music is thus a carnal medium, an image, not a language; and hence while he shares the idea that commentary on music is 'unendurable', it is for very different reasons. In commenting on a further analogy, found in Barthes's *A Lover's Discourse in Music, Voice, Language*, Engh states:

> if music ... produces effects that are singular, inexpressible, then here the very qualities that make music so very resistant to critique are being deployed as critique, aimed at rendering its object untranslatable, unable to reproduce its effects.
>
> Engh, in Solie, 1993, p.79

In other words Barthes continues the tradition that makes music un-theorisable. In this he resembles the cultural theorists who prefer dance to remain a metaphoric construct rather than a physical one. The ambiguities entailed in such views, and the ambivalence towards analysis on the part of dance theorists, theatre scholars, musicologists and theorists alike, are predicated on this slide from the real to the divine, the actual to the metaphoric. Solie reflects on the inescapable fact that it gets enormously complicated to take account of the many factors at work simultaneously – and this is my leitmotif as addressed in the music and dance specifically. Notably, Shepherd reminds us of the links between gender, vision, language and music, in which

> music comes to represent the central paradox on which industrial capitalism rests: through the appearance of various genres to individual and collective realities, music serves to reproduce the life of capitalism, yet this very function is implicitly denied through the ways in which music is understood and institutionalized in various cultural and educational processes.
>
> in Solie, 1993, p.59

The significance of Shepherd's point lies in making visible the political thread: that music, dance and theatre are institutionalised and as much constructed (even when constructed as transcendental) as is language itself. Transcendent truths are no more convincing here than they are in language. It might then be argued that what is offered in *Strange Fish* is the chance to reconceptualise Angels/Mary/Christ/Eve and the Siren as female or as gay or lesbian – an opportunity for anyone who is not white, male and heterosexual to be re-integrated, encompassed within the Church.

There are several quite distinct sets of musical ideas present in *Strange Fish*, as is revealed by the biographical sketches and interview material described in Chapter 2 and based on discussions with the composers Jocelyn Pook and Adrian Johnston and singer Melanie Pappenheim. These testimonies are compounded by characterisations of the sacred and profane within the work, embodied in Siren-like figures. It is possible to discern a continuing layer of interpretation added to each previous manifestation of these ideas, whether in movement, sound or words. For instance, the repeated refrain of the Angel's song (Melanie Pappenheim), in its variations on the first occurrence, speaks across the intervening action, and seems in many senses more important than the 'action' itself.

Strange Fish: a religious lament

For *Strange Fish*, Pook drew musical ideas from previous work and from the sound track of a film she had seen (*The Time of the Gypsies*) where 'out-of-tune voices' can be heard, apparently sung by an old lady. She also took ideas from films to which Lloyd Newson had referred, and which contained ecstatic singing.[12] This cross-cultural and liturgical thread seems to recur. Pook denies that there is any musical thematic material common through different scenes, although she recognises a stylistic similarity across these compositions and across her work as a whole.

Traces of a requiem mass evoke certain moods for many Western listeners, but in *Strange Fish* Pappenheim and Pook undermine these feelings with traces of other musical themes. In the notes of Pook's recording of another piece, *Blow the Wind/Pie Jesu*, is the following text, which gives a flavour of her work:

> after the opening entry of a deep synthesiser bass drone come the sounds of a distant children's play ground followed by the unmistakable, honeyed contralto of Kathleen Ferrier (1912–53). This motif, from a Scottish folk-song, is used throughout the predominantly modal developments, but the timbre of the sample – the nostalgic frozen snapshot of the older singer's performance – is contrasted with the vibrato-less multitracked tones of Pappenheim. For the last 30 seconds the Ferrier sample is used in canon. The repeated fragment of popular melody works the knowing listener's responses like multiple images reflected in the 1950s dressing-table mirrors of a Terence Davies film.
>
> Walters, 1997, p.39

What Walters does not say is that Ferrier herself can be constructed as a bisexual figure whose music, in its pitch and timbre, affected both homosexual and heterosexually inclined people equally, and equally powerfully.[13] Echoes of these themes can also be seen in *Strange Fish*, and I return to this idea in a later section.

The quality of elegy in *Strange Fish*, of a flowing melancholic humanity, arises from found sound (e.g. interview voices, church bells, corrugated iron or the shipping forecast) just as much as from specific melodic fragments. Together they construct 'emotive talismans that often evoke feelings of loss, melancholia and of a pervasive Englishness' (Gray, 1995, p.14). The lament suggests itself for *Strange Fish* as a musical form, being based on a descending tetrachord that refers to an endless round of suffering, interiority, introspection, despair, resistance or stoic resignation (Richardson, 1999, p.120). Richardson suggests, in his analysis of *Akhnaten*, that the fanning out of the chaconne pattern reinforces this, with the descending trumpet line being a hymn to the Sun (p.122). Stoic tranquillity becomes resignation by musical means.

The key to the religious link is to see Melanie Pappenheim as taking each of the roles described in Chapter 5 in turn and sometimes together. Firstly, she can be constructed as sharing threads of identity with the Blessed Virgin Mary, on the basis that her attentions to others (after the first scene) are solicitous, caring, supportive and warm. Threads of the *Mater Dolorosa* result from Mary's role as witness and mourner at the suffering of her son on the Cross – linked to her role as mediator or intercessor. This, too, is Melanie's role, in watching Wendy and Dale's scene of sexual disappointment (Scene 9) and then in the dying represented in Scene 11. She traces the part Mary played in both the Incarnation and the Redemption. Through the recitation and repetition of the *Ave Maria*, Mary intercedes between men, women and God, pleading the case for humanity. So, too, does Melanie.

Despite the Reformation critique of the increasing trend towards Mariolatry, and despite the return to scriptural authority, Mary continued to be assigned a significant place through a return to the earliest texts equating her goodness with faith. The paradox of being the Virgin Mary, Queen of Heaven, Queen of Angels, and yet an ordinary peasant girl was not in the end too much of an imaginative tension for Christianity to stomach. Without this 'eternal feminine' vision, and without later miraculous sightings of her, Catholic Christianity's power over women would have been seriously eroded.[14] Constructing an ambiguous role for women can be seen as a device used in many societies, where ritual is used to unsettle believers by creating sufficient uncertainty for women to require continual reassurance that they fit the model. Warner says of Catholicism that

> on the one hand it affirms the beauty and goodness of the natural world and insists that man's purpose is to cultivate fully his God-given gifts on earth; but on the other it endorses the most pessimistic world-denying self-sacrifice as the state of the elect, and accords virginity, the symbol of renunciation, the highest accolade.
>
> 1990, p.337

As veneration of Mary grew, she developed an adaptable character that could be vested with different meanings of blessedness through the centuries. Whatever the differences, it is indisputable that she has maintained to this day a special place in the hearts of many and has become the secular icon of femininity with the longest standing. This may explain why it is still so difficult to challenge.[15] Warner roots this vision of Mary in a Platonic ideal, asking why men create such beliefs and then seek to become the gods they have explicitly raised above themselves. Mary is established as the absolute standard of virtue, and a divine being who mere mortal women cannot hope to match. As Warner points out, Jungian psychology colludes in this by setting up archetypes, in this case of the Great Mother.

> The moral concepts the Virgin expresses are presented as quite natural. By emptying history from the figure of Mary, all the various silks interwoven for centuries on the sensitive loom of the mind are deprived of context, of motive, of circumstance, and therefore seem to be the spontaneous expression of enduring archetypal ideas.
>
> p.335

Thus goodness, motherhood, purity, gentleness and submission create the compound of womanhood familiar to us all. Wistfulness, modesty, grace, wonderment and humility add to this list of daunting and unmistakably feminine attributes – apparently unquestioned so that 'the interlocking of myth and ideology is camouflaged' (p.336). The Virgin sets an impossible ideal, encouraging young female Catholics into a position of 'hopeless yearning and inferiority' (p.337) if it does not provoke revolt. As Warner goes on to say,

> the process is self-perpetuating: if the Virgin were not venerated, the dangers of sex, the fear of corruption, the sense of sin would not be woven together in this particular misogynist web.[16]
>
> p.337

Matching this is an ideology of romance offered to the reader of *Strange Fish* in a manipulative, sentimental form through the angelic lyrical songs of the 'Christ' figure. Sorrow compounds the romantic message of death and resurrection, to create another powerful image: that of a sorrowing mother devoted to the son, demanding nothing for herself, at the disposal of the male, yearning for submission and (through this self-effacement) completion.

In my own structuring of the experience of *Strange Fish*, the musical links clearly invite memory of what I know of a much earlier period than our own through its use of sounds that create this sense of location in an entirely different place and time. Its ostensible subject matter and use of symbols such as the Cross makes such references inevitable. This is an integrated, spoken/sung, narrative and musical event in which each element is integral to the whole – much, it might be argued, as verbal text, sung chant and instrumental events are to the liturgy.

> Every liturgical service is a performance, from the musical point of view, involving fundamentally chants for a celebrating priest, an assisting deacon and an assembled congregation.
>
> Grove, 1980, vol. 14, p.803

The sacred voice of the Siren in *Strange Fish*

The musical traces cited here are first heard in Scene 1 and then used in a variety of forms during other scenes. As a reminder, this is the start of the piece, as I have described it:

Scene 1 – Church Scene 1: Religious observance

In the first scene of religious observance, Diana Payne-Myers faces the camera with a bank of lighted candles between her and the viewer. She is dressed in black with a black cap or scarf over her head. She looks ahead, chin slightly upturned, serious and reverential. Behind her is a large Cross on which, just visible, can be seen the outlines of a figure. Wendy Houstoun, in an orange sweater and casual trousers, drifts around at the foot of the Cross shrouded in dim light. Scattered across the field of vision are candles, placed singly and in groups. Visible also is an effigy of mother and child. When combined with a figure kneeling in prayer, and a shaft of light shining as though through a high narrow window, it suggests a church. A melodic female voice, sometimes in solo form and sometimes apparently in two-part harmony with itself, is at first disembodied. In a closer shot it can be seen to belong to the figure clothed as 'Christ'. Once the figure moves, straining against thongs, the camera closes in, and it becomes clear that this Christ is female. This 'Christ/Siren/Angel' figure is Melanie Pappenheim, who appears in various guises later on in the piece: hence this multiple designation. Wendy Houstoun walks around and watches, apparently detached, perhaps uncomprehending, perhaps dismissive of what she sees. Finally she opens a door upstage left, letting a shaft of daylight in, and departs, closing the door noisily.

The rendering of the melodic lines, in the Figures that follow, is in a loose form of plainsong, where the signs for notes record approximate rhythmic shapes rather than precise time values, 'which the singer is expected to render in a free and flowing manner' (Grove, 1980).[17]

The music in Scene 1, *On the Cross* (Pook), is based on a drone on a low G (one-and-a-half octaves below middle C) and, less present, a D, and even more indistinct, a high G. Figure 1). Vibrations on these notes create a strong sense of pulse. If counted in fours, this lasts for four bars. The tonality is set by the persistent G in the bass, against which is heard a short melodic phrase starting on a higher G, two octaves above the drone. In the original stage version the melody then falls an octave and settles on a chord of two notes, A-flat and the E-flat below it, before repeating the higher G, moving to a tone lower (F) and back to G before finally settling on D. Its mood settles on a Phrygian mode on G. The tension between A and A-flat suggests an Aeolian mode.

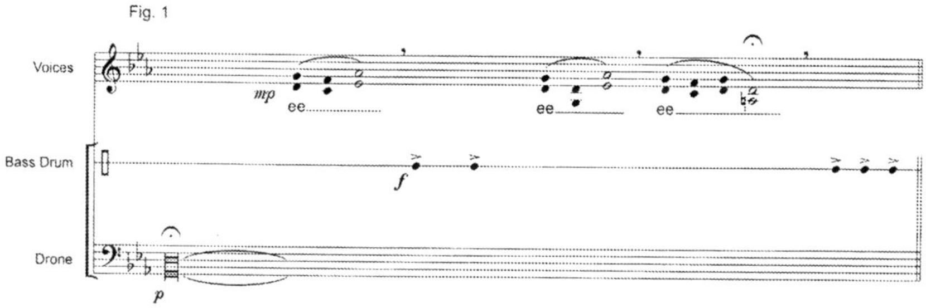

Figure 1. Melodic fragments in Strange Fish

Two drumbeats separate this phrase from the next, which picks up the interval of a fourth and moves through a series of parallel fourths starting on the G with D (the fourth below). It rises and falls through a C/G chord to finish on the starting G/D chord.

In the video version, the first vocal entry elucidates a text where words can be discerned, albeit not in any recognisable language. It is vaguely Latinate; I merely indicate in Figure 2 the crucial consonants and vowel sounds under some of the notes, more as guidance to indicate the phrase I refer to than an attempt to create an accurate rendition. Similarly the note values are a rough indication of the timing of a melody, which is mellifluous and moves easily without clear bar-line demarcations.

Fig. 2

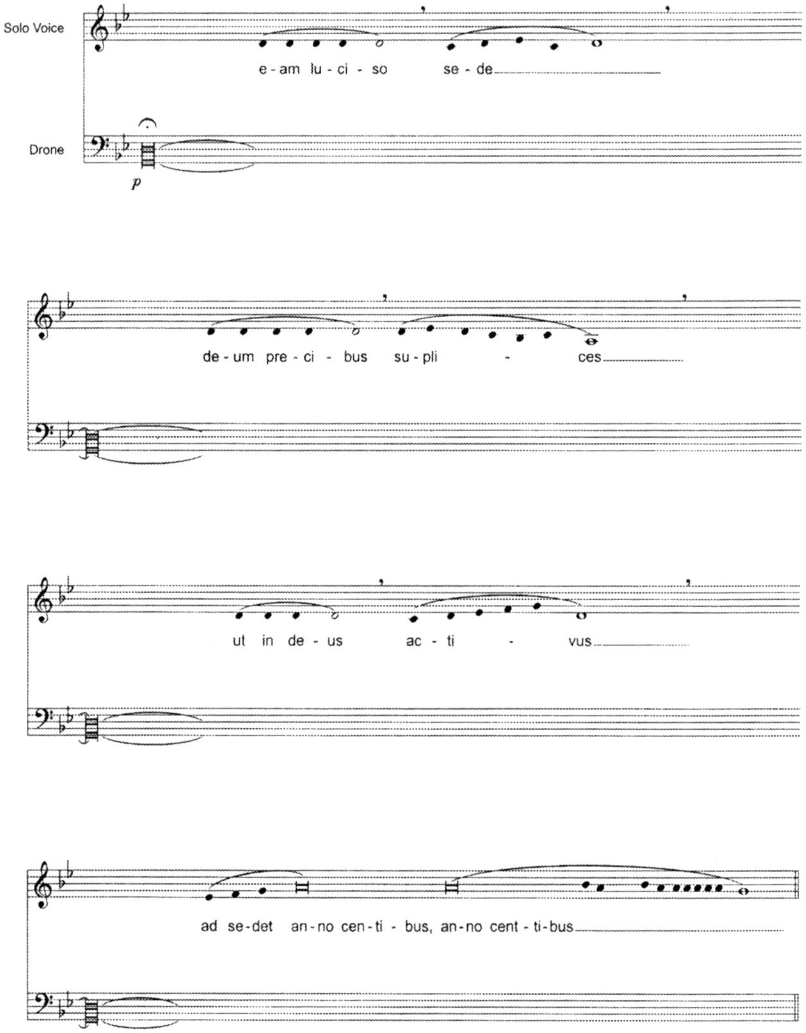

Figure 2, Approximation of the words sung

Phrase 1: eam luciso sede
Phrase 2: deum precibus supplices
Phrase 3: ut in deum activus
Phrase 4: ad sedet anno centibus, anno centibus, anno
centibuuuuuus[18]

The solo voice bases itself more securely on D rather than on G for its melodic phrases. Only in the fourth phrase does it rise to A and indulge in melismatic ornamentation, the repeated notes evoking Monteverdi. It sounds strangely subdued compared with the tape-recorded version of the stage production, which reaches higher in the vocal range and which, through the relationship of the two voices (actually the same singer with herself), creates a more excited and lively start to the piece. Continuing with the recording on the video (since this is the only available record that brings the action and the music together and that continues to be available to a new audience), Figure 3 shows the elaboration of these first phrases in a higher register in the character of a monotone.

Fig. 3

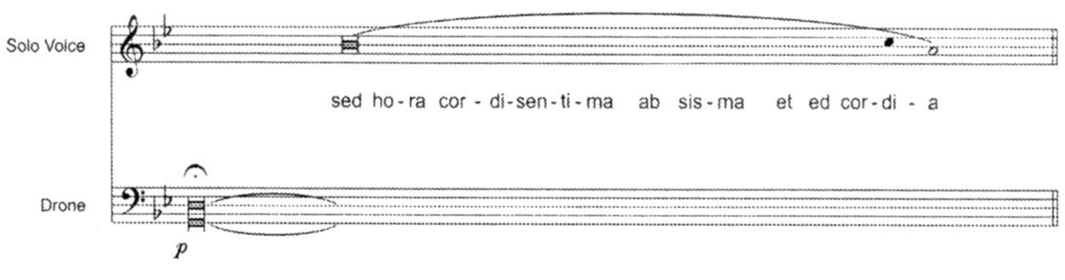

Figure 3. Elaboration of phrases

Starting from a D, this melody rises to A – taking on a much greater intensity than did the lower version with which the piece began. As with the earlier phrase, a repeated first bar gives way to a different second bar, in each case heightening the tension while remaining within the melodic confines of the modal framework.

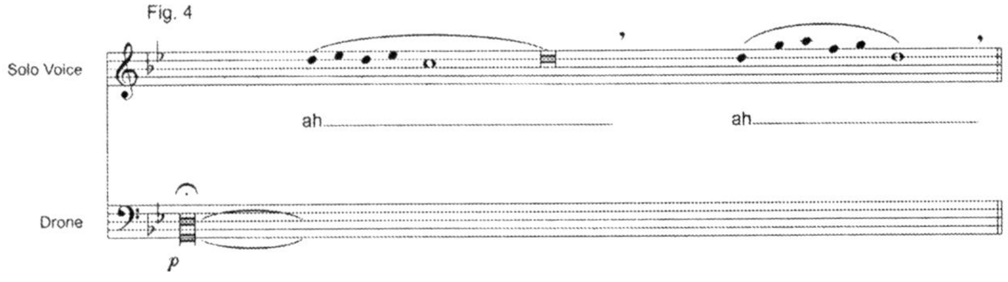

Figure 4. The Alleluia

In the melodic lines the final note is higher than the starting one, suggesting the cantor traditions still found in both the Church of England and the Jewish faith. Four reiterations of the recitative phrase follow each other with different endings – the last time more drawn out and rhythmical and in slower tempo, with increased note values. Holding the final D (Figure 4), the soprano voice takes off into a recitative on this note based around the word 'Alleluia'. During the exposition of these musical themes, Diana Payne-Myers, the nun-like figure, makes small genuflections behind a bank of candles while the woman in an orange jumper (Wendy Houstoun) approaches the foot of the Cross, wanders around a table looking at papers, and walks casually forward and across the space. The camera focuses again on the older woman whose back is now turned to the camera, and the view from her perspective is to the Christ figure, now visible, sharply lit on the Cross. The music has carried the mood thus far, punctuated with pedestrian, everyday movement; but now the Christ figure dominates, coming closer, getting bigger as the camera focuses in.

The arms are outstretched, the right slightly concave at the elbow, both hands tethered to the Cross. The bent left leg, crossed over in front of the right, as though resting on the right foot is in counter-tension to the body. The lower half inclines diagonally forward, but above the waist the body is flattened against the Cross. Emphasising the counter-tension further, the head is pulled back and down and towards the left shoulder. The extended *Alleluia* phrases accompany movement, which becomes exaggerated, the head almost resting on the extended left arm, causing a bony right shoulder to rise, the right hand to splay and the ribs to lift. The extension through the right side is increased as the left contracts and twists against it. This is a tortuous position, beloved of painters of the Christ figure – only here the figure is female.

Still singing, she contracts in the centre of her body. The head is forced further back and the elbows bend, as if she is truly hanging from the Cross. She writhes, the movement rippling up and down her torso until in even closer shot the upper half fills the screen – every rib is visible, every muscle taut and her bare flesh exposed. Appropriate in accompaniment to this, the music of Figure 4 follows an extreme trajectory that lifts it right out of the melodic range used so far, to reach a top A-flat, falling a semitone to G via F, before falling to D as if in plaintive sadness. A rapid loss of focus leads to a semitone passage that mournfully drops from a D/E melisma through D-flat to B-flat. The agony is undermined only as she continues to writhe, twist and turn around the Cross, slowly pausing with only her head visible, lying along the arm of the Cross, eyes staring at the camera. This phrase is partly ecstatic, partly predatory and entirely knowing. A revisiting of the low G–D–E-flat fragments that opened the piece gives a sense of return, but the comfort this might bring is disrupted by the opening and closing of a door, bringing this scene to an end.

If we see how far a link can be made with modal theory, then it seems unequivocal that the reciting note is D and then B-flat. If the final note, like the drone that introduces the piece, is G, it would suggest a form of mixolydian mode. It can be said without much doubt that these modal forms are highly relevant to *Strange Fish*, since even a cursory glance at the typical melodic forms would encourage such speculation. In this first scene these modes create a religious mood simply through the resonance with the music written in the medieval period. What is evident in an analysis of the first phrase of the music for Scene 1 is a shared use of characteristic tendencies of the plainsong tradition.[19]

A further shared element lies in the use of rhythm, which in plainsong follows the rhythm of speech, where the beats fall irregularly. The melody in Scene 1 is easily seen in this way, as a prose rhythm that arises from the character of the words.[20] The emphasis in using the words is partly syllabic – i.e. one syllable is given to one note. However, it is also in part neumatic – i.e. small clusters of 'two to ten or 15 notes may accompany a syllable' (*melismatic*: very florid).[21] The relationship of the G drone to the melodic focus on D, the fourth above, and finally to A, a further fourth higher, suggests modal patterns, while the melisma described above is suggested by the frequent small steps and oscillations between D and the E-flat above and the same D and the notes immediately below, down to B-flat and A.[22]

In conclusion, although the soundscape is in some senses very evidently late twentieth century in its mixing of styles, the very act of drawing on these older styles is sufficient to evoke melancholy, humility and lyrical ecstasy. And yet, as with the movement, there are conflicting echoes that create tension and extend these moods. Both the movement and music introduce subversive quirks of gesture, which suggest a parodic response to the earlier styles of dance and music. A clear example of this is described in the following section.

Juxtaposing human and sacred love

One of the most important images in my judgement, and one on which this edifice of interpretation is built, is found within the first few minutes of *Strange Fish* where 'Christ' is revealed to be female. As she moves her hips in slow undulations, pressing her spine against the Cross, her head back, the bony structure of her rib cage exposed, she lifts her undeniably female breasts in a position reminiscent of soft pornography. Sado-masochistic overtones arise from the fact that she is physically constrained by thongs. In a subtle transition she lies along the length of the horizontal strut of the Cross, evoking the Siren of Greek mythology, stretching voluptuously, the epitome of self-indulgent but dangerous sensuality.

Later on, Scene 5 is also rich in its gendered allusions. I refer to this scene as *Dissolving the self*, but it is termed *Knot dance* in the music titles. The Siren, now solely a disembodied voice and no longer a physical presence, evokes the first moments of the work, simply through a melodic trace. This 'Siren' is a gentle, tender Siren, but nonetheless a Siren (i.e. a predatory woman). Lauren Potter develops a version of the Christ figure's writhing motif, without being tied to an actual Cross, but in a subtle reference to the now-absent Christ figure. There are further echoes in the position that Potter holds, as though representing the horizontal arm of the Cross against Molina's vertical stance – the vagina and the phallus – the former stretched in painful distortion. The sacrifices women make in heterosexual relationships are obvious threads added to Christ's suffering on the Cross.

Lauren Potter bends forward at the hips but extends the back, the head again pressed backwards, in another extreme position that emphasises discomfort and unease. The vulnerability of the pose and yet its manipulative character rest on intertexts of everyday behaviour, enshrined in such stereotypes as the salesman of unsavoury goods. Undulations similar to those of the Christ figure are visible; but in this changed context of a 'love' scene in a corridor, the intertexts shift. Traces surface that suggest manipulation of a relationship, an overweening desire to be desired, and a determination to be successful. Lauren attaches herself with any available part of her body to a not-reluctant Jordi Molina. The basic spatial structure of their duet is a simple two-dimensional figure – the up/down and side-to-side frame of the Cross. By positioning the movement flat against the back wall, the two-dimensional constraint evokes a painting from the period before the discovery of perspective.

Both partners adopt the motif of stretching high, reaching with one arm up the wall and rapidly falling to the ground. Wrapping their bodies sensuously around each other, Lauren and Jordi slip and slide up and down across the wall, making the cross visible and the ecstasy of desire, devotional or human, startlingly obvious. Jocelyn Pook's music links these scenes, being based on the same plainsong musical material – the throbbing drone connoting passion and the melodic line linking human and sacred love.

Figure 5 illustrates a new version of the melody shared with Scene 1. It is in a slow 2/4 time with a melody over a C and G drone as in Scene 1, but it works within a C-minor tonality. The flattened seventh produces an Aeolian modal sound. While it shares the tonality of the first scene in its flattened A, B and E, its sense of 'home' is more around C than around the G of the first scene. The same intervals can be heard

Figure 5. A Sacred Love Song

but from a different pitch base. This is of course a fourth above the first 'key' or mode. Again there is Melanie's solo voice, clearly the same voice as Scene 1, thus linking the character of Christ (already a highly sensualised Christ) with the vocalising accompanying this very human love scene. Love of Christ, or for Christ, then, is not far from the love of another human being.

Later reiteration of these themes adds a second voice (the same voice singing with itself again) in a much higher register – accompanying the first voice and decorating the original melody with a soaring version, sometimes in octaves and sometimes in fourths. A third voice reaches a high F–G–A-flat–A, in a mood of yearning against this much more earthbound melody an octave lower. It is set free from the theme, working with and against it – a voice that speaks of excess. As if in conflict as the duet progresses, Lauren Potter clasps her hands together around the writhing body of her lover, as if it were possible to dissolve the self, dissolve this narcissistic anxiety in the endless flow of sustained, but contained, movement by returning to the womb. Crisp refers to this section as 'a transcendental study in movement curving and oiling itself through bodies' (1992), but it has deeper gendered and emotional significance as well. It is highly ambiguous in that the couple's apparent intimacy is undermined by the intensity of the grasp of the woman's hands, which can be read as a refusal to let go, a manipulative control, rather than a loving embrace. The dancer locks her hands together, encircling her partner in embraces that tend to resemble strangleholds. It is in this scene that the director's influence is again noticeable, since his choice of camera shot forces the reader to see the events through Wendy Houstoun's eyes and thus undermines the intimacy further. These are the director's intertexts, exposed and imposed on the reader, compounding the already uncomfortable message that once trapped by the Siren there can be no escape.

Figure 6 illustrates the addition of the third voice to this melody and shows the accumulation of voices through these repetitions. Jordi's slightest touch sends Lauren into a spasm of desire, a sensuous drop to the floor, only to be scooped up in Jordi's arms. Finally, slithering and sliding snakelike along the floor, they roll over and over each other, their sensuous dissolution and dependency evidence of human need. Poses held against the wall are now reiterated along the floor. Lauren's clasp remains intact but Jordi steps out of her clutches, only to return to hold her closely – caught and obsessed. This phrase is a key moment in the constantly shifting paradox of the sacred and the profane.

Fig. 6

Figure 6. A Profane Love Song

A continuation of this message is seen in Scene 9, the second Room Scene, given the title *Pointless sex and its aftermath* to the music of *Stone song*. It starts once Wendy and Dale have moved into the room. Melanie is visible behind Wendy, fully clothed, while now it is Wendy who is naked to the waist, exposed in close-up shot. Figure 7 shows the very different mode/key frame of this section: there are no flats, but a focus in the melody on A-natural through B and C, dropping to the inevitable D. Showers of stones precede lovemaking. The attitude in the body highlights defiance and detachment, rather than the passion of Christ. When the melody is repeated with the second voice, it is now in thirds, not fourths, and this more obviously harmonious sound clearly

Fig. 7

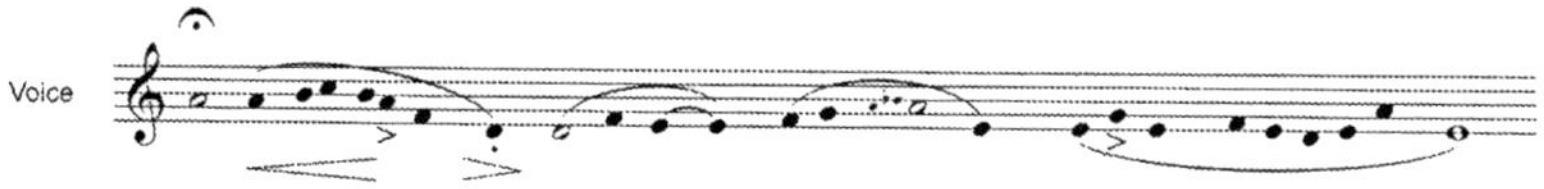

Figure 7. Evocation of Sadness

parallels the start of the lovemaking scene. There is a dangerous sense of indulgence in the music as Dale, oblivious to the turn of events, ignores Wendy to continue his relentless humping. Just as the naked Christ was suspended in silence while Melanie's melodies wove their spell in Scene 1, here Melanie is present as Mary the Mother, singing this haunting theme where Aeolian and Phrygian modes on A are evoked. She steps aside and watches.

Scene 10 (music title *Stone games*) follows without a musical break from Scene 9, with violent sounds of the shuffling of stones as Wendy thrashes around on the ground, both overlaid with Dale's endless search for satisfaction. Wendy twists around, disturbing the stones with her violent thrashing, emphasising the pain of sharp edges on her almost naked body. Her legs flail from side to side; she seeks escape or satisfaction – it is impossible to tell which, except that the stones function as a religious intertext with a very specific set of meanings.

This scene is one of retribution, woman stoned for the sin of fornication; it ties in to the figure of Mary Magdalene, the complex 'Mary' who sins, is forgiven, but carries for ever the stain of this life, despite her anointing of Jesus with precious ointments. Biblical historians suggest that there are several actual characters combined in one, and this seems entirely consistent with the need to construct symbols that reflect the dilemmas of real people. Repentance is offered to all, even to those who are beautiful, rich or live unwisely, to 'women who love too much', and especially to this privileged friend of Christ in his lifetime. Warner (1990) situates Mary Magdalene within the traditions of the harlot, Venus and penitent whore, who, after a life of excess, repents and becomes a hermit. Such a woman re-inscribes yet again the link between sin, the flesh and the female, a state of evil retrieved only by emulating the male, celibate ascetic who is removed from all pleasure of the world.

This serpent-like movement and tortuous melodic singing draws intertextually on the history of both instrument and voice. Craig-McFeely (2002) describes the history of the lute, associated since its origins with fertility, sexuality and courtesan practices. She cites the Flemish linguistic link between 'lute' and 'vagina', pursuing an argument about the dominance of lute imagery in suggestive and sexual metaphor from the fifteenth to the late seventeenth centuries. The lute, representing the serpent, was an archetype of seduction.

In *Lullaby* (Scene 11, *Baptism and absolution*) Pook's music can be heard again leading directly into the final scene (*Hell, fire and damnation*). Here the music is Aeolian, based on a B (natural) for the first time, with prominent F-sharp and C-sharp included in the melodic line (Figure 8). While the shape of the phrase as it rises and falls imitates earlier statements, the tonality is different. The vocal range is more extreme, in fact just over two octaves from a low G to a high A and A-flat, and the form is of layered threads of improvisation above a cantus firmus.

Figure 8. Lullaby

In Scene 11 the singer's image is literally inverted in a reflection in the water and then seen the right way up. At the same time a distorted version of the Siren's song is heard, in parallel to the visual inversion.

A palindromic technique is used in both *Lullaby* and *Stone song* (Melanie's accompaniment to the sexual encounter between Wendy and Dale). In *Lullaby* the use of thirds creates a closer harmony between Melanie and the sick man than was evident in sections using fourths and wider intervals. The pitch is low, the volume soft and intimate, creating a closeness of image that fits closeness of harmony. This melody is decorated an octave above by the same solo voice, echoing the previous higher pitch of Scene 5. This high voice is more obviously raga-like in its melismatic wanderings, cumulatively building sound layers containing echoes of previous melodies. The use of semitone passages seems to squeeze closeness out of the music. The title of *Lullaby* contrasts painfully with the images of death: a child going to sleep juxtaposed with the final sleep. The singer is still, it is as though the sound speaks, and the figures convey through their silences and stillnesses the devastation of their positions. There are echoes of the love duet in the position of holding another, but without sexual connotation. The holding is soft and supportive, a comforting contact, warmth that attempts to revive the shivering and faltering man. It is an echo of Mary the Mother, comforter and intercessor for us all.

On the several occasions on which Melanie sings with herself, the music evokes both angelic qualities and virginal (Marian) qualities. Wheelock argues that while patriarchal narratives can be used to silence or control women's voices, there is also evidence from the eighteenth century of these same voices being used to 'undermine and transform conventional categories of gendered expression' (in Solie, 1993, p.205). In this kind of singing in *Strange Fish* we have the minor mode representing threat and danger, not weakness and femininity; and so a more complex gendering of mode can be seen. In the eighteenth century

> the arias of grieving heroines instantiate their fidelity, the constancy of their love. At the same time, however, contemporary views of the minor mode as weak, changeable, and indecisive create a somewhat unsettling paradox in these arias: in its chromatic mutability, its wide-ranging access to remote harmonic regions, the minor mode is unpredictable, unstable, *in*constant ... [creating] a more widespread uneasiness about the constancy of women's affections.
>
> Wheelock, in Solie, 1993, p.211

Wheelock refers to the 'minor mode's audible powers to destabilize tonal order and to evoke disordered states of human consciousness' (p.219), extending the simplistic association with women and the expression of grief to the expression of crisis and hysteric reaction. Koskoff, writing on the biblical 'Miriam', talks of paraliturgical melodies, borrowed or newly composed: wordless melodies, drawing on both Jewish and non-Jewish Eastern European folk sources and created by Lubavitcher Jews to produce often ecstatic states (in Solie, 1993, p.153). This Hasidic-derived movement, documented in New York in the 1960s and 1970s, is referred to by Koskoff as 'orthodox and mystical' (p.151) in its desire for unity with the divine through joyous and enthusiastic music. In this mode, music resonates with the spiritual or divine, rather than with the mundane associations of the text. So powerful are the women's voices that men are prohibited from hearing them for fear of sexual stimulation (p.153) – a direct evocation of the Greek Siren song. On many of these accounts, women's ability to create new life is seen to place them closer than men to spiritual matters:

> but a woman's voice, especially in singing, is problematic in that it leads to promiscuity. [It] has the potential to connect the body to prohibited sexuality, and thus to the mundane world and the animal soul.
>
> Koskoff in Solie, 1993, p.153

Thus, despite my sub-heading specifying *The sacred*, it becomes clear that such notions entail their opposites and hint at the shades of intertwined meanings in between.

Profanity in *Strange Fish*

Lloyd Newson does little to disrupt traditional postures, reinforcing whore/virgin/mother constructions while using them to striking theatrical and profane effect. In a sense the final scene (Scene 12) shows us not one but two mad women. It is set in a transformed liturgical environment, where extreme desecration of conventional Christian values ensues.

In *The desecration of the Cross*, Wendy emerges from the water in a violent spurt, coughing, soaking wet, into total silence. There is only the sound of water trickling against a still background, accompanied by her soft voice calling quietly but urgently, 'Nigel!'. A continuous sound starts in the background against which this scene takes place, an excruciating, aching sound, moving between A-flat, B, B-flat and C, and returning to the tonality of Scene 1, an octave higher and with strong semitone movement, mixing conflicting thirds and seconds. Wendy calls with increasing intensity and fear as she moves down a dark corridor, lit with strips of blue light, into a scene that recalls the first one, the church or religious environment. This time it is dark, its objects in disarray, with clothes strewn across the floor and 'Christ' back on the Cross, singing an agonised discordant chant.

There is no answer to Wendy's call. Grabbing a chalice, she climbs the Cross, pulls the singer's head back and pours the wine/blood over her face, mouth and throat, and silences her by bringing their mouths together. As 'Christ' utters an almost silent scream and slides and falls from the Cross, Wendy descends, walks to the door upstage left and exits, looking back into the room as the light fades, in repetition of her exit from the first scene. This tense atmosphere settles into nothingness as the sound dissipates with a loss of any sense of key signature and security of 'home', although echoes can be heard of earlier phrases mixed with other strange, previously unheard tonalities.

Traces collide paradoxically in space here: returning Christ's supposed beneficence, throwing it back in his face; a lover's kiss for an asexual man, a lesbian kiss between two desiring women; the kiss of Judas for Christ which reveals his identity; the spear in the side, the loss of blood leading to death, and our inheritance of swallowing the 'gall',[23] of trust and belief betrayed. All these threads are present as we (you, me, the modern spectator) face our own inadequacies, our own mortality.[24] These fragments multiply across time and space to comment on each other, to begin to talk among themselves.[25]

The poignancy of similarity and difference between the beginning and the end of the work is brought about by using the same religious environment, picking up the opening moments. A reflection on the consequences of the intervening action can then take place – full of the 'preconditions' and 'moments' of the text in the manner to which Frow refers (1990). The textual contrasts are in both set and mood, from the calm, warm, softness of the iconography in the first scene, with Payne-Myers's candlelit obeisance at the foot of the Cross, to the bleak, cold, harshness of the final scene, where the Cross remains as the sole religious symbol in a scene that is otherwise one of devastation. The musical modulation from soothing seduction to higher pitches and screaming tones is sufficient to make the point. The inviting sensuality of the Christ/Siren figure, which already carried overtones of threat, menace and pain, results only in violence and violation as Wendy Houstoun in the closing scene forces her attentions on the tortured, suspended figure.

In this denouement in which the sanctity of the communion ritual is destroyed, 'Christ's' facial expression is agonised, the twisting of the body is grotesque, and she falls to the ground, in wild contrast to the languorous movements of the first scene. Wendy Houstoun is finally left alone, in the stillness and silence of the aftermath of a holocaust.[26] It is as hard to avoid an interpretation based on destruction and desecration of Christianity as it is to ignore the assumption that woman, whether Siren or screaming harridan, is its cause.

As Wendy Houstoun pours this dark red liquid over the face of the Christ figure, other associations are recalled. Outside the Christian tradition, and pre-dating it, are the associations of sexual fluids with eating – to take an example: in classical, sacrificial ritual in India. Despite shifting linguistic terrain and practices between Vedic and post-Vedic writings, O'Flaherty (1980) demonstrates the continuity of the alliance of blood, milk and semen as fluids of both male and female, but she also emphasises the closer link between milk and the breast as key to women's force, and semen as the essential quality of men. Many 'deaths' are associated with loss of these fluids, whether of semen through ejaculation (also known as *le petit mort* and celebrated in songs and poems of Western history), or of blood through menstruation (usually feared, not celebrated) or through defloration of the virgin (definitely celebrated in the 'right' context).[27] While milk is thought to be the primary, succouring fluid, the gods (male) occupy a superior position as procreative figures, adopting the analogy of milk for semen.

There is scope for considerable ambiguity in the idea that water can be converted into urine, blood and breath (O'Flaherty, 1980, p.20): butter and honey become metaphors for semen; 'the ritual ingestion of semen or its metaphorical substitutes' is a powerful image of potency (p.27). Woman is primarily the 'receptacle' (p.29); uterine blood is less significant than semen; but her danger lies in the act of intercourse where male power is lost and transferred to the female body – in extreme cases it is 'stolen' from the male (echoes of Samson and Delilah). There is much greater ambivalence towards women's menstrual blood in post-Vedic literature than towards men's semen. Mythologies of demons arising from blood, and demonesses who drink it, do not encourage a positive attitude. Neither do confusions between female 'seed' and blood in Sanskrit texts, which lead both to prohibition of intercourse during menstruation and to its opposite – that it is mandatory (p.35).

We incorporate or ingest, quite literally with the bread and wine, the Christ who died for us, thus also 'consuming' spiritual values constructed for the benefit of men. This analogy is made powerfully by Wendy Houstoun's sacrilege in forcing the 'Christ' figure to drink her/his own body and blood. Add to this the idea that the wine may represent not just the blood of a dying man, pierced in the side, but the menstrual blood of a woman, and the heresy deepens. In Daly's radical feminist terms the Eucharist is a form of deception, with women being made to swallow their own inferiority in the name of transubstantiation (1984).

The depth of sacrilege in enshrining Christ with the Siren within the female person in *Strange Fish* is thus doubly apparent, and the reader's continuing sense of shock can be explained. When the female intruder later 'kisses' or draws the breath from the female 'Christ' in the final scene, the lesbian agenda, now alive between Wendy Houstoun and 'Christ' or the 'Siren', is complete, and the ultimate challenge to male domination is made.[28] It is not just lesbianism, however, that threatens the sacred agenda. Androgyny and its asexual or multiple-sexual dilemmas are buried in these sections of *Strange Fish*, too, since the narcissistic male whom Dale Tanner portrays in the sex scene (Scene 9), and whom Jordi Molina reveals in the bar scene (Scene 4), is one of the stereotypes of androgyny. The Christ figure, too, cannot become fully sexual even in *Strange Fish* without offending even more deeply than it already does. Melanie's bisexual longing becomes androgynous loving and finally takes maternal form as she mutates from whore/Christ (Scene 1) to guiding and guardian angel (Scene 9), to mother of Jesus (Scene 11), before making clear that she (or the Church, or Christ, or Mary) is, in the end, a whore (Scene 12).

The image of a female rape of the father's temple, whether in more literal Christian story terms through the presence of the female Christ or as a challenge to Lacan's 'name-of-the-father' is strongly present, compounded by associations of women with the excess that leads to madness and hysteria – the very reason why women were not allowed power in the first place. The 'holy of holies', this 'womb-like sacred environment' with which *Strange Fish* opens, is a metaphor for the innermost sanctum of many religious traditions. It is a metaphor of the body as the temple of the soul – and in this context violent entry and destruction 'requires little elucidation' (Richardson, 1999, p.171) – it stands for a metaphorical rape of the father's religion, in the guise of Kristeva's *chora*, a place of nurturing.

Rather more unpleasant, to my mind, is that Lloyd Newson and DV8's work can be read as stating that male homosexual relationships, even if sado-masochistic, are crucially different from heterosexual relationships. Daly suggests that even sado-masochistic acts between two males allow a trading of roles between them, 'without jeopardising their status in the culture ... a crucial emotional adjunct to that agreement is their mutual derision of genital females' (1984, p. 66). Whatever if would take, in Butler's terms, to produce 'subversive discontinuity and dissonance among sex, gender, and desire', it is barely visible here (1990, p.ix). Heterosexuality and its various oppositional positions are reinforced, not disabled, on balance, which, seeking radicalism, I find disappointing.

As Wendy and the Christ figure connect mouth to mouth, another intertext from a later version of the Siren story (from Heracles the healer) is recalled, in which the Siren is a bird, a spoonbill (a relative of the crane). The spoonbill sucks the breath of dying men – an image found sometimes in English medieval carvings (Graves, 1992). This citation is not limited to Western thought or to ancient times. In Salman Rushdie's novel *The Moor's Last Sigh*, the powerful 'heroine' or 'goddess' who bewitches men is credited with the same skill. In a scene set in India in 1946, Aurora, at the age of 21, stands in the dock, accused of being a modern witch:

> burly goldtooth stevedores accused her of trying to steal their souls by literally *drawing them out of their bodies* [Rushdie's italics]
>
> 1994, p.130

Newson himself was clearly aware of the Heracles story, and refers to Wendy Houstoun sucking the breath out of Christ's body (Meisner, 1992). It is significant that neither intertext occurred to most critics of Newson's work, who generally interpreted this gesture as a kiss, and a resoundingly sexual one, thus setting up other traces in this mosaic of quotations.

Conclusion

As Auslander (1994) argues in relation to the Wooster group and its performance of blackface in the piece *L.S.D.*, these representations are highly questionable. They fail in the end to 'construct a critique of the racist implications of that convention' (p.91), and the same can be said of Lloyd Newson in gender terms. It is reasonable to ask if 'the inclusion of specifically historical and political images ... makes the production into a representation of the structure of mediatized postmodern culture itself' (p.94) rather than a stringent critique.

1 Modern American universities still promote Greek-named societies and continue to devise powerful and highly dangerous rituals for young male initiates as a result of which death is not unknown (three cases were reported in the *Los Angeles Times* in the space of three weeks in April–May, 1997).

2 I take this idea without agreeing with Butler's proposition that 'sex' is a 'gendered' category. See Case (1996, pp.13–17) for a critique of Butler.

3 My references here are solely to the video version, since the image and the sound are so closely intertwined. It would make no sense to refer to the stage recording.

4 An interesting discussion of the changes that arise from filming dance and a description of DV8's work for video can be found in Rubidge (1993).

5 Swedlund, *The Anthropometry of Barbie: Unsettling ideals of the Feminine Body in Popular Culture*, in Schiebinger (ed., 2000).

6 This is to be read in the context of the prestige of the fugal form, its complexity and detailed conventions in writing.

7 Wood is Smyth's biographer, and she writes at length about the conflict and concord of the fugal theme of lesbian desire in Smyth's music and in her writings.
8 McClary on Schubert (in Brett *et al.*, 1994) identifies his homosexuality with musical techniques that challenged narrative of a conventional kind, deflecting and exploring other ideas freely instead of driving to a conclusion – creating ambiguity, yielding to pleasure. These are notably feminine attributes as conventionally constructed. Drifting and oblique modulations between keys seems to open up alternative narratives.
9 Abbate (in Solie, 1993) intriguingly uses analysis of a 1978 film (*Mascara*) to reveal entangled motifs (from vocal characteristics to political purposes) to show how together they can question received positions. In her example, the archetypal female Salome is revealed as male – a nice inversion of Christ in *Strange Fish.*
10 In fact, changing genders and trans-gendered identities can be traced back to the earliest years of Christianity. Davis (2002) uses the construct of intertextuality to explore legends of holy women disguised as men. ' "Crossdressing" female saint'[s] were not unusual (p.4), and he reveals a substantial 'corpus of transvestite saints' lives which has attracted renewed interest" of late (p.5).
11 As White (2000) comments, 'anyone familiar with the old, English cathedral countertenor circuit will know, the presumption that men who sing high swing gay has always been veiled in closet campery and innuendo' (p.35). David Daniels is able to celebrate his own gay relationship without attracting such gossip and while standing as the figurehead of a new generation. His colleagues may be heterosexual, justifying the point that it is an aesthetic, not a physiology that makes it 'gay' in later twentieth-century parlance.
12 Pook has made three works for DV8, starting with *My Body, Your Body* (1988), then *Strange Fish* and subsequently *MSM* (1994), and one for O Vertigo Dance company – *Deluge* (1994).
13 Conference paper delivered by Elizabeth Wood at the University of California (Riverside): *Indecent Acts* in April 1997.
14 More realistically (or more cynically), the granting of ecclesiastical approbation and the systematic encouragement of an official cult may be seen as the 'effort to restrain in the legions of the Marian faithful the excesses to which Marian devotion has been especially subject' (Pelikan, 1996, p.187).
15 Marina Warner, the well-known feminist historian and critic, in her book *Alone of all her sex. The myth and cult of the Virgin Mary* (1976, 1990), addresses just this persistence in a feminist world and in her own life. The beauty of Warner's text lies in her skilful accumulation of cultural threads which, she argues, have been linked, often without much scriptural evidence, in the woven fabric that we inherit, its multiple narrative threads compounded by visual images and musical texts through the ages.

16 Warner explains this view in more detail, saying that 'the teleological view that the natural law ordains that women must bear and suffer underpins the Church's continuing indefensible ban on contraception; a dualistic distaste for the material world reinforces the ideal of virginity; and an undiminished certainty that women are subordinate to men continues to make the priesthood of women unacceptable' (1990, p.338).

17 I am indebted to Dr Stephen Goss for his advice on this section. It seems to be a rather stunning irony that this mode of plainsong, which was originally created in an oral tradition, and only later dictated to a scribe and notated, should reappear. The irony lies where the 1998 scholar finds herself taking down by ear music that was constructed straight onto tape by improvisation and mixed/ treated in various ways, without a score of any kind being produced. In reverse mode it may be possible to put this sound tape through a computer and for a written score to emerge, but that is beyond this researcher at present and would be an exercise in spurious objectivity.

18 Although it is tempting to fit actual Latin words to the sounds, I have resisted too obvious an effort, allowing the apparent syllables to emerge in written form.

19 This tradition is characterised by melody that should circle round or touch frequently upon one special note and then drop to a cadence in a florid figure. Such a figure is called a melisma. The word is used for any decorative passage in which the music is spun out with more than one note to a syllable (Grove, 1980, vol. 14, p.814).

20 'The concern of the early (11th and 12th century) Byzantine and Latin neumatic notational systems with representing nuances of dynamics as much as precision of pitch reflects something of the manner in which musical memory and oral transmission operate' (Grove, 1980, p.802). This sense, too is significant in *Strange Fish*.

21 Glorias, creeds, psalms and hymns are usually set syllabically, while the main neumatic families are tropes, introits, *Sanctus* and *Agnus Dei* melodies and communions.

22 It would be foolhardy for a non-specialist to embark on further detail in this analysis, since modality is a complex but important classificatory element. Some brief notes follow to illustrate this point, but in the end it is not significant; what is important is that this conglomeration of sound evokes for us the plainchant form, with all its overtones of mood.
But I venture to suggest that if the reciting note is D in this phrase, the mode would be based on A, although possibly based on the Ambrosian form of the D mode with a dominant A; or on the Gregorian Mode 1 extension D–D with dominant A. On the other hand, Mode 2 (or hypodorian, or later, hypoaeolian) seems to characterise the melodic line of *Strange Fish*, although it is placed against a drone G.

23 The vinegar ('gall'), not water, which Christ was apparently offered on the Cross, was an anaesthetic to counter the asphyxiation of the act of crucifixion; but he refused it.

24 Evoked, too, is Christ's translation of water into wine at Canaa, and the wedding feast in the feeding of the 5000, where five loaves and two fish become sufficient to feed the crowd.

25 Beers (1992) argues that even within modern societies assimilation has still not taken place, and indeed, in some sense cannot, because of the *male* function of sacrifice. Only if women and original sin lose their connectivity can women be accepted in this role. A male god and the sacrifice of a male child, celebrated in the Eucharist, cannot be women's business, on Beers's argument. Support for this point of view can be found in responses to the ordination of women in the US in the 1970s, which are markedly similar to reactions to the equivalent movement in Britain in the early 1990s, where women still experience severe difficulty in being accepted as priests.

26 The analogy of the holocaust is also used by Sayers (1989) in describing another of Newson's works, *Dead Dreams of Monochrome Men* made in 1988.

27 The possible death of women in childbirth does not seem to generate so much interest or concern.

28 Douglas offers a sophisticated analysis of the contradiction between male domination and the reality. Where social systems permit women to be coerced (she cites the Lele) this agreement 'is continually liable to founder on the contradiction that female manoeuvring gives to male domination' (1960, p. 149).

CHAPTER 7

An Elegy

Pedal notes in music, like insistent cultural themes, have been read as signifying infinite space, a space inhabited only by God (Poizat, 1992). The 'pedal notes' that collect around *Strange Fish* are the ideas that dance, opera, the musical lament and the requiem each invokes this ultimate silence through constant references to death, grief and loss. The voice, whether in liturgical or operatic form (and historically they are closely related), and the dancing body can be seen as objects of joy that attempt mastery of this fragile life. Poizat argues that it is neither the plot nor the visual saturation (of opera, although the same can be said of this kind of physical theatre) that creates emotional upheaval. He comments ironically (or psychoanalytically):

> there is something inescapably paradoxical about opera: producers spend enormous sums ... to create sumptuous sets and costumes, only to have the spectators, in those great moments of success, close their eyes to the display the better to be ravished by the diva's singing.
>
> 1992, p.33

The spectators of physical theatre, in contrast, are generally wide-eyed, ravished by extreme moments where the meeting of dramatic movement and music makes a rare impact. Physical theatre is rarely about the singing voice, but the analysis of musical evocations in Chapter 6 shows how the music compounds the story so far, adding further layers and traces to it. These are not just sounds and movements for today, but, as Richardson (1999) says of *Akhnaten*, liturgical forms that have a history. In his case it is the hymn: in *Strange Fish* it is the lament and plainsong, musical forms that are themselves hugely significant in inscribing fragments of Christian belief. This is Foucault's history as archaeology (1969), the laying down of many series of traces.

> The music of the hymn is archaeological not because it deals with real archaeological artefacts from ancient Egypt but because it treats the entire history of Western classical music as an archaeological site, digging up signifiers from the music past and,

> by the very act of representation, uprooting them from the semantic field that formerly nourished them.
>
> Richardson, 1999, p.201

Strange Fish trawls its own archaeological sites in movement, in narrative song and action, as Chapters 4–6 have shown. Abbate's statement applies to all three when she argues that

> narrative song may be seen as a locus of *intrusion*, at which myth writes itself into the continuity of the present, and ensures that the future either enacts myth or struggles against it, being in either case determined by it.
>
> Abbate, 1991, p. 76

Strange Fish writes itself into the present by re-enacting the myths we know while simultaneously struggling against them, maintaining through spectacle and theatricality an appearance of challenging the known. There are dramatic points of tension, which act to stun the reader into silence. Formal repetition that carries the reader along but that suddenly ceases, creating silence and stillness, is itself a gesture where the break is rich in implication. After the violent movement at key points in *Strange Fish*, silence and stillness resonate deeply – as, for example, early in Scene 1 with Melanie's immobility as Christ on the Cross; towards the end of Scene 4 where Wendy strips Lauren of her wig; and at the start of Scene 9 where Wendy stands completely still, naked to the waist. The end of Scene 10 is climactic in this regard as Nigel is pushed into a water tank, and sudden stillness, silence and cataclysmic emptiness reverberate. Jordi, too, in Scene 4, is mesmerising in his at first silent and then gently accompanied candlelit dance, its intense focus on the self reinforcing its preoccupation with presence and absence.

The traces that can be followed in *Strange Fish*, while leading to a multi-vocality of stories, myths and postmodernist constructions, finally rest on structures that are neither neutral nor monolithic. Opportunities open up to reconceptualise Christ. This Siren/Christ figure is immediately so clearly sensual, as well as female, that a challenge is inevitable to the 2000 years of history that sees a threat to spirituality from any form of sensuality, and most particularly from that of women since,

> together, the Virgin and the Magdalene form a diptych of Christian patriarchy's idea of woman. There is no place in the conceptual

> architecture of Christian society for a single woman who is neither a virgin nor a whore. Indeed, in Catholic countries the unmarried woman who has not taken the veil is a pathetic figure of fun ... the Church venerates two ideals of the feminine – consecrated chastity in the Virgin Mary and regenerate sexuality in the Magdalene. Populous as the Catholic pantheon is, it is nevertheless so impoverished that it cannot conceive of a single female saint independently of her relations (or lack of relations) with men.
>
> Warner, 1976, 1990, p.235

Disappointingly, as I read it, Lloyd Newson's work does not seem to attempt to counter this, and cynically promotes the message that conventions and beliefs continue to constrain how we make sense of what we see. My account attempts to expose these conventions and beliefs and to 're-make' the narrative of *Strange Fish* through the Siren. It is an act that opens up 'the space of contradiction ... to destabilize and finally alter the meaning of those representations' (de Lauretis, 1984, p.7). 'Finally' might be overly optimistic, but I have exposed both the 'making and the working of [the] narrative' (p.10) of the sacred and profane. For me this is as relevant for those who are heterosexually inclined as for bisexual or homosexually inclined men and women.

It would be comforting to believe that the benefits of a postmodern, pluralistic encounter lie in the recognition of difference and in accommodation to the difficult moral positions entailed in seeing and enjoying the postmodernist mixtures and interleavings of both the sacred and the profane in such works as *Strange Fish*. However, as Auslander argues, the pluralism of postmodernism is perhaps not a 'genuinely pluralistic outlook' but a form of cultural bricolage and appropriation. 'Each bit of information becomes another sign available to circulate within an economy of signs', although each sign 'does not altogether lose its particular history and integrity' (1994, p.17). This is pluralistic postmodernism as yet another level of imperialism. And yet, many theorists and artists would suggest that by entering this flow postmodernism still offers a position from which to critique culture 'deconstructively, resistantly, from *within*', whether as artist, writer or spectator (p.51).

The 'quotations' from other disciplines and other art forms relevant to *Strange Fish* come up against traces of analytical dance and theatre disciplines. In turn these merged sites explain the sometimes conflicting stylistic coding of movement and sound, and its structuring in relation to certain subject matters. The result is a contrapuntal interweaving that loops back on itself and crosses its own path, raising a host of possibilities from this mosaic of texts. In this book I have argued that the inter-related elements of music, theatre, dance and text in *Strange Fish* invite such an analysis. These elements coalesce, and to some extent conflict, around the central conflation of religious imagery with sensual and seductive music and movement, in ironic play (Chapters 2 and 3).

Responses to *Strange Fish* point to the need to develop methodological frameworks that are not as familiar in dance, music and theatre scholarship as they might be, using a dynamic cultural anthropology that attends to the individual's emotional response as well as to the rituals of cultures and the needs of groups. These approaches can then be combined with other methods, adapted from new historicism, cultural studies and literary theory and practice. From this mix a new form of theorising can be constructed: an intertextuality of theories, taking account of and exposing the performance texts, alongside the interests of the writer/reader.

This essay becomes a testing ground for a methodology for analysis in the performing arts. This is explored through a rooted analysis of the motivational and emotional aspects of *Strange Fish* allied to the events of the work, interacting directly with a culturally-based understanding of how the traces which it sets in motion acquire multiple signification for present-day readers. With a touch of irony it also offers me the chance (which I find very tempting) to return the compliment to generations of theorists, using *their* theories as metaphoric intertexts in this analysis. Metaphorical statements are very seductive, like the siren in *Strange Fish*, like the body in cultural studies, and equally dangerous.

Terry Eagleton is one of the most widely cited of recent theorists. He says, playfully, of the recovery of the body in recent radical thought, that 'few literary texts are likely to make it nowadays into the new historicist canon unless they contain at least one mutilated body' (1990, p.7). In *Strange Fish* Lloyd Newson is happy to oblige. The practices of physical theatre tend to contain many mutilated bodies in both a literal and a metaphorical sense. Putting these senses together in context is vitally important for scholars of dance, theatre and music, lest such works and such scholarship be simply incorporated yet again into another discipline in a metaphoric manner that suits the marauders rather better than the victim. I share Eagleton's concern that

> it is difficult to read the later Roland Barthes, or even the later Michel Foucault, without feeling that a certain style of meditation on the body, on pleasure and surfaces, zones and techniques, has acted among other things as a convenient displacement of a less immediately corporeal politics.
>
> p.7[1]

It is of interest here to note Barthes's use of the Siren metaphor in his discussion of intertextuality, which he refers to 'as a music of figures, metaphor, thought-worlds; it is the signifier as Siren' (1977, p.145). It is not only the Sirens in mythology who are complex and already metaphoric, but our constructions of theory, too. Theory can be seen as a metaphoric dance of the angels, transient, free from earthly constraints, a matter of imaginative play. The dangerous habit that the arts have of subverting dominant cultural messages is replicated in postmodern theoretical constructs. The prevalence of dance as a metaphor in other disciplines tempts us to find Barthes's frequent references to music and the body reassuring. But the body, dance and music occupy a peculiar place in many critical writings – the absence of music in Barthes's theoretical constructions of semiotics and its dominance in his *critique* of semiotics should give pause for thought. He is not unique. This combined neglect and 'valorisation' is commonly found, and is remarkably akin to that offered to women and to dance. As many others do, he sees music and the body as rich analogical or metaphorical material, not as subjects of study.

It remains a tantalising challenge to comprehend how dance itself comes to stand for the play between life and death, between mortality and immortality. In part it is the ability of dance to contrast human frailty, grossness and ugliness with a technically exquisite, ethereal and apparently transcendent bodily spirit. The essentially spiritual nature of (Western) views of dance is reinforced by its uses in early Christian religious practice to glorify God, through metaphors such as the dance of the angels and practices such as dancing in graveyards at night. Paradoxically, dance represents fear in the dance of death, and wickedness in the licentious practices of heretics and women, and yet these metaphors are then used both to draw on and to create superstitious 'pagan' belief.[2] The bodies of dancers, actors and musicians can seem to disappear entirely either into the ether of a New-Age spiritualism or into post-structuralism's 'body without organs' in some recent theorising on the significance of language in constructing all our experiences (Deleuze and Guattari, 1987).

I find Abbate's argument telling in relationship to dancers' bodies, since both the voice and the body have suffered in these debates. The singing voice is as crucial in *Strange Fish* as is the moving body. Bodies, like voices, can be stubborn, insisting on their own modes and meanings.

> Voice ... has suffered some battering ... through arguments that attempt to dislocate or disembody speaking subjects, in order to demonstrate how the subject is constituted through language ... But music's voices – unlike the voices assumed to reside in written texts ... cannot be summarily stilled in these terms ... its own voices are stubborn ... they manifest themselves ... as different kinds or modes of music that inhabit a single work.
>
> 1991, p.12

Much as dancing bodies are hailed as representing immortality, and are thus delightfully capable of appropriation for metaphoric purposes, equally they decompose and stand for degradation and disease. In our own time, Gilbert (1998) highlights painfully the 'body in trouble, its vulnerabilities, its betrayals and, most significantly ... how it becomes culturally inscribed by illness'. The capacity of the body to destroy itself explains both the fear of it, which leads to its metaphoricity, and also the tendency to use such illness as cancer metaphorically, to represent 'repressed desires, emotional vulnerability, psychic disharmony'.[3] Underlying this, Gilbert argues, is the construction of the body

> in the pervasive discourses of contemporary immunology, as a system rather than a machine. The body's exterior has thus come to represent a textual system that can be read and decoded ... forc[ing] us to confront the vulnerabilities of our own embodiment.

As Sontag has shown (1977, 1988), diseases such as tuberculosis, and now cancer and AIDS, if treated as 'invincible predator[s]' become mysterious, feared at a moral level, as 'ill omened, abominable ... obscene' (1991, p.9). Cancer is a 'demonic pregnancy' (p.14). It is Sontag's interest in unravelling ideas of the morbid that I adopt here. Her willingness to confront AIDS resonates with the work of DV8, the company that made *Strange Fish*.

Disease as retribution is not, however, just a modern conception. The Hutcheons see the body as the point of intersection of nature and culture, and thus of the medical and human sciences. Opera can be construed as the 'nexus of the singing body as the representation of both pleasure and pain, as desired and desiring as well as sick and suffering' (1996, p.10), and as historically obsessed with (often violent) death. It is deeply revealing of the period in the way it deals with death and love. Such diseases as syphilis, cholera and tuberculosis are historic precedents for AIDS, in 'the idea of an incurable and devastating illness suddenly attacking an entire society [which] has long been read as a divine scourge, a punishment for godlessness, evil, or sometimes a specific sin' (1996, p.14).

And here, then, is evidence of a long-standing tendency to read the dancing body as a textual system, often used to force us to confront the vulnerability of the body in dance-theatre. In dancing we invite the direct analogy of the body consuming itself, much as cancer can consume the real body. The actuality of dance, it might be said, faces us with an unwelcome vision of our own, only too limited, human bodies and lives.[4] This ties in with Shilling's comment that 'the body has its own history as a *simultaneously biological and social* phenomenon' (1993, p.202).

From this sociological position Shilling seeks to demonstrate the importance of 'taking the body seriously' (p.175).[5] The complexity of its significance, he argues, lies in its death – there is only the body. The fear arises that all other certainties have been eroded, particularly those provided by conventional religious belief. The body becomes the only bastion of security and wholeness as we tackle death – the last taboo, as it is often called.[6]

Understood in these terms, the difficulties that dance has in stabilising its images and in establishing its scholarship might be rather more deeply rooted than we like to think. Death and dance have intermingled through the history of Western culture, their metaphoric partnership matched by their mutual presence at crucial personal and cultural moments. By association, 'dance' can become a taboo, a stigmatised category, associated with the uncontrollable, abject body.

If this characterises the rather depressing actual body of dance, then the metaphoric body, meanwhile, is riding high. A more sanguine view is offered by Janet Wolff: 'since the body is clearly marginalised in Western culture, it might appear that dance is an inherently subversive activity' (1995, p.135). In my own view this does not solve the problem of stigmatism, and is compounded by conflating the 'body' with 'dance' without sufficient reference to its highly differentiated forms. It also further conflates ideas of 'woman', 'dance' and an unchanging essentialist body, with all the disadvantages that accrue from such a position.

Wolff argues that the message – theory-as-dance – has not resulted in better 'critical practice, or a useful cultural politics', despite the increased fluidity in conceptual framing that might be expected to result from the playful pluralism of these theories. Wolff attributes enthusiasm in using dance 'to do the work of radical destabilization' (p.79) to two mistaken views: firstly, that dance can somehow bypass language; and secondly, that since it is rooted in the body, it 'provides access to what is repressed in culture' (p.79). My objection, as Wolff's, but more from the position of a dance scholar, is that dance is a means to an end, annexed to other subjects, and through this process of appropriation it is denuded of any fleshly characteristics to become a series of metaphoric constructions.[7]

Clearly dance and physical theatre cannot escape being part of the social nexus. There are many perspectives on how this functions, and it has become a commonplace that people see the body as the 'foremost of all metaphors' for a society's perception of itself.[8] In this respect dance shares with anthropology a desire to undermine the disembodied objectivism of the human and social sciences by emphasising that concepts and categories that organise knowledge are neither abstract nor independent of the body, but are rooted/routed in and through it.

But in life, and in death, dance and theatre can also be seen as a play on political life to the extent that they articulate relationships between capitalism and sexuality. I have used Martin's idea that 'dance lies at the point at which reflection and embodiment meet' (1998, p.1). Neither for him nor for me is it a naïve or romantic position but one from which to argue that, by the 1990s and continuing into the start of the third millennium, a new construction of sexuality takes up the role formerly occupied by capitalist expansionism. Such a position is characterised by 'its tendency to penetrate and colonise ever-increasing areas through its commoditisation and commercialisation of social life' (Weeks, 1985, p. 22). This pervasive sexuality was firstly seen in the commodification of femininity, evident in advertising as well as in everyday behaviour. Cultural practices such as those in television entertainment and the arts have reinforced the message, but an emergent gay male aesthetic is now the 'new femininity'. Weeks, in a nice inversion of much writing on sexual practice, which tends to see cultural practices as *reflections* of sexual anxieties, suggests that sex 'has long been a transmission belt for wider social anxieties, and a focus of struggles over power, one of the prime sites in truth where domination and subordination are defined and expressed' (p.16).

On the other hand, Martin's approach to the relationship between dance and politics is to argue that dance 'generates a sense of being in the midst of a crisis, a break, a rupture, even a loss and a prospect at the same time'; yet this is only metaphoric, given its forward movement. He describes politics as 'the collision and mutual displacement of forces' and articulates the need to understand 'how the concrete labor of participation necessary to execute those ideas is gathered through the movements of bodies in social time and space ... Politics goes nowhere without movement' (1998, p.3). Lloyd Newson's work, and particularly *Strange Fish*, can be read as a passionate collision of forces – a politics of and in movement, and one that in some ways 'goes nowhere'.

A simple way to illustrate this collision of *embodied* forms of knowledge in *Strange Fish* is to recall the Christ figure, repository of all (male) authority, here in female form. Referring to branches of scholarship that see gender as both a condition of experience and an analytic category, it becomes possible to address the implications of this construction. We can ask what challenges such a figure poses to current culturally dominant ideas of 'Christ'. It is 'the body's relation to language and identity, writing and power' that is foregrounded so that women's lived experience in the body can be central to the discussion of the viewer's experience (Bell, 1992, p.96).

Susan Carlson's *Leaking Bodies and Fractured Texts: Representing the Female Body at the Omaha Magic Theatre* (1996) seems to have all the magic ingredients for cultural success that I have referred to so far, if you would forgive the pun. In this case the ingredients are 'women's bodies', 'practical and theoretical issues', 'collaboratively written plays', 'technology' and 'text', 'gender', 'identity', 'sexuality' and 'the material body'. Her themes, however, are not so sexy. They are 'feelings, blood, leaks', not such fashionable post-structuralist concepts, although derived from Hélene Cixous's feminist and political mode of analysis. They are not fashionable, since they are more usually associated with women. The body is seen here as a 'leaky borderline, a permeable passageway, a more-than-material cite [*sic*] of performance'. While there are positive aspects to these theories, there are also great disadvantages – how is it possible to welcome or value the idea of being leaky and permeable, given the resonances of these terms in our society? Not an attractive prospect and of questionable relevance for the dancing body, but an important continuation of the medicalising of the body.[9]

In summary, in the last 20 years a newly structured inter-disciplinary field, but one in some sense unchangingly metaphoric, has opened up, based on something of an obsession with the properties of the body. The focus is no longer on the spiritual metaphor of Christianity, where the body was the rather frowned-upon necessity of human existence and, by extension, of dance. In its new version 'dance' is no more real, but becomes a challenging *concept* for many other disciplines, where its evocation of late-twentieth-century bodily pleasures and disciplines creates a useful metaphor. Carried into this arena is a newly constructed and mediated body – a body for all seasons, perhaps – one that can be robust and fragile, real and metaphoric, powerful and vulnerable, whole and fragmented, at will.[10] It may be part of the distinctive strength of dance that it tends always towards ephemerality and degradation in the sense that it is thereby able to deal fluidly with complex and disturbing matters.

The assumption, or myth as it might be called, that there exists a 'natural' body underlies all such metaphoric appropriations of dance. Using constructs from 'biopolitics', Shiebinger exposes

> the privileged first-born twins of modern science: the myth of the natural body and the myth of value-neutral knowledge ... science, like other human endeavours, is guided by social priorities and cultural ideals ... definitions of woman's 'nature' came to justify her exclusion from the public realms of politics and the learned professions.
>
> 2000, p.4

It becomes incomprehensible to separate scientific definitions of 'woman' from political questions of her role in society. With the evolution of a vocabulary for specifically female parts (e.g. uterus, clitoris) came acknowledgement of the different social roles men and women should occupy – the male in public spheres and the female in the home. Physical difference is used to support (unequal) political priorities. This line continued through the twentieth century as biological knowledge increased, with myths of women's uncontrollable hormones, which prevent them from being rational. At the end of the twentieth century the search for 'gay' genes continues this attempt to find biological markers for sexual difference, an exercise that is fundamental for those who wish to justify divisions within society. Scientific sexism and racism remain dominant and disturbing discourses. At the cultural rather than anatomical level, Shiebinger argues that

> bodies have not only been prodded and poked by scientists and defined by legislatures as rights or non-rights bearing individuals, they have also come to embody – at different times and in different ways – cherished religious, scientific, and cultural ideals.
>
> 2000, p.11

Using metaphors about the body in the interests of re-vitalising other disciplines generates problems for such physical arts as dance and physical theatre. Physical theatre inhabits a shifting territory, sometimes described as 'performance', as 'visual theatre', as 'political theatre' or as 'dance theatre', each of which reflects particular positions within the cross-boundary, interdisciplinary practices that have been popular in the theatre in Europe since the early 1980s. Just as these performance practices have transgressed boundaries once thought to be fixed, scholarship has moved with them, forced to recognise the need to draw on many disciplines to inform analysis of such modes of performance. Desmond stands as an example of such change, arguing that 'dance, as an embodied social practice and highly visual aesthetic form, powerfully melds considerations of materiality and representation' (1997, p.2).

Finally, but appropriately for my subject matter, I make a cultural and aesthetic parallel between the priesthood and late-twentieth-century contemporary dance. If theatre and dance, like the priesthood and many other high-ranking professions, can be seen as a club of male-identified men (both hetero- and homosexual) who quite deliberately exclude women, the Church indeed is continuous with all other cultural practices. The amusement generated by Matthew Bourne's *Swan Lake*, for example, and its massive financial and international success, should give pause for thought. Men, pretending to be the swans that were danced by women in the original Petipa version and in almost all others since, become the prime site of a camp cabaret. The women are set up as stock pantomime characters; the men play up the ambiguity of their roles and set themselves up as gay icons, to be adored by both women and men. While Lloyd Newson does not do it in the same way, it can be argued that his work is still the kind of attack on gender categories that leaves women in a poorer position. Even women's transcendent role, beloved of Christianity, has been usurped by the gay male, as I have suggested in Chapter 6.

This is significant, since Lloyd Newson (and many gay men and lesbians of the late twentieth century) challenge the long association of effeminacy with male homosexuality and of masculinity with lesbians, shattering these crude categories through the construction of identities such as the macho gay and the lipstick lesbian. A refusal to be categorised in heterosexual terms is at the root of this.

We live in an era where gay and other identities are clearly marked. The 'gay male aesthetic', as I use the term here, does not necessarily carry an assumption that homosexual practices are the current preferences of all those who act or those who watch or listen. Rather, it is indeed an aesthetic – a set of qualities, dynamics, ways of treating subject matter, a manner of performance. A convincing argument can be made that this aesthetic has for some years dominated the British dance landscape, firstly through the increasingly de-sexualised androgyny of the female dancer, whether in classical or contemporary forms, and secondly through the dramatic rise of the male (often gay) choreographer, almost to the exclusion of the female, radically changing the gender balance that existed among choreographers of the 1970s and 1980s. Both these points support an argument that says this is a male world, not a female one, for all its greater openness to more subtle sensualities.

Lest an 'aesthetic' might seem harmless, a matter of appearances rather than social and political reality, a warning is necessary. As de Lauretis argues, if

> Nietzsche and Derrida can occupy and speak from the position of woman, it is because that position is vacant, and what is more, cannot be claimed by women.
>
> 1987, p.32

While philosophers may see these issues as a question of discursive style, women tend to see them poignantly as social constructions – of style, gender and rhetoric – which construct their own subjectivities. De Lauretis discusses gender within the frame of what she calls 'the rhetoric of violence and the violence of rhetoric' to show how violence can be, in effect, 'institutionalised' in cultural practices of the family (p.32) – and, I would add, in religion and in representation in art. Auslander's pertinent comment is that

> television culture is a culture of flow in which discourses overlap, intersect, and interpenetrate. The spectator cannot stand apart from that flow of information and imagery but exists within it and is defined by it.
>
> 1994, p.51

If violence does not result from deviance, a sick society or a breakdown in social order, it can be seen, more unpleasantly and ideologically, as a means of maintaining a certain kind of social order.[11] De Lauretis challenges both Barthes and Foucault's discourse on sexual difference, arguing that 'it consistently desexualizes women even as it reclaims the feminine position for male sexuality or proposes a utopia of free-floating desire and sexual/gender indeterminacy' (1994, p.7).

The conclusion is inescapable, from my particular readings, that this is a convincing and plausible reading of Lloyd Newson and DV8's *Strange Fish*, that it maintains the social order, hence my title for the chapter, *An Elegy*, reflecting the loss of that moment when we hoped for a more equal society.

1 Samuels (in Pople, 1994, p.162) describes Barthes's rather literal descriptions of the music 'stretching', which Barthes then relocates to the physical body and the pulse of the heartbeat. Such a view assumes an essentialist body and operates at a biological level. Samuels posits a less physical model, which, in its emphasis on movement, suggests that the musical body simply opens up a trace of another text.

2 The literature on this theme is not extensive from the dance point of view, but a useful survey can be found in Backman (1952).

3 Stacey suggests that 'the power of metaphor in the case of cancer makes the silence speak'; and Gilbert's view is that it thus 'exceeds and displaces interpretation' (1998).

4 We would prefer to hold onto the myth of eternal youthfulness (you are only as old as you feel) and the modern valuing of erotic relationships (it's never too late). This is despite the obsessions with youth culture and fashions suitable only for anorexic 16-year-olds, and certain features in the respectable newspapers, such as the *Guardian*'s 'Soulmates' and the *Independent*'s 'Independent Hearts' columns.

5 As with all fashionable ideas, the death of the body has already been announced – in this case, almost before its has opened its metaphoric mouth.

6 Feral (in Carlson, 1996) suggests that the loss of oppositional and experimental qualities signposts the need for another autopsy, this

time for 'Performance Art' carrying further the demise of the body and replacing it with the high-tech global culture.

7 As a discipline in late-twentieth-century practice and thought, in recent years dance has responded to (and structured itself within) a series of shifting metaphors. These range from those of the 1960s, where dance stood as the aesthetic aspect of a physical education to serve the dualist 'healthy mind in a healthy body' philosophy, to sharing the field with the metaphors of cultural studies and the methods of ethnography.

8 Itself (Bell, 1992, p.95) referring to Benthall and Polhemus.

9 In lighter mood, the widespread metaphorisation of the arts can be seen in an advertisement for a course run by the Office for Public Management, London, in June 1998 on 'The theatre of leadership. Manager to Director', described as 'a three-day programme using the metaphor of theatre to explore and develop the capacity of senior managers to work effectively in tomorrow's organisations'. Its contributors included the actress Joan Plowright; the opera and theatre director David Freeman; and Greg Ripley-Duggan, Executive Producer of Shakespeare's Globe, along with executives in the public services world. They explained the link by analogy between the work of a theatre director and that of a senior manager in the public service sector, in the management of public 'performances'. Rather romantically, perhaps, they characterised the working practices of directors as creating 'mutually supportive and creatively challenging environments', which can be emulated in public health settings.

10 In recent critical theory, metaphor has to be treated alongside metonymy, condensation and displacement, and some consideration of the recent history of these terms is necessary. Metaphor, while originally attributed to Latin and Greek origins as a figure of speech in which a name or descriptive term is transferred to some object to which it is not properly applicable (e.g. to 'Life as a pilgrimage (biblical)' – from the Shorter OED), has taken on the psychoanalytic associations of condensation and displacement in Freudian thinking. In its use of the prefix 'meta', it also implies a higher science of the same nature as that to which it refers – a science or theory that deals with ulterior problems, as in metanarrative.

11 de Lauretis refers here to work by Breines and Gordon (1983) in *Signs* 8:3: pp.490–531. Gender-neutral expressions (such as 'spouse abuse') mask that fact that the vast majority of perpetrators are male (1987, p.34). Foucault demonstrated that techniques had developed steadily since the end of the eighteenth century to ensure the survival of a particular social class. They comprised the development of a series of discourses around sexuality, procreation and 'perverted' behaviour, based in academic disciplines and implemented by the State (1976; 1978).

Bibliography

Abbate, C., 1991, *Unsung Voices*, Princeton UP.

Adler, K. & Pointon, M. (eds), 1993, *The Body Imaged: the Human Form and Visual Culture since the Renaissance*, Cambridge: Cambridge UP.

Adshead, J., 1980, *Dance as a Discipline*, University of Leeds, unpublished PhD thesis.

——————, 1981, *The Study of Dance*, London: Dance Books.

——————(ed.), 1988, *Dance Analysis Theory and Practice*, London: Dance Books.

Adshead-Lansdale, J., 1994, 'Dance Analysis in Performance', *Dance Research*, Vol. 12 No. 2, pp.15–20.

——————, 1997, 'The "Congealed Residues" of Dance History: a Response to Richard Ralph's "Dance Scholarship and Academic Fashion" – One Path to a Pre-determined Enlightenment?' *Dance Chronicle*, Vol. 20 No. 1, pp.63–80.

—————— (ed.), 1999, *Dancing Texts: Intertextuality in Interpretation*, London: Dance Books.

——————, 2001, 'Narratives and Metanarratives in Dance Analysis', in Berghaus (2001), pp.189–204.

——————, 2002, 'Siren Sensualities in Physical Theatre. Lloyd Newson's *Strange Fish*', in L. Austern (ed.), *Music, Sensation, and Sensuality*, New York and London: Routledge, pp.121–36.

——————, 2004, 'Ancestral and Authorial Voices in Lloyd Newson and DV8's *Strange Fish*'. *New Theatre Quarterly* Vol. XX Part 2 May, pp.117-126.

Allen, G., 2000, *Intertextuality*, London and New York: Routledge.

Arditti, M., 1993, At the Theatre of Blood, *The Independent*, 6 December.

——————, 2000, *Easter*, London: Arcadia.

Auslander, P., 1992, 1994, *Presence and Resistance. Postmodernism and Cultural Politics in Contempo.rary American Performance*, Ann Arbor: University of Michigan Press.

Ayrey, C. & Everist, M. (ed.), 1996, *Analytical Strategies and Musical Interpretation. Essays on Nineteenth and Twentieth Century Music*, Cambridge: Cambridge UP.

Backman, E.L., 1952, 1977, *Religious Dances in the Christian Church and in Popular Medicine*, London: Allen and Unwin.

Baigent, M., Leigh, R., 1982, *Holy Blood, Holy Grail*, New York: Dell.

Bailey, D.S., 1955, *Homosexuality and the Western Christian Tradition*, London: Longmans, Green.

Bartenieff, I. *et al.*, 1984, 'The Potential of Movement as a Research Tool: A Preliminary Analysis', *Dance Research Journal* Vol. 16 No. 1, Spring, pp.3–26.
Barthes, R., 1977, *Image, Music, Text*, London: Fontana.
Bartky, S. L., 1988, 'Foucault, Femininity, and the Modernization of Patriarchal Power', in E. Diamond and L. Quinby (eds), *Feminism and Foucault: Reflections on Resistance*, Borston: Northeastern UP, pp. 103-118.
Bataille, G., 1962, *Eroticism* (trans. M Dalwood), New York: Boyars, reprinted 1987.
Beaumont, C.W., 1944, 1969, *The Ballet called Giselle*, New York: Dance Horizons.
——————, 1947, *The Swan Lake*, London: Beaumont.
Beauvoir, S. de, 1971, *The Second Sex* (trans. H.M. Parshley), New York: Knopf.
Beers, W., 1992, *Women and Sacrifice. Male Narcissism and the Psychology of Religion*, Detroit: Wayne State UP.
Bell, C., 1992, *Ritual Theory, Ritual Practice*, Oxford: OUP.
Berghaus, G. (ed.), 2001, *New Approaches to Theatre Studies and Performance Analysis*, Tübingen: Niemeyer.
Best, D., 1974, *Expression in Movement and the Arts*, London: Lepus.
——————, 1992, *The Rationality of Feeling*, Brighton: Falmer.
Birtwistle, H., 2000, *The Last Supper*, Glyndebourne and the Deutsche Staatsoper, Berlin.
Bland, A., 1981, *The Royal Ballet. The First 50 Years*, London: Threshold.
Blasis, C., 1828, 1975, *The Code of Terpsichore*, New York: Dance Horizons.
Blundell, S., & Williamson, M. (eds), 1998, *The Sacred and the Feminine in Ancient Greece*, London: Routledge.
Bouldrey, B. (ed.), 1995, *Wresting with the Angel: Faith and Religion in the Lives of Gay Men*, New York: Riverhead.
Bremmer, J., 1987, *Interpretation of Greek Mythology*, Sydney, Australia: Croom, Helm.
Bremmer, J. (ed.), 1989, *From Sappho to de Sade. Moments in the History of Sexuality*, London: Routledge.
Brennan, M., 1992, 'Raw piranhas', *The Herald*, Glasgow, 4 June.
Brett, P., Wood, E. & Thomas, G.C., 1994, *Queering the pitch. The New Gay and Lesbian Musicology*, New York: Routledge.
Brown, D. 2003 *The Da Vinci Code* UK: Bantam
Bryant, C. & Jary, D. (eds), 1991, *Giddens' Theory of Structuration. A Critical Appreciation*, London: Routledge.
Burnside, F., 1992, 'Home Thoughts from Abroad', *Dance Theatre Journal*, Vol. 9 No. 3, Spring, pp.30–3, 42.

Burt, R, 1995, *The Male Dancer*, London: Routledge.

————, 1998, 'Dance, Gender and Psychoanalysis', *Dance Research Journal*, Vol. 30 No. 21, Spring, pp.34–53.

Butler, J., 1990, *Gender Trouble. Feminism and the Subversion of Identity*, New York: Routledge.

Caldwell, R., 1989, *The Origin of the Gods. A psychoanalytic study of Greek Theogonic Myth*, Oxford: OUP.

Campbell, P. (ed.) 1996, *Analysing Performance*, Manchester: Manchester UP.

Carlson, S., 1996, 'Leaking Bodies and Fractured Texts: Representing the Female Body at the Omaha Magic Theatre', *New Theatre Quarterly* Vol. 12 No. 45, pp.21–9.

Case, S.E. (ed.), 1995, *Performing Feminisms. Feminist Critical Theory and Theatre*, Baltimore and London: John Hopkins UP.

————, 1996, *The Domain-Matrix. Performing Lesbian at the End of Print Culture*, Bloomington: Indiana UP.

Case, S.E., Brett, P. & Foster, S.L. (eds), 1995, *Cruising the Performative. Interventions into the Representation of Ethnicity, Nationality, and Sexuality*, Indiana: Indiana UP.

Clarke, M. and Crisp, C., 1989, *London Contemporary Dance Theatre. The First 21 Years*, London: Dance Books.

Claid, E., 1998, *Yes, No, Maybe. The Practice of Illusion in Dance Theatre Performance*, University of Surrey: unpublished PhD thesis.

Clements, A., 2000, (Programme) Notes on Birtwistle's *The Last Supper*.

Comstock, G.D. & Henking, S.E., 1997, *Que(e)rying Religion. A Critical Anthology*, New York: Continuum.

Connor, L., 1997, *Spreading the Gospel of the Modern Dance. Newspaper Dance Criticism in the US 1850–1934*, Pennsylvania: University of Pittsburgh Press.

Connor, R.P. *et al.*, 1997, *Cassell's Encyclopedia of Queer Myth, Symbol, and Spirit*, London: Cassell.

Constanti, S., 1987, 'Easing the Load', *Dance Theatre Journal*, Vol. 5 No. 2, Summer, pp.26–9.

————, 1992, 'Ship of Fools', *The Spectator*, 8 August.

Cook, N. & Everist, M. (eds), 1999, *Rethinking Music*, Oxford: OUP.

Craig-McFeely, J., 2002, 'The Signifying Serpent. Seduction by Cultural Stereotype in Seventeenth-Century England', in L. Austern (ed.) *Music, Sensation, and Sensuality*, New York and London: Routledge pp.219–317

Cranitch, E., 1992, 'DV8 Strange Fish', *City Limits*, 23–30 July.

Creed, B., 1993, *The Monstrous Feminine. Film, Feminism and Psychoanalysis*, London: Routledge.

Crisp, C., 1992, 'Strange Fish', *Financial Times*, 31 July.
Crisp, C. & Clarke, M., 1974, *Making a Ballet*, New York: Macmillan.
Culler, J., 1983a, *Barthes*, London: Fontana.
——————, 1983b, *On Deconstruction. Theory and Criticism after Structuralism*, London: Routledge.
Daines, A., 1987, 'DV8. The Place: Spring Loaded Season', *New Dance*, Vol. 40, p.27.
Daly, M., 1984, *Pure Lust. Elemental Feminist Philosophy*, London: The Women's Press.
Davidson, G., 1967, *A Dictionary of Angels Including the Fallen Angels*, New York: Free Press.
Davidson, J., 1998, *Courtesans and Fishcakes. The Consuming Passions of Classical Athens*, London: Fontana.
Davis, S.J., 2002, 'Crossed Texts, Crossed Sex: Intertextuality and Gender In Early Christian Legends of Holy Women Disguised as Men', *Journal of Early Christian Studies* Vol.10, No.1, pp.1–36.
Deleuze, G. & Guattari, F., 1987, *A Thousand Plateaus*, Minnesota: University of Minnesota Press.
Derrida, J., 1967 (trans. A. Bass, 1978) 'Force and Signification' from *Writing and Difference*, Chapter 1 pp.3–30, London: Routledge Kegan Paul.
—————— (ed. D. Attridge), 1992, *Acts of Literature*, London: Routledge.
Desmond, J. (ed.), 1997, *Meaning in Motion. New Cultural Studies on Dance*, Durham (North Carolina) and London: Duke UP.
Dolan, J., 1993, *Presence and Desire. Essays on Gender, Sexuality, Performance*, Michigan: Ann Arbor.
Doniger, W., 1998, *The Implied Spider*, New York: Columbia UP.
Douglas, J.D. (ed.), 1974, *New International Dictionary of the Christian Church*, Exeter: Paternoster.
Douglas, M., 1966, *Purity and Danger*, London: RKP.
Dromgoole, N., 1992, 'The things that couples do to each other', *The Sunday Telegraph*, 2nd August.
Dworkin, A., 1987, *Intercourse*, London: Arrow.
Eagleton, T., 1990, *The Ideology of the Aesthetic*, Oxford: Blackwell.
Eco, U., 1979,1984, *The Role of the Reader: Explorations in the Semiotics of Texts*, Bloomington: Indiana UP.
Eliade, M., 1982, *A History of Religious Ideas*, Chicago: University of Chicago Press.
Ellison, M. 1999, 'New York seeks to ban Britart sensation', *The Guardian*, 24 September.
Finaldi, G., 2000, *The Image of Christ*, catalogue of the exhibition *Seeing Salvation*, National Gallery Company, London, and US: Yale UP.

Foster, S.L. (ed.), 1995, *Choreographing History*, Bloomington, Indianapolis: Indiana UP.

————, 1996a, *Choreography and Narrative. Ballet's Staging of Story and Desire*, Bloomington, Indianapolis: Indiana UP.

————(ed.), 1996b, *Corporealities: Dancing Knowledge, Culture and Power*, London: Routledge.

————, 2001, 'Closets Full of Dances: Modern Dance's Performance of Masculinity and Sexuality' in J. Desmond (ed.), *Dancing Desires. Choreographing Sexualities On and Off the* Stage, Wisconsin: University of Wisconsin Press, pp.147–207

Foucault, M., 1969, *L'Archéology du savoir*, trans. 1972: *The Archaeology of Knowledge*, London: Routledge (1992).

————, 1975, *Surveiller et punir*, trans. 1997: *Discipline and Punish*, London: Penguin (1991).

————, 1976, *La Volonté de savoir*, trans. 1978: *The Will to Knowledge. The History of Sexuality* Vol 1, London: Penguin (1992).

————, 1978, *L'Usage des plaisirs*, trans.1985: *The Use of Pleasure. The History of Sexuality* Vol 2, London: Penguin (1992).

Frow, J., 1990, 'Intertextuality and Ontology', in Worton and Still (1990), pp.45–55.

————, 2006, *Genre*, London and New York: Routledge

Frymer-Kensky, T., 1992, *In the Wake of the Goddesses. Women, Culture and the Biblical Transformation -of Pagan Myth*, New York: Free Press.

Fuss, D. (ed.), 1991, *Inside/Out. Lesbian Theories, Gay Theories*, New York/London: Routledge.

Gardner, S., 1994–5, 'Expressive Positions' *Writings on Dance*, Summer, pp.72–5.

Geertz, C., 1973, *The Interpretation of Cultures*, New York: Basic.

Giddens, A., 1976, *New Rules of Sociological Method. A Positive Critique of Interpretative Sociologies*, London: Hutchinson.

————, 1987, *Social Theory and Modern Sociology*, Cambridge: Polity.

————, 1991, *Modernity and Self Identity*, Oxford: Polity.

Gilbert, R., 1998, review of Jackie Stacey's *Teratologies: A Cultural Study of Cancer*, London: Routledge. In *The Times Higher Education Supplement*, 16 January.

Goellner, E.W. & Murphy, J.S. (eds), 1995, *Bodies of the Text. Dance as Theory, Literature as Dance*, New Jersey: Rutgers.

Gombrich, L., 1997, Personal communication.

Gordon-Seifert, C., 2002, 'Heroism Undone. The Erotic Manuscript Parodies of Jean-Baptiste Lully's *Tragédies en Musique*', in L. Austern (ed.) *Music, Sensation, and Sensuality*, New York and London: Routledge, pp.137–63.

Gottschild, B. Dixon, 1996, *Digging the Africanist Presence in American Performance*, Connecticut: Greenwood.
Graves, R., 1992, *The Greek Myths*, London: Penguin.
Gray, L., 1995, 'Jocelyn Pook', *The Wire*, October, p.14.
———, 1997, 'Romantic pragmatist', *Gramophone*, pp.38–9.
Grayburn, P., 1990, *Gertrud Bodenwieser 1890–1959*, Guildford: University of Surrey.
Grosz, E., 1995, *Space, Time, and Perversion. Essays on the Politics of Bodies*, New York and London: Routledge.
Grove, 1980, *see* Sadie.
Harpe, B., 1992, 'Strange Fish', *The Guardian*, 24 July.
Hathorn, R., 1977, *Greek Mythology*, Lebanon: American University of Beirut.
Hutcheon, L., 1989, *The Politics of Postmodernism*, London and New York: Routledge.
———, 1998, *The Poetics of Postmodernism*, London and New York: Routledge.
Hutcheon, L. & Hutcheon, M., 1996, *Opera: Desire, Disease, Death*, Lincoln and London: University of Nebraska Press.
Huxley, M. & Witts, N. (eds), 1996, *Twentieth Century Performance Reader*, London: Routledge.
Jacobus, M., Fox Keller, E., & Shuttleworth, S. (eds), 1990, *Body/Politics. Women and the Discourses of Science*, New York: Routledge.
Jay, K. (ed.), 1995, *Lesbian Erotics*, New York and London: New York UP.
Johnson, B., 1980, *The Critical Difference*, Baltimore: Johns Hopkins.
Johnson, M., 1987, *The Body in the Mind. The Bodily Basis of Meaning, Imagination and Reason*, Chicago: University of Chicago Press.
Johnston, A., 1997, Interview conducted with the author.
Jordan, S., 1992, *Striding Out*, London: Dance Books.
———, 2001, *Moving Music: Dialogues with Music in Twentieth-Century Ballet*, London: Dance Books.
Karina, L. & Kant, M., 1996; 1999, *Tanz Unterm Hakenkreuz*, Berlin: Henscher.
Kake, N., 1994, *Postmodernism and Performance*, London: Macmillan.
Kermode, F., 1997, review of L. Steinberg, *The Sexuality of Christ in Renaissance Art and in Modern Oblivion* (revised edn), Chicago: University of Chicago Press. In *The London Review of Books*, 3 April.
Kirstein, L., 1971, *Movement and Metaphor*, London: Pitman.
Knight, D., 1990, 'Roland Barthes: an Intertextual Figure', in Worton & Still, pp.92–107.

Koritz, A., 1995, *Gendering Bodies/ Performing Art. Dance and Literature in Early Twentieth Century British Culture*, Michigan: University of Michigan.

Kuhn, A., 1985, *The Power of the Image*, London: Routledge, Kegan Paul.

Langer, S., 1967, *An Introduction to Symbolic Logic*, New York: Dover.

Lark, C., 1999, *The Body Finds a Voice: An Investigation into the Dual Identity of Physical Theatre in Dance and Drama*, University of Surrey: Unpublished PhD thesis.

Lauretis, T. de, 1984, *Alice Doesn't. Feminism, Semiotics, Cinema*, London: Macmillan.

——————, 1987, *Technologies of Gender. Essays on Theory, Film and Fiction*, Bloomington, Indianapolis: Indiana UP.

——————, 1994, *The Practice of Love. Lesbian Sexuality and Perverse Desire*, Bloomington, Indianopolis: Indiana UP.

Lebrecht, N., 1997, 'Crossed off the crossover chart', *The Daily Telegraph*, 9 April, p.21.

Leitch, V.B., 1983, *Deconstructive criticism. An advanced introduction*, London: Hutchinson.

Lepecki, A., 1995, 'If I can't dance I don't want to be part of your revolution; Review of bodies of the text' in *Ballet International/Tanz Aktuell*, Vol. 8 No. 9, pp.68–70.

Levene, L., 1992, 'Fish out of water', *The Independent*, 11 July.

Lodge, D., 1988, *Modern Criticism and Theory: A Reader*, London: Longman.

Lycouris, S., 1996, *Destabilising Dancing: Tensions Between the Theory and Practice of Improvisational Performance*. University of Surrey: Unpublished PhD thesis.

Lyotard, J.F., 1979, trans. 1984, *The Postmodern Condition: a Report on Knowledge*, Manchester: Manchester UP.

Mackrell, J., 1992, 'Underwater group therapy', *The Independent*, 11 July.

——————, 1994, 'As seen on television', *The Independent*, 8 January.

——————, 1995, 'Truly, badly, but terribly manly', *The Guardian*, 22 September.

Marinis, M. de, 1993, *The semiotics of performance*, Bloomington: Indiana UP.

Martin, J., 1933, 1969, *The Modern Dance*, New York: Dance Horizons.

——————, 1939, 1965, *Introduction to the Dance*, New York: Dance Horizons.

Martin, R., 1998, *Critical Moves. Dance Studies in Theory and Politics*, Durham (North Carolina) and London: Duke UP.

McClary, S., 1991, *Feminine Endings: Music, Gender and Sexuality*, Minnesota:

Meinhof, U.H. & Smith, J. (eds), 2000, *Intertextuality and the Media*, Manchester: Manchester UP.

Meisner, N., 1992, 'Strange Fish', *Dance and Dancers*, July, pp.10–13.

———, 1995, 'Real men don't drink snowballs', *The Times*, 13 September.

Mitchell, M. & Leavitt, D., 1998, *Pages passed from Hand to Hand. The Hidden Tradition of Homosexual Literature from 1748 to 1914*, London: Chatto & Windus.

Moi, T. (ed.), 1986, *The Kristeva Reader*, Oxford: Blackwell.

Moore, C.-L., 1999, *The Choreutic Theory of Rudolf Laban*, University of Surrey: Unpublished PhD thesis.

Morgan, E., 1972, *The Descent of Woman*, London: Corgi.

Morris, G. (ed.), 1996, *Moving Words. Re-Writing Dance*, London: Routledge.

Mulvey, L., 1989, *Visual and Other Pleasures*, London: MacMillan.

Newson, L., 1992, 'Lloyd Newson about *Strange Fish*', *Dance and Dancers*, July, pp.10–13.

———, 1993, 'Lloyd Newson on...dance', *Dance Now*, Vol. 2 No. 2, Summer, pp.11–13.

Newson, L. & Hinton, D., 1993, *Strange Fish*, BBC/RMArts video; 2007 Arthaus Musik DVD.

Nugent, A., 1992, 'It's a strange fish indeed', *The Stage*, 13 August.

O'Flaherty, W. D., 1980, *Women, Androgynes and Other Mythical Beasts*, Chicago: University of Chicago Press.

Orbach, S., 1997, 'A place at the Table of Despair', *The Times Higher Education Supplement*, 19 December.

O'Toole, D., 1992, '*Raw Fish*', *The List*, Glasgow, 5–18 June.

Pappenheim, M., 1997, Interview conducted by the author.

Parry, J., 1990, 'Outside Dance', *Dance Theatre Journal*, Vol. 8 No. 3, Autumn, p.43.

———, 1992a, 'Sex as holy communion', *The Observer*, 2 August.

———, 1992b, '*Strange Fish*', *Dance Now*, Vol. 1 No. 3, Autumn, pp.22–7.

———, 1996–7, 'Dance on the edge', *Dance Now*, Vol. 5 No. 4, Winter, pp.67–75.

Pelikan, J., 1996, *Mary Through the Centuries*, New Haven and London: Yale UP.

Percival, J., 1992, 'Vivid portrayal of the search for love', *The Times*, 1 August.

Poesio, G., 1993, *The Language of Gesture in Italian Dance from Commedia Dell'Arte to Blasis*, University of Surrey: Unpublished PhD thesis.

Poizat, M., 1992, *The Angel's Cry: Beyond the Pleasure Principle in Opera*, Ithaca,New York: Cornell UP.

Pook, J., 1997, Interview conducted by the author.

Pook, J. & Johnston, A., 1992, Music for *Strange Fish* recorded by Pook and Johnston.

Popalisky, D., 1998, 'The Male Dancer': review of Burt 1995. In *Dance Research Journal* Vol. 30 No. 1, Spring, pp.76–9.

Pople, A. (ed.), 1994, *Theory, Analysis and Meaning in Music*, Cambridge: Cambridge UP.

Porter Abbott, H., 2002, *The Cambridge Introduction to Narrative*, Cambridge: Cambridge University Press.

Preston Dunlop, V., 1999, *An Extraordinary Life*, London: Dance Books.

Pritchard, J. (compiler), 1996, *Rambert. A Celebration*, London: Rambert Dance Company.

Ralph, R., 1985, *The Life and Works of John* Weaver, London: Dance Books.

————, 1995, 'On the light fantastic toe: Dance scholarship and academic fashion', *Dance Chronicle*, Vol. 18 No. 2, pp.249–60.

Reinelt, J. & Roach, J. (eds), 1992, *Critical Theory and Performance*, Ann Arbor: University of Michigan Press.

Richardson, J., 1999, *Singing Archaeology. Philip Glass's Akhnaten*, Hanover and London: Wesleyan UP.

Riffaterre, M., 1990, 'Compulsory Reader Response: The Intertextual Drive', in Worton & Still (1990), pp. 56-78.

Robertson, A. & Hutera, D., 1988, *The Dance Handbook*, London: Longman.

Rubidge, S., 1993, 'DV8 Physical Theatre on television', in Jordan, S. & Allen D. (eds), *Parallel Lines*, Arts Council of Great Britain, pp.204–07.

Rushdie, S., 1994, *The Moor's Last Sigh*, London: Vintage.

Ruyter, N., 1979, *Reformers and Visionaries*, New York: Dance Horizons.

Sadie, S., 1980, *The New Grove Dictionary of Music and Musicians*, London: Macmillan.

Sarup, M., 1988, *Post-Structuralism and Postmodernism*, Hemel Hempstead: Harvester.

Sayers, L., 1989, 'Dance Theatre at Dance Umbrella', *Dance Theatre Journal*, Vol. 6 No. 4, Spring, pp.28–30.

Schechner, R. & Appel, W., 1990, *By Means of Performance: Intercultural Studies of Theatre and Ritual*, Cambridge: Cambridge UP.

Schiebinger, L. (ed.), 2000, *Feminism and the Body*, Oxford: Oxford UP.

Searson, C., 1997, 'Our friends Electra', *Classic FM Magazine*, pp.49–51.

Sedgwick, E.K., 1990 *Epistemology of the closet*, Berkeley: University of California Press.

Seymour, P.A.H., 1999, *The Birth of Christ. Exploding the Myth*, London: Virgin.

Shilling, C., 1993, *The Body and Social Theory*, London: Sage.
Showalter, E., 1998, *Hystories*, London: Picador.
Smith , W. & Cheetham, S., 1880, reprinted in 1968, *Dictionary of Christian Antiquities*, New York: Kraus.
Solie, R. (ed.), 1993, *Musicology and Difference: Gender and Sexuality in Music Scholarship*, Berkeley: University of California Press.
Solway, A., 1985, Lloyd Newson interview, *New Dance* No.34, Autumn, pp.10–11.
Solzhenitsyn, A. I., *The Gulag Archipelago*, New York: Harper Row.
Sontag, S., 1961; 1987, *Against Interpretation*, London: Deutsch.
——————, 1977, *Illness as Metaphor* London: Penguin reprint 1991.
——————, 1988, *Aids and its Metaphors*, London: Penguin reprint 1991.
Stebbins, G., 1986; 1977, *The Delsarte System of Dramatic Expression*, New York: Dance Horizons.
Steinberg, L., 1983; 1996, *The Sexuality of Christ in Renaissance Art and in Modern Oblivion*, Chigaco: University of Chicago Press.
Stravinsky, I., 1947, *Poetics of Music*, Cambridge, Massachusetts: Harvard UP.
Thomas, H. (ed.), 1993, *Dance Gender and Culture*, London: St Martin's Press.
_______, 1995, *Dance, Modernity and Culture*, London: Routledge.
Thorpe, E., 1992, 'Power of eight', *The Evening Standard*, 31 July.
Tompkins, J.P., 1980, *Reader-Response Criticism: From Formalism to Post-structuralism*, Baltimore: Johns Hopkins UP.
Turner, V., 1969, *The Ritual Process: Structure and Antistructure*, London: Routledge, Kegan Paul.
—————(ed. E.L.B .Turner), 1985, *On the Edge of the Bush. Anthropology as Experience*, Arizona: Arizona UP.
———, 1990, 'Are There Universals of Performance in Myth, Ritual and Drama?', in Schechner & Appel, 1990.
Usher, R. & Edwards, R., 1994, *Postmodernism and Education*, London: Routledge.
Vernon-Warren, B. & Warren, C., 1999, *Gertrud Bodenwieser and Vienna's Contribution to Ausdruckstanz,*. Netherlands: Harwood.
Walker, B.G., 1983, *The Women's Encyclopedia of Myths and Secrets*, New York: Harper Row.
Walser, R., 1993, *Running with the Devil. Power, Gender and Madness in Heavy Metal Music*, Hanover and London: Wesleyan UP.
Walters, J.L., 1997, *Blow the Wind/Pie Jesu*, notes in *Gramophone*, p.39.
Warner, M., 1976, 1990, *Alone of All Her Sex: The Myth and Cult of the Virgin Mary*, London: Picador.

Watson, K., 1992a, 'Personal, political and positively perverse', *The Guardian*, 30 April.

———, 1992b, *Strange Fish* programme notes, DV8.

———, 1995, 'Straight and narrow-minded', *The Observer Review*, 10 September, p.11.

———, 1997, 'Bound to Please', *Dance Now*, Vol. 6 No. 2, Summer, pp.8–15.

Weaver, J., 1706, 1971, *Orchesography: Or the Art of dancing, by Characters and Demonstrative Figures*, London: Gregg.

Weeks, J., 1985, *Sexuality and its Discontents., Meanings, Myths and Modern Sexualities*, London: Routledge.

Weller, P., 2001, 'The ears have it', review of Jocelyn Pook's first UK tour, *The Guardian*, 9 March.

Whetstone, D., 1992, 'Different kettle of fish', *Newcastle Journal*, 13 July.

White, M., 2000, 'Proud to sing high. David Daniels stepping into the limelight', *BBC Music Magazine*, August, pp.32–5.

Winterson, J., 1985, *Oranges are Not the Only Fruit*, London: Vintage.

Wolff, J., 1990, *Feminine Sentences. Essays on Women and Culture*, Oxford: Polity.

———, 1995, *Resident Alien. Feminist, Cultural Criticism*, Oxford: Polity.

Worton, M., 1986, 'Intertextuality: To Inter Textuality or to Resurrect it?', in Kelley, D. & Clasera, I. (eds), *Cross-references, Modern French theory and practice of criticism*, Leeds: Society for French Studies, pp.14–23.

Worton, M. & Still, J. (eds), 1990, *Intertextuality: Theories and Practices*, Manchester: Manchester UP.

Index

Lightning Source UK Ltd.
Milton Keynes UK
09 June 2010

155261UK00003BA/2/A

9 781852 731175